THE STRONG EYE OF

SHAMANISM

THE STROПG EYE OF
SHAMANISM
A Journey into the Caves of Consciousness

ROBERT E. RYAN, J.D., Ph.D.

Inner Traditions
Rochester, Vermont

Inner Traditions International
One Park Street
Rochester, Vermont 05767
www.InnerTraditions.com

Library of Congress Cataloging-in-Publication Data

Ryan, Robert E.
     The strong eye of shamanism : a journey into the caves of
consciousness / Robert E. Ryan
        p.   cm.
        Includes bibliographical references and index.
        ISBN 0-89281-709-7 (pbk. : alk. paper)
        1. Shamanism—Psychology.   I. Title.
BL2370.S5R93 1999   98-47208
291.1'44—dc21   CIP

Printed and bound in Canada

10 9 8 7 6 5 4 3 2

Text design and layout by Kristin Camp
This book was typeset in Janson with Berliner Grotesk and Mason™Sans
as display faces

FOR
LINDA, BOBBY, AND BILL

CONTENTS

ACKNOWLEDGMENTS

For permission to reprint excerpts of their published works, I wish to gratefully acknowledge the following sources: Harry N. Abrams, Inc., for excerpts reprinted from *Treasures of Prehistoric Art* by André Leroi-Gourhan, published by Harry N. Abrams, Inc., New York, all rights reserved; Holt, Rinehart and Winston for excerpts from *Apache Odyssey: A Journey Between Two Worlds* by Morris E. Opler, © 1969 by Holt, Rinehart and Winston, reprinted by permission of the publisher; Inner Traditions International for excerpts from *Aboriginal Men of High Degree: Initiation and Sorcery in the World's Oldest Tradition* by A. P. Elkin, © 1997, 1994 by University of Queensland Press, reprinted by permission of Inner Traditions International; William Morrow & Company, Inc., for excerpts from *A Forest of Kings: The Untold Story of the Ancient Maya* by Linda Schele and David Freidel, © 1990 by Linda Schele and David Freidel, by permission of William Morrow & Company, Inc.; Princeton University Press for excerpts from Mircea Eliade, *Shamanism: Archaic Techniques of Ecstasy*, © 1964 by Princeton University Press, reprinted by permission of Princeton University Press; W. W. Norton & Company, Inc., for an excerpt from *Sonnets to Orpheus* by Rainer Maria Rilke, © 1942 by W. W. Norton & Company, Inc., renewed © 1970 by M. D. Herter Norton, reprinted by permission of W. W. Norton & Company, Inc.; Temple University Press for excerpts from *The Shaman and the Jaguar: A Study of Narcotic Drugs Among the Indians of Colombia* by Gerardo Reichel-Dolmatoff, © 1975 by Temple University Press, reprinted by permission of Temple University Press; Waveland Press, Inc., for excerpts from *Flesh of the Gods: The ritual use of hallucinogens*, edited by Peter T. Furst, © 1972, reissued 1990. Reprinted by permission of Waveland Press, Inc. All rights reserved.

For permission to reproduce photographs I wish to thank the following sources: Fig. 2A courtesy of Mme. Yvonne Vertut, Jean Vertut, photographer. Fig. 2B courtesy of the Musée National de Préhistoire (M.N.P.), Les Eyzies de Tayac, France. Fig. 4 courtesy of the Musée de la Préhistorie, Mas d'Azil, Mr. Alteirac, Conservateur, and Mado Goncalves, Assistant Promotion, Comité Départemental du Tourisme d'Ariège Pyrénées, Foix, France. Fig. 5 courtesy of the Collection of Musée de l'Homme, Paris, France. Fig. 7 courtesy of the Agence Photographique de la Réunion des Musées Nationaux (© photo RMN), Jean Schormans, photographer, Réunion des Musées Nationaux, Musée des Antiquities Nationales, St. Germain-en-Laye, France. Figs. 6, 8A, 8B courtesy of the Agence Photographique de la Réunion des Musées Nationaux (© photo RMN), Loic Hamon, photographer, Réunion des Musées Nationaux, Musée des Antiquities Nationales, St. Germain-en-Laye, France. Fig. 9 courtesy of the Ulmer Museum, Ulm, Germany, Kurt Wehrberger, M.A. Figs. 18, 19, 20 courtesy of the French Government Tourist Office, New York. Figs. 21 and 23 courtesy of N. Aujoulat, Centre National du Préhistoire, Ministère de la Culture, Perigueux, France. Fig. 24 courtesy of Dr. Kathleen Stuart Strehlow, South Prospect, Australia, based upon a commissioned painting by John A. Gardner, FSRF after original photograph of subject taken by T. G. Strehlow. Fig. 25 courtesy of Mr. Eldon Leiter from his private collecton, Eldon Leiter, photographer. Figs. 30, 31 courtesy of Temple University Press. Fig 33 courtesy of Charlie Ugyuk, artist, Taloyoak, Northwest Territories, Canada, "Harpooned Shaman," 1988. Fig. 35 courtesy of the Cleveland Museum of Natural History, Marvin Cade, photographer. Fig. 43A courtesy of the Agence Photographique de la Réunion des Musées Nationaux (© photo RMN), M. Beck-Coppola, photographer, Réunion des Musées Nationaux, Musée des Antiquities Nationales, St. Germain-en-Laye, France. Fig 44A courtesy of the Agence Photographique de la Réunion des Musées Nationaux (© photo RMN), Loic Hamon, photographer, Réunion des Musées Nationaux, Musée des Antiquities Nationales, St. Germaine-en-Laye, France. All illustrations, unless otherwise noted, drawn by Linda Stitt Ryan.

I also wish to thank especially my wife, Linda, for endless patience in organizing, typing, illustrating, and other indispensable assistance in the production of this work.

LIST OF FIGURES

Chapter 1

AN INTRODUCTION TO THE STRONG EYE

As all men are alike (tho' infinitely various),
  So all Religions &, as
all similars, have one source.
The true Man is the source, he being the Poetic Genius.
                                            William Blake

"We have lost our immediate feeling for the great realities of the spirit—and to this world all true mythology belongs," Carl Kerényi warns us.[1] Joseph Campbell echoes this thought when he observes that today we live "in a terminal moraine of myths and mythic symbols," a massive accretion of fragmented forms left by previous ages that we lack the power to rearticulate.[2] Not only are the forms shattered but the sensibility that produced and understood them has also withered. Shamanism, one of the earliest and most basic expressions of this sensibility, has in particular suffered from this disability. Despite the progress made by modern Western culture in our encounter with and effort to understand the riches of the many civilizations that ethnology and archaeology have revealed over the past century, a cloud of opprobrium has long hung over the figure of the shaman. To the religious missionaries who often first encountered this figure, his "religious" practices seemed more nearly to place him within the camp of the Devil. To practitioners of the emerging science of medicine, with its rigid presuppositions, these archaic healers seemed to be ridiculously inept and often counterproductive. And to minds dominated by the materialist paradigms prevailing since the Enlightenment, the worldview of the shaman, which often seemed to fly in the face of "plain material facts," was simply incomprehensible.

As a result, the shaman has often been regarded as a quack or a charlatan, someone who relied upon trickery, sleight of hand, or intimidation of the gullible and superstitious to maintain his position in society. The situation was worsened by the fact that shamans, for various reasons, often were people characterized by physical or mental abnormalities. Shamanism was frequently associated with periods of neurosis, schizophrenia, or some sort of "initiatory madness." In addition, shamans often spoke a secret and incomprehensible language they claimed to share with the animal world. They dressed in a complex garb decked with paraphernalia the use or symbolic meaning of which was entirely unfathomable to the outsider, and they consequently appeared as the epitome of the absurd. They claimed supernatural abilities, such as clairvoyance, magical flight, and the ability to dismember and rearticulate the body parts of the initiates to their profession. Moreover, as people of their own cultures became alienated from their traditions under the impending influence of modernity, they often treated the formerly revered shaman as something of an embarrassment, a risible figure, a sad remnant of traditions no longer understood. As a final blow, this epigone of primordiality often became an alien within his own culture.

Persistent anthropological and ethnological fieldwork, however, began to show that shamanism was a phenomenon dating back to the very horizons of our knowledge of man as a myth-producing being. This work revealed a phenomenon apparently extremely widespread and persisting into our own time in provocatively similar manifestations across far-flung regions of our globe. This durative power and ubiquity strongly suggested that the phenomenon must have some human significance that scholarship was missing, a quality that attracted and held the human mind, or an aspect of it, almost everywhere and always but had become opaque to modern Western intelligence. With continued research, aspects of significant form began to crystallize. This process took a quantum leap forward when, in 1951, Mircea Eliade published his work, *Le Chamanisme et les techniques archaïques de l'extase*, later translated into English (1964) as *Shamanism: Archaic Techniques of Ecstasy*. We could not do better than to use a few of his observations as a point of entry for our discussion. Shamanism is a complex, significant, and enduring expression of the human spirit that defies any brief, synoptic definition. However, we may establish a few touchstones, a few firm points to anchor our probing into a world at first so alien and "other." "A first definition of this complex phenomenon," Eliade explains to us, "and perhaps the least hazardous, will be: shamanism = *technique of ecstasy.*"[3] The shaman is the great master of ecstasy.[4] Ecstasy on the plane of archaic religions is a transcendence of or being carried beyond one's individual self, and, as such, the shaman becomes the mediator between the individual human mind and the archetypal, transpersonal realm beyond it, potentially open in dream, vision, and trance. Breaking through to the plane of the transpersonal is most often experienced and represented as soul flight, "a trance during which his [the shaman's] soul is believed to leave his body and ascend to the sky or descend to the underworld."[5] Here the shaman experiences something akin to the divine and gains access to a matrix of generative force and power, returning with a supernatural power that he acquires as a result of direct personal experience. The shaman's soul journeys to its source, the source of all soul, and this gives his function in society a larger scope. The shaman's larger concern is, in Plato's terminology, "the tendance of the soul." "This small mystical elite," Eliade tells us, "not only directs the community's religious life but, as it were, guards its 'soul.' The shaman is the great specialist in the human soul; he alone 'sees' it, for he knows its 'form' and its destiny."[6] At death the shaman serves as psychopomp, leading the deceased soul to its destination, a journey for which the shaman has prepared the way by traveling it himself. Perhaps more important, he serves the living soul. "Through his own preinitiatory and initiatory experiences, he knows the drama of the human soul, its instability, its precariousness; in addition, he knows the forces that threaten it and the regions to which it can be carried away. If shamanic cure involves ecstasy, it is precisely because illness is regarded as a corruption or alienation of the soul."[7]

The shaman's trance state, or its variations, is unqualifiedly recognized as a transformation of consciousness or an altered state of consciousness—sometimes spontaneous, sometimes deliberately induced—in which the shaman personally encounters an ontologically prior reality, a realm of essence, the formal power within the outer sheath of what we see as reality. It is important to realize in our society, whose religious forms are most often based on a remote historical revelation and the written word, that shamanism everywhere clings to a nucleus of direct, intense, and numinous personal experience. Thus, Eliade perceptively observes that it is more nearly correct to classify shamanism as a form of mysticism rather than to group it with what are commonly called religions, and that as such the ecstatic experience upon which shamanism is based is coeval and "coexistent with the human condition, in the sense that it is an integral part of what is called man's gaining consciousness of his specific mode of being in the world."[8]

And it is precisely here that this intensely personal experience paradoxically opens into the universal and archetypal. In shamanism a universal grammar of symbols emerges that must be regarded as being more basic and essential than any locally conditioned cultural styles and can be explained only as reaching back to man's deepest psychological and even biological foundations. As Joseph Campbell tells us, "The phenomenology of shamanism is locally conditioned only in a secondary sense. . . . And since it has been precisely the shamans that have taken the lead in the formation of mythology and rites throughout the primitive world, the primary problem of our subject would seem to be not historical or ethnological, but psychological, even biological; that is to say, precedent to the phenomenology of the culture styles."[9] While all mythologies are clothed in the local or ethnic ideas of their particular time and place, "actually, however, there is a formative force spontaneously working, like a magnetic field, to precipitate and organize the ethnic structures from behind, or within, so that they cannot finally be interpreted economically, sociologically, politically, or historically. Psychology lurks beneath and within the entire historical composition, as an invisible controller."[10]

We must remember, however, that as Carl Jung has cautioned, "psychological" does not mean "merely psychological," for the psyche has its own deep roots, roots that both Jung and the shaman trace back to the formal source of human experience. In gaining access to the deep structures of the psyche, the shaman galvanizes archetypal formal principles, "the formative force spontaneously working like a magnetic field," to marshal the local expressions of his time and place into universal forms. For, as Campbell has said with regard to the traditional forms of shamanism, this force "moves within, and is helped, or hindered, by historical circumstance, but is to such a degree constant for mankind that we may jump from Hudson Bay to Australia, Tierra del Fuego to Lake Baikal, and find ourselves well at home."[11] The validity of this observation becomes strikingly apparent when we begin to examine in more detail the antiquity, ubiquity, durative power, and constancy of the shamanic phenomenon.

Shamanism has a historical pedigree that may reach back to and even beyond the moment of the transition from the Lower to the Upper Paleolithic age and seems to offer the first concrete proof of the earliest forms of its presence, perhaps as early as thirty thousand years ago, in the Ice Age caves of southern France and northern Spain. And, indeed, its roots may lie even deeper, for Eliade perceives it as being continuous with some of the very oldest fragmentary religious structures that we can trace and asserts that "nothing justifies the supposition that, during the hundreds of thousands of years that preceded the earliest Stone Age, humanity did not have a religious life as intense and various as in the succeeding periods."[12] Specifically with regard to the traces of shamanism surviving in these caves, Eliade notes, "What appears to be certain is the antiquity of 'shamanic' rituals and symbols. It remains to be determined whether these documents brought to light by prehistoric discoveries represent the first expressions of a shamanism *in statu nascendi* or are merely the earliest documents today available for an earlier religious complex, which, however, did not find 'plastic' manifestations (drawings, ritual objects, etc.) before the period of Lascaux."[13]

The ubiquity of shamanism is as striking as its antiquity. We find it in such diverse areas as Aboriginal Australia, Siberia, Malaya, the Andaman Islands, North America—particularly in the western and circumpolar regions—Central and South America, parts of Africa, and elsewhere. Its remnants are often encountered in the world's most remote and "forgotten" regions, that is, among the Ona of Tierra del Fuego at the extreme tip of South America or in the North American Arctic of the Eskimo, in the inaccessible Vaupés region of Colombia, where the Tukano still maintain relatively undisturbed lifeways, or in the remote regions of southern Africa inhabited by the !Kung Bushmen. At the same time, recent advances in translation of the hitherto unfathomable Mayan system of writing reveal a society strongly focused on shamanic cultural structures. Scholars see pronounced shamanic elements in Norse mythology as well. And classical scholars E. R. Dodds, Erwin Rohde, W. K. C. Guthrie, and Walter Burkert all see shamanic figures moving dimly behind Greek myth, religion, and philosophy.

Perhaps even more uncanny are the structural and functional similarities among these far-flung cultural manifestations. According to Eliade, "Shamanism is the most archaic and most widely distributed occult tradition."[14] Even a scholar as thoroughly immersed in universal mythic forms as Eliade candidly admits, while examining shamanic initiation in Siberia, "Now it is disconcerting to note that this peculiarly Siberian and central Asian pattern of initiation is found again, almost to the letter, in Australia."[15] Studying the Warao Indians of Venezuela, Johannes Wilbert notes that there is "a remarkable correspondence . . . not only in general content but specific detail" between the shamanic neophyte's quest for power among the Venezuelan Warao and the Wiradjuri of Australia, two very widely separated cultures. With regard to his work with the Warao, Wilbert states, "It will have been immediately apparent to anyone familiar with the literature on shamanism that the Warao experience contains much that is near-universal, or at the very least circum-Pacific."[16] He enumerates extensive parallels between Warao shamans and those of Australia, Indonesia, Japan, China, Siberia, native North America, Mexico, and South America.

Indeed, the shamanic phenomenon is increasingly recognized as presenting detailed similarities in structure and function in its numerous manifestations across the face of our planet. According to Eliade, the similarity between Australian and Siberian initiation practices confirms both the authenticity and antiquity of such shamanic rites.[17] The problem becomes how to account for this similarity. Is it due to migration and diffusion? Or is it the product of the archetypal structures of the human mind, which generate similar responses to the universal human predicament independently? Or do both necessarily play a part? Roger N. Walsh neatly capsulizes the problem:

> If migration is the answer, that migration must have begun long, long ago. Shamanism occurs among tribes with so many different languages that diffusion from a common ancestor must have begun at least 20,000 years ago. It is difficult to explain why shamanic practices would remain so stable for so long in so many cultures while language and social practices changed so drastically. This makes it seem unlikely that migration alone can account for the long history and far-flung distribution of shamanism.[18]

Whether it is the product of diffusion or is of independent origination in parallel structures in different parts of the world, shamanism could not have survived for so long if it did not reflect the deep and abiding source of form in the human mind, the common "formative force" that gives shape to structures that fascinate and hold the human mind.

Why should shamanism be of interest in an age of space travel and computer networking? In the first place, any cultural form that has a possible origin over thirty thousand years ago must significantly expand our understanding of humans and the human mind. If shamanism is rooted in the early Upper Paleolithic period, it is one of the oldest, if not the oldest, cultural-religious forms to survive into the modern world while still maintaining a significant complex of structural and functional features that we can trace back over this immense period of time. Moreover, this age-old grammar of symbols and traditions still has human significance. In understanding this archaic form of experience and expression, we witness the seedbed of many of the world's most significant mythologems. As Åke Hultkrantz observes, "The oldest Orpheus tale was probably the narrative of a shaman's ecstatic journey to the land of the dead to fetch the soul of a seriously ill person."[19] Campbell maintains that the relationship of the shaman's inner experiences to myth is an extremely important theme. Given the enormously long period of time that the shaman guarded and gave voice to the mythological lore of mankind, "the inner world of the shaman must be assumed to have played a considerable role in the formation of whatever portion of our spiritual inheritance may have descended from the period of the paleolithic hunt."[20] And Eliade notes, "It is likewise probable that the pre-ecstatic euphoria [of the shaman] constituted one of the universal sources of lyric poetry." He goes on:

> The shaman's adventures in the other world, the ordeals that he undergoes in his ecstatic descents below and ascents to the sky, suggest the adventures of the figures in popular tales and the heroes of epic literature. Probably a large number of epic "subjects" or motifs, as well as many characters, images, and clichés of epic literature, are, finally, of ecstatic origin, in the sense that they were borrowed from the narratives of shamans describing their journeys and adventures in the superhuman worlds.[21]

Moreover, shamanism, which emphasizes techniques conducive to illumination, provides a valuable introductory chapter to diverse traditions. Understanding shamanism sheds light on the possible origins of the meditative techniques we find in yoga. And A. C. Graham indicates with regard to the earliest forms of Chinese "inward training" that "the meditation practiced privately and recommended to rulers as an arcanum of government descends directly from the trance of the professional shaman."[22]

"Western consciousness is by no means the only kind of consciousness there is," Carl Jung reminds us; "it is historically conditioned and geographically limited, and representative of only one part of mankind."[23] In the Western world, our orientation is outward, toward the manipulation of the material world. Better than any previous society we have learned how to let the machine perform this work for us; now it is increasingly obvious that it also does our thinking and imagining for us. Wittingly or not, we pattern our life and society after it; they are increasingly mechanized, standardized, impersonal, fragmented, and repetitive. As Friedrich Schiller long ago noted, "Eternally chained to only one single little fragment of the whole, Man himself grew to be only a fragment; with the monotonous noise of the wheel he drives everlastingly in his ears, he never develops the harmony of his being, and instead of imprinting humanity upon his nature he becomes merely the imprint of his occupation, of his science."[24]

In a sense, shamanism points us in another direction. The shaman combines the roles of doctor, priest, philosopher, mythographer, artist, and psychiatrist. This was no doubt easier in "simpler" societies than it is today. But, as I hope we shall see, understanding shamanism suggests a level of psychic integration where we can recognize a natural point of convergence for these now disparate human functions, functions that badly need to reinforce one another rather than assert their individual and exclusive superiority.

Historically, shamanism evolved slowly and remained rooted in the deep structures of the mind, instinct, and nature. It reaches back not only into the depths of time but also into the depths of the psychological and physiological continuum. While the modern Western human being looks obsessively outward, the shaman cultivates what the Australian Aborigines call the "strong" or "inward" eye. And it is through this vehicle that he discovers the principles of both human experience and continuity with the creation. The shaman's world unfolds from within, and consequently his journey is inward, toward what he experiences as the inner source of form, a necessary and universal world of essential and paradigmatic reality.

The archaic mind in general has been less inclined than we seem to be today to grant automatically an ontological priority to the world of sense experience. That we remain so steadfastly wedded to what William Blake called the "outward Creation" is somewhat paradoxical. Much of modern philosophy, psychiatry, and physics seems to point us in an opposite direction, one that may help us understand the claims of the strong eye. Let us follow this train of thought for a few pages in an effort to give credibility to the strong eye in a world whose current orientation is so utterly opposite. Let us briefly examine a pattern in modern thought that leads us away from an exclusive concern with the peripheral world of material reality and moves us toward an understanding of the deep formal structures of the human mind that give our reality its shape and meaning, a shape and meaning ultimately understood as the expression of an inwardly experienced source.

Nietzsche warned us against what he called the fallacy of the "immaculate perception." Contrary to the tenets of naive realism, the formal principles that shape our reality are within the human mind, and we have no access to a reality existing prior to or apart from these constitutive mental functions. Nietzsche's predecessor, Schopenhauer, treated this folly of the "immaculate perception" with gleeful derision. "One must be forsaken by all the gods to imagine that the world of intuitive perception outside . . . had an entirely real and objective existence without our participation, but then found its way into our heads through mere sensation, where it now had a second existence like the one outside," he scoffed.[25] Bryan Magee neatly summarizes this position in his book, *The Philosophy of Schopenhauer*:

> The brain no more "learns from experience" to create a perceived world out of the data transmitted to it by the sense organs than the blood corpuscles "learn from experience" to take up carbon dioxide from the body's tissues and void it in the lungs. On the contrary, it is necessary for the brain already to have carried out its characteristic function before there can be any experience. . . . The *prerequisites* of experience could no more be among the *objects* of experience, and therefore derivable *from* experience, than a camera could directly photograph itself, or an eye could be one of the objects in its own field of vision.[26]

According to Schopenhauer, "Thus the *understanding* is the artist forming the work, whereas the *senses* are merely the assistants who hand up the materials."[27]

This facet of the thought of Schopenhauer and Nietzsche received its impetus from Kant's critical work and his thorough exploration of the constitutive role the human mind plays in our everyday experience. Kant's work is most frequently recognized for shattering our pretension to a knowledge of a self-subsistent, independently existing material reality. Moses Mendelssohn characterized him as "the all-pulverizer" in recognition of his work's devastating effect. Other philosophers, however, have recognized a salutary direction of thought emerging from Kant's critical itinerary. According to Karl Jaspers, it serves to free us "from the natural faith in the self-subsistence of the world as the whole and exclusive reality,"[28] and Ernst Cassirer recognizes that it shifts the focus of our attention to the formal powers of the mind. "Instead of measuring the content, meaning, and truth of intellectual forms by something extraneous which is supposed to be reproduced in them," Cassirer tell us, "we must find in these forms themselves the measure and criterion for their truth and intrinsic meaning. Instead of taking them as mere copies of something else, we must see in each of these spiritual forms a spontaneous law of generation; an original way and tendency of expression which is more than a mere record of something initially given in fixed categories of real existence." Such human forms as myth, ritual, and artistic expression must now be viewed as "forces each of which produces and posits a world of its own. In these realms the spirit exhibits itself in that inwardly determined dialectic by virtue of which alone there is any reality, any organized and definite Being at all." For Cassirer these symbolic forms are "not imitations, but *organs* of reality, since it is solely by their agency that anything real becomes an object for intellectual apprehension, and as such is made visible to us."[29] Finally, as "organs of reality," such expressions of the mind must be seen as "forms of its own self-revelation" rather than slavish reproductions of sense experience.[30]

Ernst Cassirer was greatly influenced by F. W. J. Schelling, who articulated an extremely relevant and now largely ignored theory of mythological expression. For Schelling, "the general organon of philosophy—and the keystone of its whole arch—is the *philosophy of art*," and myth represents the most important aspects of art.[31] He called mythology "absolute poesy, as it were the poesy en masse," which, drawing upon the formative force of the unconscious and the formal power immanent in the creation itself, universalized the content of art and fathered forth a product that in "profundity, permanence and universality is comparable only with Nature herself."[32] As "poesy en masse," myth epitomizes the inner lawfulness of artistic creation. It is as if the substance of mythology, being passed again and again through the human mind, assumes the very shape of the formal principles of that mind itself and crystallizes through its repeated exemplars a sort of general morphology of what mankind experiences as universal and necessary in the dark urgings of that preformal consciousness that connects man back to the creation itself.

Unlike so many of his predecessors who saw the human intellect as set apart from nature and even as posed against it, Schelling had a more holistic vision. The human autonomic system, instinct, and the unconscious are invested with the same formative force that animates the natural world. Our intellect did not simply spring into existence like Athena from the head of Zeus. It is the product of a long teleological process of which it is the expression and to which it is still related. Human creativity is, in important part, a product of the unconscious, just as the generation, growth, and maintenance of the human body emanate from a source anterior to the hubristic human consciousness, which it both creates and sustains. To underline the relationship between the self-generating form that grounds both the natural and human worlds, Schelling referred to nature as "slumbering [unconscious or, better, preconscious] spirit" and to the objective world as "the primitive, as yet unconscious, poetry of the spirit." The word *poetry* harks back to its Greek meaning, "to make," and emphasizes the unconscious formative force shared by human creativity and that of the natural world. Thus, human creativity in art and myth arises from this unconscious formative force with the same necessity and universality as do the products of nature and in its timelessness and universality of form becomes their correlative.

And just as humankind, no matter the penury of its circumstance, is always driven to produce art, so is the tendency to create mythic and religious forms not only innate but also necessary, ineluctable, and even involuntary. It is, for Schelling, nothing less than the process by which forms of the Divine impose themselves on human consciousness:

> Peoples and individuals are only *instruments of this process, which they do not perceive as a whole, which they serve without understanding it.* It is not in their power to cast off these ideas, to accept them or not to accept them: for these ideas do not come from outside but are within the mind and men never know how they arise: for they come from the innermost consciousness, on which they imprint themselves with a necessity that permits no doubt as to their truth.[33]

According to Schelling, "In substance the human consciousness is that which naturally *(natura sua)* postulates God. Because the original relationship is a natural one, consciousness cannot depart from it without inaugurating a process that leads back to it."[34] Thus, human consciousness cannot help manifesting itself as a process, as expressing an innate purposiveness, which leads it to experience a greater informing force, and this very process is, according to Schelling, mythology. Mythology, like Schelling's power of aesthetic intuition and for similar reasons, "can come to rest only in the infinite."[35] Thus, mythological expression has its own teleological directedness. It is "a tool of the gods" which necessarily leads back to its source in the Divine.[36]

For Schelling, the universality of myth is both the expression and guarantee of its reflection of the preconscious inner lawfulness of mankind's creativity. "Greek mythology . . . arose among a people and in a manner both of which make it impossible to assume any thoroughgoing intentionality."[37] Although it is the product of diverse individuals at different periods, it manifests an unmistakable "harmony with which everything is unified into a single great whole."[38] This paradox of a thoroughgoing unity derived from diverse sources and from diverse times can be resolved only if mythology is understood as the "work of one common formative impulse" shared by all humankind.[39] Thus, for Schelling, the question haunting the literary criticism of his time as to whether Homer was one poet or many is too empirically and too narrowly stated:

> Mythology and Homer are one and the same; Homer was already involved in the first poetic products of mythology and was, as it were, potentially present. Since Homer, if I may put it this way, was already spiritually—archetypally—predetermined, and since the fabric of his own poetry was already interwoven with that of mythology, it is easy to see how poets from whose songs Homer might be put together were each able to have a hand in the whole, though completely independently of one another, without suspending its harmony or departing from that initial identity. What they were reciting was a poem that was already there, though perhaps not empirically.[40]

"There was a myth before the myth began," said Wallace Stevens. And for Schelling there is only one true mythic poet repeatedly incarnated in human history, writing the one true mythic poem in various exemplars and with different inflections but with the lineaments of a thoroughgoing unity of expression.

By following the mind inward, Schelling was one of the first thinkers in the modern West to recognize the germinal role played by the human preconscious in the formation of significant human experience, particularly as it manifests in the production of artistic and mythic religious forms. The preconscious is an expression of the formal power immanent in the creation that produced it. In the recognition of beauty and mythic form, we awaken deep mental structures that share their formal capacity with the cosmos that produced them. And in expressing these structures, we evoke a creative power that, grounded in nature, in turn has "a profundity, permanence and universality . . . comparable only with Nature herself." This aspect of the preconscious mind has its own inner purposiveness that, both spontaneously and necessarily, produces symbols capable of leading back to their source, a source the mind experiences as Divine. Mythic symbols are thus, truly, "tools of the gods."

In the work of Carl Jung, these philosophical observations are given a scientific underpinning and are extended into the field of psychology. For while Jung was early influenced by Kant and Schelling, the fundamental principles of his theory came from a long process of methodically probing deep into the minds of his contemporary analysands. And again we can detect the same direction of thought moving from the "ready-made" material world to the deep formal structures of the human mind and their ultimate relationship to an inwardly experienced source.

J. J. Clarke, in *In Search of Jung*, asserts, "Jung's most important contribution to modern thought, in my opinion, lies in his recognition of the reality of mind and in his recovery of the idea of the psyche as a cosmos equal and complementary to the physical world."[41] According to Jung, "The psyche is the world's pivot"; it is "the one great condition for the existence of a world at all."[42] "What most people overlook or seem unable to understand is the fact that I regard the psyche as *real*," he remarks. "They believe only in physical facts."[43] However, "'physical' is not the only criterion of truth:

there are also *psychic* truths which can neither be explained nor proved nor contested in any physical way."[44] These truths have to do with the reality of the psyche and are not addressed to the reality of the physical world:

> Because the unconscious is not just a reactive mirror-reflection, but an independent, productive activity, its realm of experience is a self-contained world, having its own reality, of which we can only say that it affects us as we affect it—precisely what we say about our experience of the outer world.[45]

In exploring the world of inner experience, he discovered that it, too, had its own formal structure and that it spoke in a once familiar, but now largely obscured grammar of primordial symbols and images. Jung recognized a striking resemblance between the dream and fantasy images of his patients and the materials revealed in archaic traditions. "I can only say that there is probably no motif in any known mythology that does not at some time appear in these configurations,"[46] he observed and further noted, "We can find psychic forms in the individual which occur not only at the antipodes but also in other epochs with which archaeology provides the only link."[47] And he asserted:

> We take our stand simply and solely on the facts, recognizing that the archetypal structure of the unconscious will produce, over and over again and irrespective of tradition, those figures which reappear in the history of all epochs and all peoples, and will endow them with the same significance and numinosity that have been theirs from the beginning.[48]

Jung began to discern a universal psychic heritage existing in mankind and postulated that myth-forming structural elements must be active in the unconscious mind. Thus, starting with what he called "individual psychic facts" concerning modern patients, "which not I alone have established, but other observers as well," and comparing these with material from folklore, myth, and history, Jung felt he was able to "demonstrate the uniformity of psychic events in time and space."[49]

One of Jung's best descriptions of this concept is in his "Psychological Commentary on *The Tibetan Book of the Dead*":

> Among these inherited psychic factors there is a special class which
> is not confined either to family or to race. These are the universal
> dispositions of the mind, and they are to be understood as analo-
> gous to Plato's forms *(eidola)*, in accordance with which the mind
> organizes its contents. One could also describe these forms as *cat-
> egories* analogous to the logical categories which are always and
> everywhere present as the basic postulates of reason. Only, in the
> case of our "forms", we are not dealing with categories of reason
> but with categories of *imagination*. As products of imagination are
> always in essence visual, their forms must, from the outset, have
> the character of images and moreover of *typical* images, which is
> why, following St. Augustine, I call them "archetypes". Compara-
> tive religion and mythology are rich mines of archetypes, and so is
> the psychology of dreams and psychoses. The astonishing paral-
> lelism between these images and the ideas they serve to express
> has frequently given rise to the wildest migration theories, although
> it would have been far more natural to think of the remarkable
> similarity of the human psyche at all times and in all places. Ar-
> chetypal fantasy-forms are, in fact, reproduced spontaneously any-
> time and anywhere, without there being any conceivable trace of
> direct transmission.[50]

In what Jung called the collective unconscious lie the "deep-
rooted, well-nigh automatic, hereditary elements that are ubiqui-
tously present, hence the impersonal or transpersonal portions of
the individual psyche."[51] Thus, "the existence of the collective un-
consciousness means that individual consciousness is anything but
a *tabula rasa*. . . . it is in the highest degree influenced by inherited
presuppositions. . . . [It] comprises in itself the psychic life of our
ancestors right back to the earliest beginnings," he observed.[52] "The
collective unconscious contains the whole spiritual heritage of
mankind's evolution, born anew in the brain structure of every individual."[53] "To me it is a vast historical storehouse."[54] Furthermore, "every civilized human being, whatever his conscious development, is still an archaic man at the deeper levels of his psyche.

Just as the human body connects us with the mammals and displays numerous relics of earlier evolutionary stages . . . so the human psyche is likewise the product of evolution which, when followed up to its origins, shows countless archaic traits."[55] Thus, Jung was able to say, "Together the patient and I address ourselves to the 2,000,000 year old man who is in all of us," that representative of the legacy of our ancestral life.[56]

For Schelling, we remember, mythic forms are "tools of the gods," acting with their own purposiveness to reconnect man with his own vital center, a center reaching back into the cosmos. Jung found much the same thing on the psychiatrist's couch. The archetypal symbol is experienced by the psyche as vitally meaningful. It precipitates a transformation of consciousness that is "the natural analogue of religious initiation ceremonies," uniting man with the transpersonal aspect of his mind, which reaches back into the world of instinct and nature itself.[57] This transformation activates the symbolic propensities of the unconscious, promoting the emergence of further salutary symbols. The production of such symbols expresses a priori latent structures within the mind and is "evidently an *attempt at self-healing* on the part of Nature, which does not spring from conscious reflection but from an instinctive impulse."[58]

The unconscious can be reached and expressed only by symbols, and art, myth, dream, and fantasy, with their symbolic propensities, are effective psychopomps, leading the mind to an anamnesis of the origins of psychic life. The result of this anamnesis (an "unforgetting" or rediscovery) is, on the one hand, an accession to power and vitality resultant from this integration. On the other hand, the mind experiences a perception of something akin to essential form and divinity at the heart of the creation and begins to sense an underlying acausal pattern of continuous creation. The two aspects coalesce in spontaneous images, often taking the form of a mandala and emphasizing a unifying centrality surrounded by a symmetrical quaternary or circular structure suggesting a microcosmic-macrocosmic identity between creature and the cosmic creation, of "Deity unfolding in the world, in nature, and in man."[59] "The experience of an archetypal symbol results in a sense of relationship to the interior workings of life, a sense of participation in the movements of the cosmos," Ira Progoff explains. "The individual at such moments feels his individuality to be exalted, as though he were transported for an instant to a higher dimension of being."[60] Jung sums up the core of the experience for the individual: "He is of the same essence as the universe, and his own mid-point is its centre."[61] This "anamnesis of origins" does not simply reach back to the deep structures within the psyche itself but leads to the experience of a very real relationship between the preconscious mind and the formal patterning principles of the creation, the origin itself.

Jung felt that the results of his psychological research, which indicated a level of psychic experience connecting man interiorly back to the cosmic ground, bore a telling affinity to the discoveries being made in modern subatomic physics. Here physical reality could no longer be explained in terms of the older Newtonian causal paradigms but also seemed to be the continuous unfolding of a unified acausal pattern of reality, a formal pattern in which it seemed, at least since the work of Werner Heisenberg, that the human mind participated. And, indeed, today the "nonlocal" character of quantum states still suggests a holistic worldview somehow coordinated by a "noncausal," or implicate, order unfolding in creation.

Jung, in his work "Synchronicity," quotes Chuang-tzu, "If you have insight 'you use your inner eye, your inner ear, to pierce to the heart of things.'"[62] We have seen how for a few modern Western observers this inner eye reveals a reality with its own structure, where the individual opens into the universal and transpersonal and where the principles of art, myth, religion, psychic integration, and a penetration of the cosmos converge. In general, however, the modern Western human being, the dreamer wedded steadfastly and unwittingly to his dream, becomes daily more dispersed in materiality. "It is not a matter of giving him sight. He possesses that. But he is facing in the wrong direction and does not look where he ought. That is the problem." So observed Plato at the beginning of Western culture. "Education is not what some people declare it to be," he asserts. "They say that they put into the soul knowledge that was not there before, like putting sight into blind eyes. . . . But our present argument shows that this power is present in the soul of all, the instrument wherewith everyone acquires knowledge. . . . And the art of education is then concerned with this very question: how the man shall most easily and completely be turned around."[63] For Plato this process of turning man completely around, which tellingly takes place in a cave that reveals itself to be the portal to the Otherworld, was also expressed as the awakening of the inward-looking "eye of the soul."

Curiously, the world's shamans have also turned the eye inward to discover the reality of "the psyche as a cosmos equal to and complementary to the physical world," a realm marked by its own inner lawfulness and purposiveness, which is experienced as an expression of the creation itself. And they may have done so for tens of thousands of years. As we proceed with our study of shamanism, we have the uncanny sensation that the pattern of linear progress paradigmatic for Western consciousness, for the few who can see beneath the surface, is bending back upon itself to form the image of the eternal recurrence of the same. The snake bites its tail to form the circular image of the uroboros, archaic symbol of unified consciousness. We find ourselves immersed in "the psychic life of our ancestors right back to the earliest beginnings" and discover that it is *our* psychic life, for "every civilized human being, whatever his conscious development, is still an archaic man at the deeper layers of his psyche." In a real sense we enter into a dialogue with "the 2,000,000 year old man who is in all of us" and, opening the strong eye, are able to trace the lineaments of an inward journey from the profane world of peripheral effects to the central formal principles of our mind, themselves the eternal expression of the transpersonal "creationtime" realm. And this is, as we shall see, the eternal journey of the shaman, a journey that is strikingly the same "at the antipodes and in other epochs with which archeology provides the only link."

Chapter 2

POESY EN MASSE

There was a myth before the myth began,
Venerable and articulate and complete.
Wallace Stevens

"Only as the genius in the act of creation merges with the primal architect of the cosmos can he truly know something of the eternal essence of art," Nietzsche tells us. "For in that condition he resembles the uncanny fairy tale image which is able to see itself by turning its eyes." And starting approximately thirty thousand years ago, we find tangible evidence of man's turning his eyes inward to the creative source, the primal architect of the cosmos, and offering the homage of beauty in an art of enduring magnificence. Throughout northern Spain and southwestern France, Ice Age man adorned cave walls with painted, incised, and, sometimes, sculpted animal figures of incomparable beauty, a beauty that challenges the achievements of our twentieth-century art and our glib assumptions about the progressive development of human sensibility.

It is difficult to conceive of a sophisticated art of such antiquity. We stretch our minds to reach back twenty centuries to the life of Christ and the beginnings of the New Testament Bible, and perhaps another twenty or so to Sumer and Babylon and the Epic of Gilgamesh. Beyond this time we become swamped by the centuries. Yet some idea of the age of this art is given by the title of a seminal study of this subject by the Abbé Henri Breuil—*Four Hundred Centuries of Cave Art*—and we can gain a degree of perspective from the chart of the chronology of the Upper Paleolithic (Figure 1) of the vast time spans involved and how the mere two-thousand-year period that we denominate "anno Domini" is dwarfed by it.

Breuil dated significant portions of this cave art back to the Aurignacian period. More recently, André Leroi-Gourhan, using more modern methods for assigning dates to this art, but admittedly hindered by a paucity of reliable information and the unscientific and haphazard techniques of the early cave explorers, determined that these early works previously regarded as Aurignacian should be assigned to the period between the Gravettian and Solutrean. "Evidences from before 20,000 B.C. are scanty, consisting of slabs decorated with extremely crude engraved or printed figures," he concluded.[1] According to him, the cave art was produced from this time and continued throughout the Solutrean and Magdalenian periods. Then, about ten thousand years ago, the whole development seems to come to an end, with other cultures having no relationship to that of the hunters of mammoth and reindeer replacing it.[2]

Very recently, however, significant aspects of Leroi-Gourhan's painstaking chronological work may have been dealt a shocking blow. First, divers off the coast of France near Marseilles found an underwater entrance to a cave now referred to as Cosquer. During the Ice Age the sea level was substantially lower than it is today, a portion of the earth's water being then appropriated by glaciers, and significant coastal areas were accessible that are today under water. After following approximately 490 feet of watery darkness through the narrow tunnels into which the cave entrance leads, the divers surfaced into magnificently embellished inner chambers. The earliest portions of this site, consisting of stenciled images of the human hand, were deemed to be about twenty-seven thousand years old, followed by a later period of animal representations dating from about 18,500 B.P.[3]

More startling was the discovery of Chauvet Cave in the gorges of the Ardèche River, a tributary of the Rhone, in southeast France. It was discovered in late 1994, but the find was not made public until about one year later. Here were more than two hundred animal depictions, in the form of both paintings and engravings, of a beauty described as equaling or exceeding the most famous

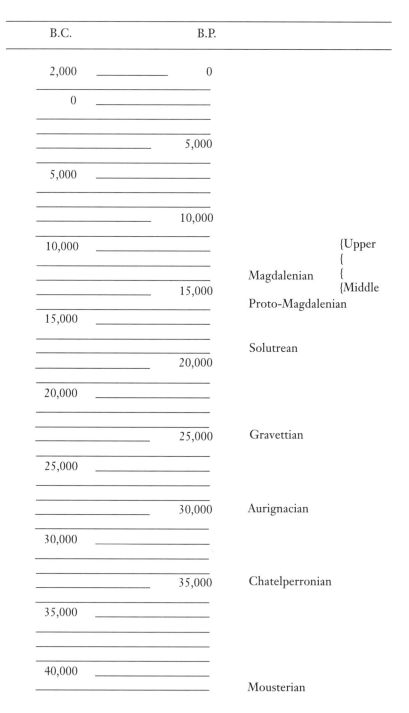

B.C.		B.P.	
2,000	————	0	
0	————		
	————	5,000	
5,000	————		
	————	10,000	
10,000	————		{Upper
	————		{
	————		Magdalenian {
	————	15,000	{Middle
	————		Proto-Magdalenian
15,000	————		
	————		Solutrean
	————	20,000	
20,000	————		
	————	25,000	Gravettian
25,000	————		
	————	30,000	Aurignacian
30,000	————		
	————	35,000	Chatelperronian
35,000	————		
40,000	————		
	————		Mousterian

FIGURE 1. *Chronology of the Upper Paleolithic.*

Paleolithic caves yet known. The style and technique are extremely sophisticated. After stylistic analysis, a tentative dating between seventeen and twenty-one thousand years ago or earlier was considered plausible for such work, which, taking into account its sophisticated style, must be seen as seriously straining against the upper level of Leroi-Gourhan's chronology. More recent testing has led to what *Time* magazine described as a "stone-age bombshell."[4] Radiocarbon tests at three laboratories revealed the work to be not approximately twenty thousand years old, as thought, but thirty thousand or more years of age, a full thirty centuries older than Cosquer and approximately 150 centuries older than the art of the famous cave at Lascaux. And according to Jean Clottes, further tests on torch marks within the cave now help support these results.[5]

The site may also give us an even deeper glimpse into the prehistory of human religion. For in this cave was found the skull of a bear positioned on a rock in the middle of one gallery, suggesting purposeful placement and perhaps an underlying ritual. The discovery echoes an earlier one in a cave at Montespan of a kind of clay altar riddled with holes. According to the author of the find, Norbert Casteret, the skull of a bear cub was lying before the altar. Some commentators see this as suggesting a ritual wherein a decapitated bear's head with the animal's hide still attached was placed upon the altar for ceremonial purposes.[6] In the Gisement du Régourdou very near Lascaux, there is what appears to be a reliquary shrine containing bear skulls dating to a much earlier age, perhaps about 75,000 B.P., and near it was found the buried body of a Neanderthal man.

Joseph Campbell, Johannes Maringer, and others, long before the discovery at Chauvet, tentatively related the Montespan find to a series of discoveries in high mountain grottoes in Switzerland and Germany, where, apparently, Neanderthal peoples had stored bear skulls and certain bones in protected arrangements that suggest a ceremonial use.[7] At one site they were safeguarded behind an intentionally constructed stone wall, some with small stones arranged around them, others were placed on slabs. At another cave site such skulls were arranged in nichelike recesses in the cave wall. The mountain altitude of the grottoes as well as the stone implements and faunal remains suggested that the finds dated back to the late Riss-Würm interglacial period, when these high ranges could have been occupied. If this theory is correct, it would yield a date not later than about 75,000 years ago. While the finds and the conclusions based upon them have had their detractors, they are provocative enough to justify closing this look deep into prehistory with the words of Emil Bächler, the discoverer of several of these cave shrines:

> The purposeful collection and arranged preservation of the cave-bear skulls and long bones behind dry walls *(Trockenmauern)* set up along the sides of the caves; and more especially, the hermetic sealing away of the skulls, either in crudely built stone cabinets, protected by slab coverings, or in repositories walled with flagging, allow for no other conclusion, after the realistic consideration of every possibility, but that we have here to do with some sort of Bear Cult, specifically a Bone-offering Cult, inspired by the mystical thoughts and feelings of an Old Paleolithic population; thoughts involving transcendental, super-sensual ideas. Many ethnological parallels testify to a broad distribution of bone-offering cults in the historic period, especially among the hunting peoples of the north. And so, it seems we may be confronting here what is truly a First, in the elder Paleolithic: the original offering cult, namely, of mankind.[8]

Eliade has shown that the symbolism of bone and skeleton as a return to essence and consequent rebirth is ancient and widespread and, as we shall see, plays an integral role in shamanism. And so does the bear, in certain areas of the world, as the shaman's master animal and as the subject of sacrifice. If Bächler's conclusions are well-founded, perhaps we can glimpse a continuous cultural thread extending back seventy-five thousand years or more.

Let us return to the Upper Paleolithic and the period of the cave art we have been discussing. André Leroi-Gourhan notes with regard to this period that "Paleolithic man seems to have been under the sway of a complicated religious system which induced him to decorate his implements and the walls of his caves with symbolic figures, sometimes realistic, sometimes abstract to an astonishing degree."[9] And he repeatedly emphasizes that this system of belief itself manifests an astounding durative power and continuity of subject matter over vast periods of time. He finds a religious symbolism "absolutely continuous in development from the earliest artistic manifestations down to the end of the Magdalenian period." "The first thesis that we shall defend here," he tells us, "is that the evolution of European Paleolithic art is homogeneous and continuous and that it implies the cultural continuity and homogeneity of the human groups that produced it. One or another type of weapon may have come in from the east or the south and been enthusiastically adopted while the thread of the religious traditions upon which artistic traditions were founded remained unbroken."[10]

Moreover, according to Leroi-Gourhan, this continuity implies its own substantial prehistory. When the first cave sanctuaries were established, both the figurative system and the ideology it represents had already been in existence for several millennia.[11] Therefore, no matter what the final dating of Cosquer or the sophisticated art of Chauvet is ultimately determined to be, each points in two directions. On the one hand, they indicate a substantial, but as yet largely invisible, prehistory during which this complex symbolic system evolved and, on the other hand, a durative power that maintained its hold on the human mind for a period that may once again begin to approximate the Abbé Breuil's four hundred centuries.

Let us say a few brief words about the culture that produced this art and the "complicated religious system" it expresses. The humans primarily responsible for this cultural development have come to be referred to as Cro-Magnon, an early representative of what we deem to be modern Homo sapiens in this part of the world. They were probably approximately the height of today's contemporary human, perhaps more sturdy of build in certain periods and possessed of a slightly larger cranial capacity. At the horizon of the Upper Paleolithic period, Neanderthals gradually gave way to these Cro-Magnons in this area of Western Europe, and the twenty-five thousand years of the Cro-Magnon people's existence saw the development of a vast cultural whole extending from Russia to the Pyrenees. The Cro-Magnons were nomadic hunters with tents constructed of skins and huts from branches or even from mammoth bones. They produced fine foliate flint points and spears, spear throwers, and harpoons. They also made tools of bone, ornaments consisting of perforated teeth and shells, and pendants of finely carved animal bone. They buried their dead with apparent ceremonial purpose, sprinkling the bodies with ochre and dressing them in their clothing, with their finest ornaments and weapons or tools accompanying them to the grave. Burial sites show that the people knew how to make proper garments and moccasins tailored with bone needles. There is evidence that they had early instruments of percussion struck by bone drumsticks as well as flutes made of perforated bird bone. They made fat-burning lamps from naturally hollowed or deliberately shaped stones to light the night and the cave recesses. The discovery of isolated hearths, with no trace of culinary use, outside areas where tents were probably placed at the encampment of Pincevent suggested to Leroi-Gourhan that they may have even possessed a sort of sweat bath.[12]

As with so many ancient cultures, much more concerning these people may have been lost to time. Leroi-Gourhan, not one given to wild flights of fancy, sums up as follows:

> There is good reason to suppose that what has come down to us is the merest shadow of their actual achievement, for we find dozens of palettes for grinding ocher colors in places where there are not wall paintings, and at the strata where artifacts have been excavated Paleolithic ocher is found in fifty-pound deposits. . . . We may in our mind's eye summon up admirably painted skins of horses or bison, marvelous wood sculptures, and dancing and singing people, their bodies painted with intricate designs in black, red, and white—all the panoply and vivacity of the great Magdalenian rituals, the major part of which must remain forever unknown.[13]

Yet, in addition to the cave art, what we still possess is enough to convince us of the Cro-Magnon's cultural sophistication and aesthetic sensitivity. The culture is known for having produced remarkable, highly stylized "Venus" figurines, typically with large, pendulous breasts and a marked emphasis on the abdomen and pelvic regions—often at the expense of other features. The so-called Venus of Willendorf is a well-known example. And at Laussel, in Dordogne, in the area of many well-known cave sites, was found a similar figure carved upon the convex face of a block of limestone with the effect that the central areas of the ample body swell out toward the viewer. Her left hand rests upon her abdomen, and in her right she holds at shoulder level the horn of a bison.

In addition, Cro-Magnons often decorated their implements, weapons, and certain other objects, significant examples of which survive. Chief among these are the so-called pierced staff, also known as the *bâton de commandement;* the spear-thrower, or hooked rod; the spatula; and the half-rounded rod. Opinions differ as to the uses for which these objects were intended. The terminology is imprecise, and such designations are more or less arbitrary because the actual use to which these objects were put is often different from what prehistorians at first supposed, or it is still unknown. For instance, Leroi-Gourhan informs us, the so-called hooked rods may indeed have been spear-throwers, although some seem to lack a "seat" for holding the base of the spear.[14] They are often finely carved and adorned at the top with an animal representation, frequently a horse or, in some instances, a bird. Alexander Marshack points out with regard to the pierced staffs that early theories presumed that these batons were employed either for bending and straightening shafts or to soften leather thongs by running them repeatedly back and forth through the hole. After microscopic analysis, he concluded that some baton holes did show friction wear, yet many other batons were simply too fragile for such rough use.[15] He notes, quoting Paolo Graziosi, that "often the fragility, delicacy and beauty of the decorations seem hardly compatible with practical and frequent use," an observation that appears to be true when one views such artifacts at the museums in Les Eyzies or St. Germain-en-Laye.[16] In each case, the general size and shape of the object, its richness and delicacy of decoration, coupled with its sometimes fragile configuration and its iconography, all strongly suggest a ritual use. In fact, Marshack notes the probable ceremonial use of some of these batons and even tentatively surmises that they "may have been used by the shaman" in some ritual application.[17] Indeed, as we shall see, some of these objects correspond quite closely to the traditional accoutrements of the shaman. Similar batons or rods mark the shaman's vocation in a wide range of areas. The bird-topped staff is an extremely widespread shamanic emblem, and the Siberian shaman sometimes carried a horse-headed baton symbolically related to the horse sacrifice. Marshack notes that certain batons seem to portray the act of animal sacrifice, one of which appears to show dancing shamans in chamois masks and robes participating in what may represent a horse sacrifice.[18] Finally, many of the batons are patently phallic in character (Figures 2a–b and 3), which, barring an obscene use, is hardly compatible with practical application and strongly suggestive of a ceremonial usage.

In this regard, Leroi-Gourhan notes that the spatula-shaped items may have been suspended or fastened to wood or to animal skins, and he compares them to the decorations on costumes and accessories of Siberian shamans.[19] They also resemble the "soul catchers" of the North American shaman. The half-rounded rods are probably surviving halves of rod-shaped objects similar to the shaman's baton. Thus, despite conflicting opinions as to their employment, each form seems to lend itself to a ceremonial and arguably shamanic use. And, according to Leroi-Gourhan, each form of mobiliary art contains the same religious symbolism that we find

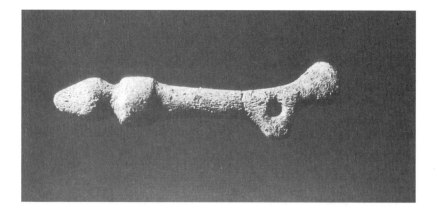

FIGURE 2A. *Phallic baton from Saint-Marcel.*

FIGURE 2B.
*Phallic baton
fragment from
La Madeleine.*

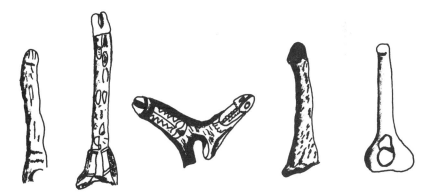

FIGURE 3. *Drawings of phallic batons or baton fragments.*

in the caves. I present several examples here both to show their aesthetic qualities and because they have a significance character-istic of much of this art, which will be developed as we proceed (Figures 4–8A–C).

Before we leave the topic of mobiliary art, we might briefly look at another Upper Paleolithic work found in south-central Germany. Carved from mammoth ivory, it probably dates back thirty-two thousand years and represents a therianthropic figure, a human body with a lion's head or, perhaps, a human being wearing a lion mask. As Alexander Marshack points out, it may well be an early representation of the animal-masked shaman, who will become a recurrent figure in the pages to come (Figure 9).[20]

FIGURE 4. *Upper Paleolithic baton or spear-thrower with top in the shape of a bird, replica of fragment reconstructed by Breuil, Le Mas d'Azil.*

UPPER PALEOLITHIC BATONS OR SPEAR-THROWERS

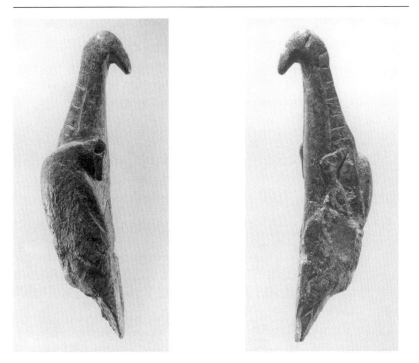

FIGURE 5. *Bird figures, fragment from top of baton, two views. Les Trois Frères.*

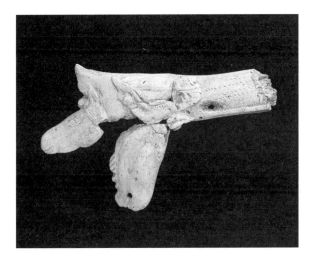

FIGURE 6.
*Two horses' heads
and horse's skull,
fragment, Le Mas
d'Azil. St.
Germain-en-Laye,
Musée des Antiqui-
ties Nationales,
© photo RMN—
Loic Hamon,
photographer.*

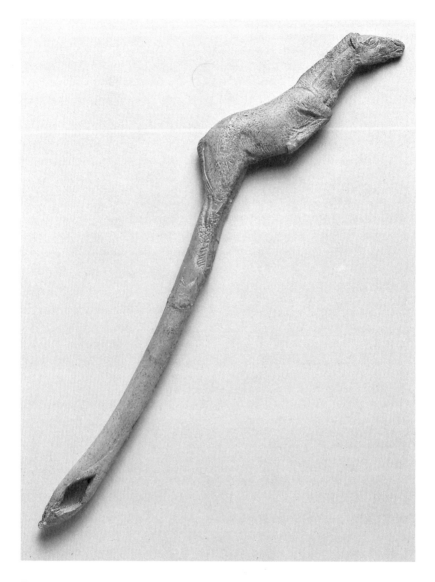

Figure 7. *Leaping horse, Bruniquel. St. Germain-en-Laye, Musée des Antiquities Nationales, © photo RMN—Jean Schormans, photographer.*

FIGURE 8A. *Baton fragment from Lorthet. Deer and salmon engraved on reindeer antler. St. Germain-en-Laye, Musée des Antiquities Nationales, © photo RMN—Loic Hamon, photographer.*

FIGURE 8B. *"Unrolled" representation of a portion of the above baton fragment. © photo RMN— Loic Hamon.*

FIGURE 8C. *Drawing of unrolled baton fragment.*

FIGURE 9. *Ivory carving of lion-headed shamanlike figure, Hohlenstein, Germany.*

It is, however, on the walls of the Ice Age caves—particularly in the recesses symbolic of their deepest revelations—that, I believe, the figure of the shaman makes its first appearance within a matrix of symbols that support its identity. Already we can recognize certain of the lineaments of a familiar figure. To date, a number of anthropomorphic characters have been discovered on the walls of these caves that share, in varying degrees, shamanic characteristics. Some appear to be extremely crude and enigmatic (Figures 10–13), and others are represented only by an anthropomorphic head with eyes and nose but no mouth, figures that have been termed "ghosts" (Figure 14). From others, however, particularly from those most clearly portrayed, certain characteristic features emerge. There is the therianthropic form, suggestive of the interface between the human world and the sacred revelation of the power of nature and the cosmos that the caves symbolize. The figures are often provided with a pair of bovid or cervid horns. Frequently, they are bending forward with what some commentators interpret as faces elongated into animal muzzles, which look like images of masked men. In certain images the mask suggests the head of a bird.

Anthropomorphs of the Caves

Figure 10. *Pech-Merle.*

Figure 11. *Cougnac.*

Figure 12. *Cougnac.*

Figure 13. *Sous-Grand-Lac.*

The forward-bent posture of creatures with animal masks and other theriomorphic features may be suggestive of "dances in imitation of animal movements."[21] Many of the creatures are phallic or ithyphallic, with pronounced or erect penises. We can take the famous "Sorcerer" of Les Trois Frères Cave as a most graphic example (see Figure 22) and the markedly ithyphallic figure at Lascaux (see Figure 23) as another, both of which we shall examine later. Another example from Les Trois Frères (Figure 15) is interesting in its portrayal of a horned, ithyphallic figure dancing on human legs among a throng of animals and apparently playing a bowlike instrument. He manifests all the qualities of the "Lord of Beasts" and is suggestive of an early anticipation of the Orpheus story about the musician who charmed the animal world into an unnatural state of harmony and, shamanlike, rescued souls from the Otherworld. Other interesting figures have been found at Le Gabillou (Figure 16), again at Les Trois Frères (Figure 17), and most recently at Chauvet where, visible from the entrance to a portion of the cave containing magnificent

FIGURE 14. *Ice Age "ghosts."*

Shamans of the Caves

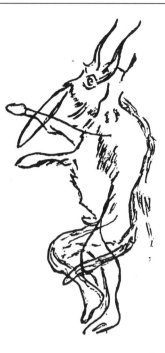

FIGURE 15. *Les Trois Frères.*

FIGURE 16. *Le Gabillou.*   FIGURE 17. *Les Trois Frères.*

animal portrayals, there is a depiction very much resembling those described above. The figure has a bison head or mask and a bisonlike upper body but is clearly shown with the legs of a human being. Its legs are bent, suggesting dance, and it seems to be approaching what appears to be a vulva positioned at the level of its waist. These figures crystallize features that came to characterize the shaman for millennia. He is frequently horned, masked, dancing, ithyphallic, therianthropic, variously combining animal and human traits, master of animals—"a kind of entranced demiurge in direct contact with the animal world," as Mario Ruspoli describes these figures.[22]

But it is the caves themselves that speak most articulately of the presence of what we shall come to recognize as a shamanic structure of consciousness. We remember from chapter 1 that the philosopher Schelling described mythology as "poesy en masse," the product of the genius of mankind speaking universally as one voice over the eons. In such works human creativity reaches back to and reflects its transpersonal formal source, which, passing again and again through the human mind, assumes its very shape. The result is both necessary and universal and manifests a permanence and profundity rivaled only by nature itself.

This process is precisely what we encounter in these caves, for they become images of the deep structures of the human mind in its encounter with the creative force that informs it. It is no wonder, for there is no more striking example of poesy en masse than these caves. Here the generations, sometimes over periods encompassing thousands of years, returned again and again with their art to pay tribute to and through the creative depths of the human preconscious, which, like nature itself, spontaneously creates forms susceptible of impressing the conscious mind as beautiful. Here the human being experienced something in the creative soul akin to the cosmos. And it is here in the shared capacity to produce the beautiful that humans could first give life to a sense of affinity with that force informing the creation, forever bringing forth its teeming abundance of forms into the world. "The artist and the shaman," observe Anne Baring and Jules Cashford, "were probably one and the same, as artists ever since have consistently claimed. Through their magical power to recreate the animal on the walls of the temple caves, they—the artist-shamans—connected the tribe with the source of life that animated both human and animal, becoming themselves vehicles of that source, creators of the living form like the source itself."[23]

Even more importantly, the caves themselves, their natural structure and man-made embellishments, become the precise objective correlative of the shaman's inward journey. They serve as immense *yantras*, meditative and initiatory "tools," which both reflect and effect the transformation of consciousness that lies at the heart of shamanism. In this chapter we shall gain only a preliminary understanding of this aspect of the cave's function, which I hope will gather flesh and life as we proceed through our larger discussions of shamanism. Properly understood, these caves are, indeed, "tools of the gods."

The first point to notice in this regard, and perhaps the most easily overlooked, is the naturally prepossessing quality of the cave itself and the resonances it spontaneously stirs in the human mind. As Joan Vastokas perceptively recognizes, "The visual and evocative context of the site itself cannot be ignored as a source of inspiration. Indeed, in many cases, it is quite likely that the site is iconically prior to and ritually more important than the pictorial images with which it is covered."[24] The caves in the Franco-Cantabrian region are naturally impressive structures, deep, maternal, and mysterious, varying from immense grottoes to barely passable long, dark, narrow, and low passageways. Pillared with stalactites and containing expansive walls often gleaming with white calcite, the cave itself is often an awesome structure naturally symbolic of the penetration of that level of consciousness where man "is made to feel that the very womb of things speaks audibly to him."[25]

In leading the mind from the everyday light world of external experience to its maternal core, the cave journey fosters an inward relocation of the focal point of reality. It opens the inward, or strong, eye to the formative sources of human experience. Over the eons, generations of artists recognized in these inspiring structures the very image of the mind that was penetrating them, and they utilized the caves accordingly. They adeptly put the varied features of individual caves to their most effective use, and one of the most impressive findings in many of the caves is the extent to which their revelations were deliberately placed in the furthest cave recesses or in some grotto or other area that especially lent itself to an experience of the sacred, such as we shall see at Les Trois Frères or Lascaux. Leroi-Gourhan well describes the perilous journey in the Etcheberriko-Karbia cave hidden in the mountains of the Basque country:

> The entrance to the cave is huge and would seem admirably suited for a fine set of wall decorations; but to reach the sanctuary a veritable expedition with full speleological equipment is required. One must toil for more than an hour, crossing little lakes, moving along narrow ledges, and climbing over slippery stalagmites several yards long, before reaching a low entrance that opens on a very narrow tunnel; the tunnel ends at a sheer cliff more than six feet high with no handholds. The sanctuary begins only on the other side of this cliff! It is even harder to get to the end: beyond the first composition, one must climb down a stalagmite fifteen feet high, skirt the edge of a precipice, and work down a twenty-seven foot cleft to find the next composition. The last composition, a horse painted at the bottom of the cleft, is so placed on the edge of a sheer drop that we can only suppose that a colleague was holding the artist by the back of his garments over the void.[26]

Here we might recall Gerard Manley Hopkins's poetic image of the human mind, for this cave journey is, indeed, a trip back into the mind of man.

O the mind, mind has mountains; cliffs of fall
Frightful, sheer, no-man-fathomed. Hold them cheap
May who ne'er hung there.

Narrow tunnels, sheer precipices, the trial of a long, dark, and dangerous journey through the disorienting underground maze must have been calculated to shock the initiate's mind from its normal preoccupations and arouse a condition of expectancy tinged with both awe and dread. Sensory deprivation, temperature extremes, severe exertion, the physical immobility involved in crawling through narrow passages were all entailed in the cave journey and are known to help effect a transformation of human consciousness conducive to inner revelation. When one begins to realize the considerable labor involved in embellishing such barely accessible inner sanctuaries—pigments and other supplies were secured, sometimes from distant sources, scaffolding was hauled into and erected deep within the caves to reach certain elevated areas, and a store of lamps and implements for painting and engraving was established in the cave recesses—one begins to realize the immense and deliberately conceived initiatory significance these caves must have had for the people of this time.

The artists appropriately utilized other features of the caves to elicit other emotional responses. The most characteristic are, of course, the immense grottoes—"the Sistine Chapels of the Paleolithic," as they have been called—wherein exquisite organic form emerges in all its elegance from the eternal silence of the rocky walls (Figures 18–21). The horse, bison, mammoth, ibex, ox, hind, and stag were among the animals most commonly portrayed, but there were also bears, rhinoceroses, lions, and others. It is a mistake to see these portrayals as a crude form of hunting magic. As several authors note, the animals portrayed and the frequency of their portrayal do not reflect the victims of the hunt that typically constituted the Cro-Magnon menu. Moreover, in only a small percentage of the portrayals is there any sign of hunting or killing, and these indications are often ambiguous.

FIGURE 18. *Scene from Rotunda at Lascaux.*

FIGURE 19. *Panel of the Crossed Bison at Lascaux.*

In fact, when one sees these majestic beasts, it is difficult not to view them as a testament to the formal power of the cosmos, an elegance of organic form that everywhere opens upward to the mystery of its source, just as do the august human forms Michelangelo painted twenty thousand years later. The artists employed the contours of the cave's surface in a masterful fashion to achieve a three-dimensional effect. Walls and cave ceilings are often simultaneously decorated. At many sites the beasts are of an imposing size and often elevated on the cave wall to further impress the viewer with their majesty. And while the artist sometimes used a ridge on the cave wall as an illusional ground surface for the animals to tread (as at Lascaux), many simultaneously have what has been termed a "free floating" quality "independent of scene or surface,"[27] a kind of "aerial suspension."[28] Perhaps this is in part achieved by the sinuosity of line, particularly the critical dorsal curve, which gives "the impression that the animal is being projected forward and upward."[29] This free-floating quality combines paradoxically with the earthy volume of the animals, which is itself portrayed against the unchanging rock surface from which they emerge. The result is a form sensed as being halfway between the void of eternity and the world of time and change, a world of self-generating essential form appearing before one's eyes. In this sense, we can agree

Scenes from Axial Gallery at Lascaux

Figure 20.

Figure 21.

with Erich Neumann that "each of these painted animals is a numinosum; it is the embodiment and essence of the animal species. The individual bison, for example, is a spiritual-psychic symbol; he is in a sense the 'father of the bison,' the idea of the bison, the 'bison as such' and this is why he is an object of ritual." The animal portrayals capture "the numinous heart and center" of the creative power and plenitude of the cosmos in its most formidable expression.[30] They are, as we shall see, "power animals" connecting human consciousness with its formal ground.

The artists have in many instances most effectively used the natural structure of the cave to heighten the effect of these hierophanies of power. A number of the caves themselves seem to have been chosen as vehicles of initiation because entering them required crawling through a long, low, and narrow entryway. This is a repeated feature of the caves, as if deliberately intended to impress the initiates, squeezed into the smallest area, that they were indeed entering another realm. Likewise, the inner grottoes of the caves are often reached immediately as the entrant emerges from the sensory deprivation of a long tunnel or narrow passage. We shall see that these observations are particularly true of the entry into the Sanctuary at Les Trois Frères and the Apse and Shaft at Lascaux. Moreover, the experience of this disorienting ordeal and resultant revelation may have been heightened by other effects. As the Abbé Breuil recognizes, "All these complicated hidden passageways lent themselves to extraordinary effects which would be inexplicable to uninitiated novices, who must have been deeply impressed. . . . The effect of songs, cries or other noises, or mysterious objects thrown from no one knows where, was easy to arrange in such a place."[31]

Deep within the caves we do find evidence suggestive of certain rites, particularly those of initiation. Within the Shaft at Lascaux have been found numerous lamps, perhaps left as we might today leave a candle before a sacred altar. At other caves, human footprints have been found. While the Ice Age people of this area of necessity generally wore some form of shoe or moccasin, these imprints almost always revealed a naked foot, perhaps again as some sects remove their shoes in the temples of God. Noting the fact that practically all the footprints appear to have been made by young people, Leroi-Gourhan contends that this argues strongly in favor of some sort of initiation ceremony.[32]

And deep within the cave of Le Tuc d'Audoubert, at the end of a gallery 770 yards from the cave entrance, where there are to be found two coupling bison modeled in clay, is a series of suggestive prints. In the once soft clay of a puddle-shaped depression now covered by a thin film of stalagmite, there are about fifty heel imprints apparently left by one or more youths who visited this sacred area. The form of the prints, made by walking with the weight placed on the heels, has suggested to some viewers rites of initiation. Herbert Kühn, describing his encounter with these curious vestiges of Paleolithic ritual within Le Tuc d'Audoubert, notes, "Since there are no other imprints than those of heels, it is obvious that this must have been a dance-floor, used for some sort of cult-dance . . . [perhaps] a bison dance." Later he relates, "We followed the traces, the footprints. These lead to the rock walls and they lead to five different spots. Everywhere we found phallic engravings, symbols of life, birth, beginning," images deep within the cave of the creative source itself expressed in sexual imagery.[33] And with regard to this rite performed deep within this cave before the sculptures of bison deities, Joseph Campbell likewise asks, "Was this the buffalo dance of some young initiate?"[34] In support of this theory, he draws our attention to the dancing bisonlike figures of Les Trois Frères and Le Gabillou (Figures 15–17). And to this we can now add the evidence of the magnificent dancing shaman in bison form found recently at Chauvet.

In addition, various enigmatic symbols accompany the postulant on his inward journey. In a number of caves, hand images are found in certain locations upon the cave walls. Some are "positive," that is, they are made by placing a hand coated with pigment against a wall, thus leaving an imprint. Most, however, are negative, made by applying or blowing pigment around the hand, leaving its outline, or silhouette, on the cave wall. The best-known group of such images is from the early Gargas Cave, recently dated at approximately 26,800 B.P., where there are 231 red and black hand depictions.[35] Chauvet and Cosquer have also been found to contain numerous images of human hands.

The signficance of the hands remains problematic. They seem to be a testimony to the presence of the Paleolithic visitor, the early signature of individual participation. Touching the mystery of the cave walls implies participation and even union with the mystery and the leaving of the print suggests an enduring participation. This has led some to again see the hand images as evidence of initiation and this impression is supported by the fact that many, by their size, seem to be those of youths, reminding us of the youthful footprints discussed earlier. It is interesting to note that in some shamanic societies, where rock paintings are attributed to the shamans, placing the hand upon them is regarded as an access to power.

At Gargas, the hands portrayed often appear to have fingers or portions of them cut off. This is also true of Cosquer, another early site, and several other sites. This naturally suggests ritual mutilation or dismemberment, and some commentators have supported this position. Such rites are consistent with and complement the symbolism of the cave journey as a form of self-mortification and sacrifice of the former or profane self in the process of initiation. With regard to the negative hand images, however, Leroi-Gourhan and others point out that it may be that the hand was placed against the wall with a finger or fingers folded downward and then stenciled in silhouette by blowing pigments around this configuration. While this may have been the technique used, at least at times, it does not help us explain the meaning of the symbolism. Rituals of dismemberment are common throughout the world's shamanic traditions, particularly in their rites of initiation. Such dismemberment can include severing the fingers at the various joints, the results of which appear to have been memorialized in the rock paintings of some societies. If the hands do not reflect actual mutilation, it may well be that they are reflective of an older or perhaps more esoteric practice undergone exclusively by shamans and only symbolically undertaken, in mimesis of the original act, by the initiate— just as some cultures today symbolically shoulder the cross in an Easter passion without submitting to crucifixion or as ancient kings adroitly found substitute practices for ritual regicide, which was then carried out only symbolically.

Eliade recognizes shamanic rites of dismemberment as symbols of initiation and of the transcending of the "old self," a part of which is symbolically sacrificed and left behind. This sacrifice is the prelude to a larger initiatory process involving a return to the well-spring of the creation and a rejuvenative rebirth from the source of form and power. This sense of participation in the all-creative source helps explain another puzzling aspect of the caves. It seems that many who entered paid tribute to and attempted to participate in the creative power that gave birth to the majestic animal forms portrayed within the cave. One of the most regularly encountered features of the caves studied by Leroi-Gourhan was what he termed "the panel of unfinished outlines," areas covered with sketchy, tangled figures, various shapes and animal forms, often incomplete but sometimes very delicately executed. They tend to be present in the vicinity of the first large composition of animal paintings in each cave, and if there are several compositions, there is generally one such panel in each area. In some caves they accompany the images of hands, and at others they adjoin areas of rock worn and polished by repeated rubbing. Leroi-Gourhan informs us that at Lascaux they seem to have been begun very early, additions being made throughout the life of the sanctuary. He concludes that since they are to be found even in the earliest decorated caves, their presence was certainly related to the early community's religious life and to the very conception of the sanctuary.[36] They imply rites in which figures of the same type as those in the large compositions, but often executed with much less skill, were superimposed one atop the other generation after generation. While many portrayals evidence an inartistic hand, at times the figures are gnomically reduced to their simplest expression, the cervicodorsal curve. Because this sinuous curve, shaped like a horizontal *S* with one loop considerably larger than the other, forms a recurrent structural motif for many of the animal representations over much of the long period of this art, this minimalist reproduction becomes almost a graphic shorthand representation of the most essential forms of the cave art. It captures the essence of formal creation, a sense of the very rudiments of form emerging from the cave walls. But whether crudely copied or adroitly suggested with an almost Picasso-like economy of form, each figure is an offering by virtue of which all who entered the cave paid tribute to and participated in the same power that generated the arresting forms of the great paintings on the cave walls.

Another enigma of the inward journey is the puzzling series of "signs" that adorn the cave walls. The entrant is confronted with rows of red or black dots, grid shapes, lines, parallels, ovals, rect-angles, branching and nested convergent lines, and other inten-tionally constructed compositions. At first these markings were thought to be primitive images of huts, animal snares, weapons, and so on. The long and painstaking work of Leroi-Gourhan, how-ever, revealed the rudiments of a primitive symbolic system com-posed of abstract signs. So impressed was Leroi-Gourhan with the system that shortly before his death he is reported to have said, "At Lascaux I really believed they had come very close to an alphabet."[37] He saw these signs as being of great significance, "the most fascinating area of Paleolithic art, the one which contradicts all customary ideas as to the simple-minded visual naturalism of the mammoth hunters."[38] He considered it a mark of their ad-vanced intelligence that they could work simultaneously with two systems of expression, one employing realistic representation and the other abstract forms. His careful analysis revealed that the signs, particularly the dots and short strokes, were purposely placed at the beginnings of the decorated areas of the caves, in their deep recesses after the representational figures came to an end, and in areas of transition between different topographical features of the cave structure, such as narrow passages and the entrance to cham-bers.[39] This has led commentators to speculate that the forms rep-resent phosphenes, light patterns naturally produced within the eye that accompany transformations of consciousness at the early stages of hallucinogenic experience or trance. We shall say more of this experience later.

For Leroi-Gourhan, these patterns had a different significance (though, in fact, one that is ultimately compatible with and perhaps reinforces the phosphene hypothesis). "Statistically," he observed, "they proved to belong to two sets: one of single dots, rows of dots, short strokes and barbed-signs; the other of ovals, triangles, rect-angles and brace-shaped signs." Drawing his cue from what he re-garded as very early examples of cave art and from mobiliary art, where sexual representations are quite apparent and frequent in occurrence, he concluded that they were divided into masculine and feminine groupings. "When each set of signs was analyzed separately, it leaped to the eye that the ovals, triangles, and quadrangular signs were all more or less abstract variations on the vulvas which appear among the earliest works of prehistoric art. As for the dots and strokes, it was obvious that they are male signs, although their degree of abstraction is beyond any simple similarity of form."[40]

Moreover, these signs were constructed in patterns of complementarity, the two sets matching and balancing each other throughout the caves. This finding was consistent with two additional sets of symbols Leroi-Gourhan had carefully studied. He found that the animal representations employed a similar sexual complementarity, based, however, on animal type rather than the depiction of gender. And he likewise observed:

> The cave as a whole does seem to have had a female symbolic character, which would explain the care with which narrow passages, oval-shaped areas, clefts, and the smaller cavities are marked in red, even sometimes painted entirely in red. This would also explain why these particular topographic features are marked with signs from the male set, which thereby become complementary. A few dots in the last small chamber of an immense cave then take on the same significance as the more complex groupings on the big panels, and this would account for the care with which, almost invariably, Paleolithic men placed some mark at the cave's innermost recess.[41]

Here we might also note that images of vulvas have been found in many caves, and we might also bring to mind the phallic images encountered by Kühn surrounding the coupling bison deep within the cave at Le Tuc d'Audoubert. More generally, the symbolism of the maternal cave would logically complement the ithyphallic quality that we have noticed as characteristic of the shamanlike creatures of the caves and the costumed shamans who may have led its initiatory penetration, perhaps carrying the phallic ceremonial batons we earlier discussed.

For some commentators, these symbols have suggested a sort of fertility cult employed to increase the animal species, and no doubt this may be an aspect of the symbolism. If it was a fertility cult, however, the fertility had a cosmogonic scope, for the hieratic aspects of the cave animals suggest that they are the animals of eternity and not of time. We know that one of the oldest and most widespread mythologems represents the cosmic creation in terms of balanced, complementary sexual opposites. Myths of the sundering of a primal androgyne (Ymir or Purusha), of the father-mother of the gods (such as the Aztec Ometéotl), or of male and female world parents (such as An and Ki in Sumer, Geb and Nut in Egypt, or Rangi and Papa among the Maori) are familiar examples. We might also note the coupling deities of the Hindu or Buddhist Tantric pantheons who give rise to the world, or yin and yang, which give birth to the ten thousand things—familiar expressions of a type whose examples could be multiplied almost endlessly. All represent the expression of the self-generating form that is the mystery behind the majesty of the creation, which is here so vividly symbolized in the essential forms of the animal world. One is reminded of the Bṛihadāraṇyaka Upanishad of ancient India, which speaks of the primal androgyne, Prajā-pati, who at the beginning of time becomes differentiated into male and female principles that proceed to create the cosmos, similarly symbolized in the forms of the great animal species:

> She [the now separate female principle] thought, "How can he unite with me after having produced me from himself?" Well, let me hide myself. She became a cow, the other became a bull and was united with her and from that cows were born. The one became a mare, the other a stallion. The one became a she-ass, the other a he-ass and was united with her; and from that one-hoofed animals were born. The one became a she-goat, the other a he-goat, the one became a ewe, the other became a ram and was united with her and from that goats and sheep were born. Thus, indeed, he produced everything, whatever exists in pairs, down to the ants.
>
> He knew, I indeed am this creation for I produced all this. Therefore he became the creation. He who knows this as such comes to be in that creation of his.[42]

Radhakrishnan glosses this last portion as, "He who knows this becomes himself a creator like Prajā-pati," the very source of creation. Or, as Joseph Campbell translates the last line, "One who thus understands becomes, himself, truly a creator in this creation."[43]

Thus, in an ancient vision, all creation proceeds through paired opposites emanating from the source of the creation itself.

Conversely, the penetration of these complementary principles represents a return to the cosmogonic source. When we understand the complementarity of yin and yang, we are told, the ten thousand things return to their origin, which they have actually never left. As Eliade has repeatedly shown, the shaman's journey is itself a return to the cosmogonic source. In the process, he unites with and transcends the duality symbolized by the sexual principles. "For the shaman unites in himself the two contrary principles; and since his own person constitutes a holy marriage, he symbolically restores the unity of Sky and Earth [the world parents], and consequently assures communication between Gods and men."[44] In penetrating the maternal cave with its eloquent forms that everywhere testify to their source, the ithyphallic shaman and his initiates are symbolically returning to the miracle and mystery of the generative source of all form. He becomes the conduit of that plenitude and power with which he is united, "truly a creator in this creation." The shaman taps the common formative force that animates both the cosmos and the human mind, especially, as Schelling and Jung point out, in its artistic and mythic productions.

It is in the far recesses, the deep structures of the cave, that we typically find the revelation of the shamanic presence. We may take the Sanctuary at Les Trois Frères as a most striking example. Herbert Kühn describes his approach to this *sanctum sanctorum:*

> The ground is damp and slimy, we have to be very careful not to slip off the rocky way. It goes up and down, then comes a very narrow passage about ten yards long through which you have to creep on all fours. And then again there come great halls and more narrow passages. In one large gallery are a lot of red and black dots, just those dots.

After passing this gallery, the ordeal of another tunnel commences:

> The tunnel is not much broader than my shoulders, nor higher. I can hear the others before me groaning and see how very slowly their lamps push on. With our arms pressed close to our sides, we

wriggle forward on our stomachs, like snakes. The passage, in places, is hardly a foot high, so that you have to lay your face right on the earth. I felt as though I were creeping through a coffin. You cannot lift your head; you cannot breathe. . . . And so, yard by yard, one struggles on: some forty-odd yards in all. Nobody talks. The lamps are inched along and we push after. I hear the others groaning, my own heart is pounding, and it is difficult to breathe. It is terrible to have the roof so close to one's head. And the roof is very hard: I bump it, time and again. Will this thing never end? Then, suddenly, we are through, and everybody breathes. It is like a redemption.[45]

And indeed it is a form of "redemption." They find themselves standing in a colossal hall, and letting their light travel along the walls, they see vividly depicted those beasts who roamed this area of France thousands and thousands of years ago. There are mammoth and rhinoceros, bison, wild horse, bear, wild ass, reindeer, wolverine, and musk ox as well as smaller beasts not often seen upon the walls of prehistoric caverns—snowy owls, hares, even fish. "No modern artist can do anything better—or even as good," Kühn proclaims.[46]

This is the chamber known as the Sanctuary of Les Trois Frères. It consists of a bell-shaped alcove containing panel after panel of figures, a welter of swarming life-forms upon the cave walls. It is the heart of the entire cave system at Les Trois Frères, the culmination of the cave's series of decorations. Here also, in close proximity, is a panel of unfinished outlines. And near the top of the alcove, on a ceiling that dominates the Sanctuary with its magnificent animal portrayals, we encounter the figure of the "Sorcerer" of Les Trois Frères (Figure 22). "It is not surprising to find so hypersymbolic a figure on the highest and innermost point of a chamber that is decorated with hundreds of figures, in the arrangement of which Magdalenian symbolism is displayed with a richness unattained elsewhere," Leroi-Gourhan observes.[47]

Here he stands some fifteen feet above the level of the floor, ominously watching—a most numinous image, as if presiding over all. This thirty-inch-high figure variously known as the Sorcerer of Les Trois Frères, the God of the Cave, or the Animal Master is painted in black paint to set him apart from the other denizens of

FIGURE 22. *"Sorcerer" of Les Trois Frères.*

this inner world. As various commentators have pointed out, he seems to possess the antlers and ears of a stag; the round staring eyes of an owl, or perhaps a lion; animal forepaws; feline genitals; and a horse- or wolflike tail. The dancing feet, however, are distinctly human, and as he rises to a semierect position, his penetrating eyes look out from behind what appears to be a human beard, though some believe the lionlike eyes suggest a mane. Among the animals portrayed directly beneath this creature is a dying bear punctured by many weapons. As Campbell observes, because the other animals portrayed in this area are not wounded, "this bear is evidently in a special symbolic role."[48]

What are we to make of the sudden epiphany of this part-human and part-animal hybrid cast against a panoply of the animal kingdom deep within the maternal cave? If we are able to believe that the deep structures of the human brain manifest a certain continuity over the millennia—and this is a central premise of this book—then the work of the psychologist Carl Jung might aid our inquiry. Jung found that "'divine' beings, part animal, part human" make frequent appearances in dreams and analysis as well as in the world's mythologies.[49] In a manner parallel to the sudden revelation of this figure at the end of the long, confining tunnel, as "archetypes" such figures appear spontaneously, with their own necessity and autonomy, and are laden with spiritual significance. They are symbols of transformation that lead the libido in certain directions, depending upon the "preparedness" of the conscious mind for such revelation. As part human and part animal, such therianthropic images represent the borderline between the conscious mind and the unconscious, the personal and the transpersonal. Jung further points out that the "unconscious, . . . as the matrix of consciousness, has a maternal significance," hence the propriety of this manifestation within the cave interior.[50] Lancelot Law Whyte summarizes this insight in a manner that highlights its significance within the context of a cave art celebratory of natural creation. He points out:

> In the unconscious mind lies the contact of the individual with the universal powers of nature. The springs of human nature lie in the unconscious, for it links the individual with the universal, or at least the organic. This is true, whether it is expressed as the union of the soul with the divine, or as the realm which links the moments of human awareness with the background of organic processes within which they emerge. But the fascination of the idea arises because it is felt to be the source of power, the home of the *élan* which moves us.[51]

Jung termed this point in the human psyche the "psychoid" level. According to Ira Progoff:

> In Jung's scheme of thought, the *psychoid* level of the unconscious represents the point at which the psyche is so close to the animal world as not yet to be differentiated from it. It still is directly connected to the realm of nature in its mode of functioning, and it is thus the aspect of the human organism that can be most directly experienced as part of nature. . . . Our individual contact with the

psychoid level of our human nature involves an inner experience of the deep ground of the Self experienced subjectively within ourselves and also objectively as part of the whole realm of nature.[52]

And as we have repeatedly noted, it is precisely this affinity with the creative source that these caves of power represent. As such, the part-human and part-animal archetype is a "uniting symbol," bringing the human consciousness into fruitful contact with its deeper roots. The effect of the experience of such symbols, for the initiated mind, is salvific. On the one hand, the integration it represents is a tapping of a source of psychic power, a power experienced as continuous with "the whole realm of nature." On the other hand, it points to the transpersonal world beyond our strictly individuated existence, a world characterized by universal or essential form.

We can now recognize how this uniting symbol in the cave recesses parallels Eliade's description of the cosmogonic function of the shaman as uniting the world creative polarities and in this way returning to the source of creation. The ithyphallic shaman's penetration of the maternal cave of power is a return to the deep structures of the human mind, the formal source of our experience, and, at the same time, to the cosmogonic source. For the revelation of the cave art is that the two sources, human and cosmic, have concentric centers and that their shared center is inwardly encountered and experienced by opening the eye of the soul, the inward-pointing strong eye. Here human creative power is experienced as continuous with nature's creative power and the formative force that infuses the cosmos. The caves, like the shaman himself, are conduits of power, the power of the psychoid realm. And they are simultaneously the portals to the transpersonal realm marked by the shaman's return to origin and to the enduring reality of the deep structures of the mind to which he is traditionally carried in trance. Thus, we should not be surprised if the central revelation of perhaps the most important of all the caves might indeed be an entranced shaman.

Within the famous cave at Lascaux lies a precipitous shaft approximately sixteen feet deep, the most inaccessible point in the cave, generally thought to have been reached by Ice Age visitors only with the aid of a rope. Herein lies one of the most controversial visions in all prehistoric art (Figure 23). Mario Ruspoli describes his encounter with this scene: "It is impossible for someone who has never descended to this point to imagine the dense, mystic, impressive atmosphere that reigns in a place so charged with occult power. One experiences a sort of metaphysical shock and begins to speak in a hushed voice, almost a whisper, while the light travels along the vertical walls and reveals the famous scene."[53]

As was the case at Les Trois Frères, the cave has been well employed to prepare, or condition, the mind for this parietal epiphany. The visitor will have already passed through the Rotunda, with its signs and great scenes of animal art and myth, and perhaps traversed the Axial Gallery as well. He or she will have crawled on all fours through the long and low fifty-five-foot Passageway area, with its sloping floor of claylike sand surrounded by white calcite walls adorned with painted polychrome figures and a tangle of numerous other obscure engravings. This confining passage opens suddenly to a more spacious area, which marks the juncture of the portions

FIGURE 23. *The Shaft at Lascaux.*

of the cave appropriately referred to as the Apse and Nave in tribute to their sacred nature. "The Apse and the Shaft (which is an extension of it) form the strangest and most mysterious part of the cave, and the part which remains most vividly in the imagination. It is the place with the most signs, images and symbols—though these are sometimes very difficult to make out. It is also the most sacred place in the cave," Ruspoli tells us. "Here ritual ceremonies were performed, though all trace of them has vanished with the passing of thousands of years."[54] Here, at this sacred center we again find, as we would expect, a panel of unfinished outlines or scrawls where there are crowded together hundreds of small engraved figures along with an array of various signs. These figures, Leroi-Gourhan notes, must have been begun very early, with additions having been made throughout the life of the sanctuary.[55] More than one thousand engravings line the Apse. And in the Shaft have been found items that either were witness to ritual ceremonies or were votive offerings: lamps, charcoal, a few fragments of bone and antler, and flint blades and spears decorated with signs.[56] Despite its inaccessibility, the Shaft "was much frequented and was apparently the most sacred place in the sanctuary, rather like the crypt of an ancient church."[57]

The heart of the mystery, however, lies with the figures depicted within the Shaft. Here we find a great bull bison, apparently severely wounded by a spear, with its entrails protruding from the wound. He is juxtaposed with a prostrate man. The man is crudely drawn, as are many anthropomorphs in prehistoric cave art, but has several salient and curious features. He wears what appears to be a bird mask, and his hands resemble the feet of a bird. His phallus is emphasized, and it is erect. An object that may be a throwing stick lies at his feet, and beside him is a staff or baton that has the image of a bird at the end with a head much like that of the man. There is also a rhinoceros that seems to be walking away from the scene. The six dots behind the rhinoceros's tail have been thought to indicate defecation, but similar arrangements of dots in other portions of the cave imply that this is a sign, though its meaning is obscure. The significance of the rhinoceros is much debated, and many think it bears no relation to the bison and man complex.

With regard to the bison and the prostrate man, opinions differ widely. All recognize that it must have had a central and probably

sacred significance, but as to the nature of this significance no consensus has been reached. Leroi-Gourhan sees it as a depiction of a
man knocked to the ground by the bison, perhaps a scene with
some underlying mythological or allegorical meaning now opaque
to us.[58] In support, he points to analogous depictions in mobiliary
and cave art that constitute what he has referred to as the "wounded
man" theme. The Abbé Breuil similarly sees it as a depiction of a
man killed during a hunt, perhaps by the departing rhinoceros.[59]
These interpretations, however, fail to explain effectively some of
the most obvious features of the scene. The bison is wounded, not
the man. Why does the man have birdlike features? What is the
purpose of the bird-topped staff that is so clearly depicted? Why
does he lie with his penis erect? And precisely what is it about this
scene that would justify its central position of veneration within
the holy of holies of this cave shrine?

Mary Settegast makes the provocative suggestion that the scene
has cosmogonic implications—the world-creating death of the first
man and the primordial animal, later to be represented by the bull
rather than the bull bison. She calls to our attention Gayomart and
the bull as well as the Vedic Purusha, whose name, she contends,
combines the words for man and bull.[60] Likewise, it is tempting to
see this panel in the womb of the cave as the remote nucleus for the
various dead and reborn gods with their association with the bull—
Dionysus, Osiris and the Apis bull, or the twice-born Shiva and
Nandi. But this must remain only temptation, for while general
cosmogonic features do, I believe, inhere in the scene, they lie within
a different context, and the complex of symbols surrounding this
portrayal seems to point more immediately in another direction.

We might take our first cue from the bird-headed staff that lies
next to the prostrate man. As we shall see such a staff is a widespread symbol of the shamanic vocation. And, indeed, some observers believe, along with Joseph Campbell, that this is a shaman
"rapt in a shamanistic trance."[61] Marshack edges tentatively in this
direction: "I have suggested that it is possible that the composition
represents a shaman in trance, but there is no proof."[62] By examining this image in light of the world's shamanic traditions, however,
as we shall do in chapter 6, proof can indeed be found, though of a
different kind from that which Marshack was seeking. And from

this perspective the grammar of symbols in this and the other caves again becomes articulate and bespeaks a consistent vision. The general initiatory structure of the cave journey, the location for the depiction of this scene in the Shaft, the staff, the man's erection, the bird-man himself, the slain bison, the maternal womb of the cave, the symbolism of the signs, and the surrounding animal forms all begin to coalesce and draw into their orbit related symbols that not only spell out a consistent vision of the structure of shamanic consciousness but also display a truly striking durative power existing in structurally and functionally parallel forms worldwide and into our own century.

In the chapters to follow we shall examine these structures in a larger context with the twofold purpose of amplifying our understanding of the specific symbolism of the Paleolithic caves and of illustrating and understanding a symbolism as old as modern Homo sapiens. In the next chapter we shall examine the symbolism of the inward journey as it is expressed in many forms of shamanism. We shall then note the manner in which it leads to the transpersonal reality represented by the luminous cave as a portal to the Otherworld. Next we shall see how these same symbols endure in structurally and functionally parallel forms in certain examples of shamanism found around the globe in witness of and tribute to the uncanny lasting power of the shamanic symbolic structure, which "in profundity, permanence and universality is comparable only with Nature herself." And, finally, ourselves initiated into the world of these symbolisms, we shall be able to perceive the overall shamanic structure of consciousness so well reflected in these ancient caves and to understand the placement, structure, and function of the symbols in the mysterious Shaft at Lascaux.

Chapter 3

THE INWARD JOURNEY

"A BREAK WITH THE UNIVERSE OF DAILY LIFE"

*Behind our existence lies something else that becomes
accessible to us only by our shaking off the world.*
Arthur Schopenhauer

With this background we begin the shamanic journey to the interior realm that the Ice Age caves so well symbolized. Appropriately, the summons to the shamanic vocation traditionally comes from within, and it typically speaks to the shaman with a compelling necessity. This sense of a necessity that cannot be refused often manifests itself in the experience of being "called," or chosen, for the profession by inner forces. Roger Walsh aptly employs a passage from the Gospel of Thomas to capture this sense of almost fatal election in the shaman.

If you bring forth what is within you,
What you bring forth will save you.
If you do not bring forth what is within you,
What you do not bring forth will destroy you.

While the shamanic novice may sometimes appear aberrant and alienated from his general community, his condition everywhere manifests a certain teleology that over the eons his community has learned to channel and harness as a special gift and a sacred force. Mary Schmidt tells us, "In the tribes I have examined, one aspect receives consensus, that shamans 'are the unusually gifted or perceptive members of their community.'"[1] They are, according to Eliade, "those who experience the sacred with greater intensity than the rest of the community—those who, as it were, incarnate the sacred, because they live it abundantly, or rather 'are lived' by the religious 'form' that has chosen them (gods, spirits, ancestors, etc.)."[2]

The tension of being chosen, being wrenched from the solace of an easy conformity within a tightly solidified community, and at the same time a sense of something deeper, something that opens fissures within that reality, often precipitates a crisis. It is of the essence of shamanism that by its own inner dynamic it turns crisis to cure and in so doing reveals the mind's own curative powers. There is a certain inevitability, the vague presentiment of an inner lawfulness not to be resisted, at the inception of the shaman's journey. As Schmidt explains to us:

> No doubt the calling alarms a child, and many would be reluctant to shoulder this demanding gift. Social isolation, a plague of odd thoughts, and the likelihood of personality alteration all characterize the fledgling shaman's experience, yet there is an inevitability about the movement. Shamans-to-be encounter raw glimpses of something numinous and demanding, some threat or promise in their own landscape of dreams.[3]

Heraclitus's observation that "man's character is his fate" or "his demon" holds particularly true for the shaman. Indeed, the shaman may be our earliest incarnation of the demonic man, and understanding this ancient concept may help us understand the shaman's character and his calling. "It is not what outwardly befalls a man but what he fundamentally *is* that constitutes his demon," Ernst Cassirer tells us.[4] Paradoxically, however, the demonic has always also characteristically referred to intensely experienced inner realities that seem to come from another world. It represents the "inexorable bond between the human life and the beyond," according to Paul Friedländer, "a realm 'intermediate' between the human level and the divine, a realm that, because of its intermediate position, 'unites the cosmos with itself.'"[5] In this sense, those who call the shaman and lead his initiation are at the same time both inner forces and denizens of the Otherworld: spirits, deceased ancestors, or departed shamans. Even his living masters work from the inside outward, if you will, galvanizing emergent realities innate in the shaman that it is his destiny to bring forth.

A Tungus shaman of Siberia, Semyonov Semyon, tells of his initial experience as follows:

> When I shamanize, the spirit of my deceased brother Ilya comes and speaks through my mouth. My shaman forefathers, too, have forced me to walk the path of shamanism. Before I commenced to shamanize, I lay sick for a whole year: I became a shaman at the age of fifteen. The sickness that forced me to this path showed itself in a swelling of my body and frequent spells of fainting. When I began to sing, however, the sickness usually disappeared.[6]

Here the crisis manifests itself in actual physical illness. And it finds its resolution, as it must ineluctably, in the shamanic vocation.

Such occurrences are by no means rare and can be related to the sense of being predestined or compelled to be a voice for the sacred. Often the call comes in the form of premonitory dreams. These are dreams that, as Eliade points out, may become mortal illnesses if they are not correctly understood and readily obeyed:

> An old shaman is called in to interpret them; he orders the patient to follow the injunctions of the spirits that provoked the dreams. "Usually a person is reluctant to become a shaman, and assumes his powers and follows the spirit's bidding only when he is told by the other shamans that otherwise death will result."[7]

Shamans throughout the world report that refusal of the call results in sickness or even death. "A shamanic vocation is obligatory," Eliade emphasizes; "one cannot refuse it."[8] "When I had no more strength left to suffer, finally I agreed to become a shaman," one shaman explained. "And when I became a shaman, I changed entirely."[9] Likewise, our Tungus shaman tells us, "My shaman forefathers, too, have forced me to walk the path of shamanism," and he relates his illness to the period prior to his accepting the call. The call of the forefathers and the illness are one and the same until the summons is acknowledged, for it is also the "sickness that forced me to this path," and it is similarly the voice of the sacred that is curative. Finally, it is the inwardly experienced forces of the interior world that are the impetus to his shamanizing, a phenomenon that we shall encounter repeatedly. When he shamanizes, the voice of his brother, Ilya, speaks through his mouth, and it is the dead shaman forefathers who compel him to his profession. From the beginning it is this interior world that summons the shaman.

With respect to receiving the shamanic vocation, Eliade informs us that there are traditionally three ways to become a shaman: first, by spontaneous vocation—a "call" or "election"; second, by hereditary transmission of the shamanic profession; and, third, by personal "quest" or, more rarely, by the will of the clan.[10] The sense of being selected by the sacred, however, persists in each. In the case of hereditary transmission of the shamanic vocation, it is the souls of the ancestral shamans who choose a young man in the family.[11] In societies where the personal quest is a predominant feature, the Sioux chief Maza Blaska tells us:

To the Holy Man comes in youth the knowledge that he will be holy. The Great Mystery makes him know this. Sometimes it is the Spirits who tell him. When a spirit comes, it would seem as though a man stood there, but when this man has spoken and goes forth again, none may see whither he goes. Thus the Spirits. With the spirits the Holy Man may commune always, and they teach him holy things.[12]

Thus the postulant of the sacred is summoned to his inward journey, a journey at first purposefully disorienting, meant to loosen the hold of the "outward Creation" on the novice and effect a relocation of the focal point of reality. The shaman travels from the familiar light world to one initially dark and forbidding, but one that is paradoxically meant to become the source of a more significant illumination. And here we remember the caves we discussed as the objective correlative of the shamanic experience—the perilous disorienting initial phase of crawling through utter darkness, reduced to slithering serpentlike to an unknown interior destination, and the carefully devised conditioning, lowering the threshold of consciousness through exhaustion, sensory deprivation, and potentially other techniques conducive to revelation while simultaneously exposing the postulant to the mythic images and signs preparatory to a final epiphany, a destination signaled by a radical expansion of the cave confines and an equally radical expansion of consciousness. These experiences parallel the traditional phases of the inceptional period of the shaman's training, his initiation or the initial steps of the shamanic quest.

The first moments of the inward journey both express symbolically and help effect what Eliade refers to as "a break with the universe of daily life" and initiate the transformation of consciousness that is essential to shamanic realization.[13] Eliade tells us that whether the shaman becomes such by spontaneous vocation, hereditary transmission, or personal quest, "a shaman is recognized as such only after having received two kinds of instruction. The first is ecstatic (e.g., dreams, visions, trances); the second is traditional (e.g., shamanic techniques, names and functions of the spirits, mythology and genealogy of the clan, secret language)."[14] There are two correlative thrusts of attack in this first phase of the training process; one aims to break the bonds by which traditional assumptions about reality, both physical and social, hold the would-be shaman and the other to "dissolve" the profane structure of personality and give birth to another of an entirely different orientation.

In her article "Crazy Wisdom: The Shaman as Mediator of Realities," Mary Schmidt emphasizes that as part of the training process the shaman enters a liminal stage often found in initiatory structures worldwide, where the neophyte experiences separation from traditional forms and categories of ordinary social life.[15] Men dress as women, wear animal heads, and otherwise juxtapose the ordinary with the extraordinary. The result is that "the familiar categories for organizing experience have broken down and do not fit the situation. . . . In the liminal state, such social categories are juxtaposed in odd ways so that the child initiate becomes aware of them as merely mental constructs."[16]

"When the surface has been cleared, things can grow out of the depths," as Jung once declared. No longer thrall to the pedestrian, the candidate begins to realize that there may be other structures of reality competing with and perhaps more significant than the manner in which man traditionally organizes his world. He perceives that these everyday structures may in fact be "merely mental constructs" not without a validity of their own, but paralleled by alternate forms of reality. As Michael Harner points out, the shaman may recognize the everyday world of ordinary reality and at the same time a realm of the real, and even "more real," revealed by the shaman's newly acquired form of consciousness.[17] The shaman "exists in two worlds," says Åke Hultkrantz, "and acknowledges the validity of both, his mastery deriving from his ability not to confuse the two."[18] "What is real for me is not real for you," points out another shaman.[19]

The shaman increasingly learns to look inward for the source of reality, a reality that he begins to experience as continuous with the formal principles of the cosmos. We remember from chapter 1 that archaic man generally does not share our own prejudice, which tends automatically to vest the material creation with an ontological priority. A philosophically inclined shaman might agree with Schopenhauer that the brain no more "learns from experience" how to form a world than the blood corpuscles learn from experience how to take carbon dioxide from the body's tissues and void it in the lungs. The seedbed of experience is within and its principles are innate. The preconscious formal principles of the mind form the rudiments of our experience and hand the product over to consciousness. The essential aspects of this process are as unconscious as the heartbeat and normally hidden from our awareness. The shaman, however, attains this knowledge not through philosophy, but immediately through his experience in ecstatic training, that is, through vision, dream, and trance, which opens the inward eye and penetrates the preconscious mind.

The world's shamanic cultures have traditionally employed several psychological and physiological techniques to foster this process. Richard Noll tells us that "many of them are considered extreme by our culture's standards: pain stimulation, hypoglycemia and dehydration, forced hypermotility such as long periods of dancing, acoustic stimulation (particularly drumming), seclusion and restricted mobility, sleep deprivation, hyperventilation and the ingestion of hallucinogens. Practicing any of these techniques would induce an alteration in one's state of consciousness."[20] Opinions differ as to the role played by drugs in inducing the transformations of consciousness essential to the shaman's journey. Eliade contends that narcotic use is a vulgar substitute for "pure" trance, a mechanical and debased method of reproducing ecstasy that attempts to imitate a model that is both earlier and exists on another plane of reference.[21] Despite this contention, however, among historical shamanic communities the use of drugs does, indeed, seem widespread, and drug-induced, or perhaps drug-aided, transformations appear to be more important and more prevalent than was once believed. In *Flesh of the Gods*, Peter T. Furst and his contributing authors offer convincing proof of the use of various narcotic and hallucinogenic substances in many different shamanic cultures and over long periods of time. We shall have more to say about this later, but we wish to draw attention briefly to the observations of Weston La Barre. He notes that "ecstatic-visionary shamanism is, so to speak, *culturally programmed for an interest in hallucinogens and other psychotropic drugs,*" and he postulates the very great antiquity of man's ritual utilization of plants with psychotropic properties, going back to Mesolithic and even Paleolithic times, based upon evidence of their early and wide diffusion in both the Old World and the New.[22] Thus, it now appears to be clear that often the shaman employs not only the various techniques mentioned in relation to traditional and ecstatic modes of training but also various hallucinogenic substances to access progressively deeper and deeper structures of consciousness.

Noll further notes that to these more exotic procedures can be added simpler techniques, such as isolation and exposure to darkness, which block visual and auditory diversions. This tends to increase receptivity to vision, and, employing a telling phrase, he informs us, "The attention feels as if drawn backward towards the brain."[23] While spatial descriptions of visionary experience should generally be regarded as metaphors, in an effort to establish a psychophysiological model of trance experience, Michael Winkelman interestingly indicates that such states do, in a sense, draw us backward toward or even into the brain, for they relate to the "deeper" or older parts of our brain. He maintains that the various techniques used in shamanic practice (hallucinogens, rhythmic auditory stimuli such as drumming and chanting, fasting and nutritional deficits, social isolation and sensory deprivation, meditation, extensive motor activity such as prolonged dancing or physical stress, and others) trigger activities that rely upon the hippocampal-septal region of the mind—"part of the phylogenetically older part of the brain" that "includes terminal projections from the somatic and autonomic nervous systems." These activities tend to stimulate patterns of response that can lead to "erasure of previously conditioned responses, changes of beliefs, loss of memory and increased suggestibility."[24] In other words, they help foster the "break with the universe of daily life" characteristic of this stage of the inward journey.

We remember that some scholars surmised that the Paleolithic caves were employed for purposes of initiation. Eliade notes that, indeed, the process of ecstatic and traditional training undergone by the shaman, when seen as a whole, clearly has a traditional initiatory structure:

> This twofold teaching [ecstatic and traditional], imparted by the spirits and the old master shamans, constitutes initiation. Sometimes initiation is public and includes a rich and varied ritual; this is the case, for example, among some Siberian peoples. But the lack of a ritual of this sort in no way implies the lack of an initiation; it is perfectly possible for the initiation to be performed in the candidate's dreams or ecstatic experiences.[25]

The fact that the initiation can be performed in the shaman's dreams or ecstatic experiences is important. It highlights the extent to which the initiation, even with its more traditional training techniques, relies upon spontaneously enlisted, innate propensities within the human mind. It is best envisioned as an anamnesis, an "unforgetting" of mental faculties deep within the unconscious. The essential schema is capable of producing itself automatically and, as such, has a certain inner purposiveness and universality. "It reproduces a traditional mystical pattern," that is, a pattern of initiation. This implies crisis; the death of the profane man; a return to the creative source, both within the mind and within the cosmos; and a rebirth with enhanced power from this source:

The total crisis of the future shaman, sometimes leading to complete disintegration of the personality and to madness, can be valuated not only as an initiatory death but also as a symbolic return to the precosmogonic Chaos—to the amorphous and indescribable state that precedes any cosmogony. Now, as we know, for archaic and traditional cultures, a symbolic return to Chaos is equivalent to preparing a new Creation. It follows that we may interpret the psychic Chaos of the future shaman as a sign that the profane man is being "dissolved" and a new personality being prepared for birth.[26]

On the personal level, the experience of this dissolution of personality is radical and profound. While it is often fostered by traditional means, it can also occur in dream and vision. And these dreams and visions often spontaneously generate symbols that image the same dissolution of the structures of the profane consciousness that the various techniques discussed earlier help effect. These symbols are autosymbolic. They image the very mental processes undergone by the psyche that produces them. It is, Jung has noted, as if the psyche is able to glimpse introspectively the changes it is experiencing and reproduce them in symbols.

We have offered the witness of the Tungus shaman, who lay sick for an entire year until his profane personality was literally "dissolved" into becoming the voice of the sacred. His story continues describing the visionary experiences of his personal transformation:

After that, my ancestors began to shamanize with me. They stood me up like a block of wood and shot at me with their bows until I lost consciousness. They cut up my flesh, separated my bones, counted them, and ate my flesh raw. When they counted the bones they found one too many; had there been too few, I could not have become a shaman.

He continues, "The same thing happens to every Tungus shaman. Only after his shaman ancestors have cut up his body in this way and separated his bones can he begin to practice."[27] Hardly could we imagine a more graphic and radical vision of the dissolution of the old persona. The shaman-to-be is stood up like a block and shot

at with bows by the shaman ancestors until he loses consciousness. His flesh is cut up and eaten and his skeleton dismembered
to the last bone. Surely this must simply be the aberrant dream of
a man with the curse of a too vivid imagination. But we note that
he tells us that this is typical of every Tungus shaman. And we see
the same phenomenon in the trance experience of another Siberian shaman, Kyzlasov, who had lain ill for a full seven years before he became a shaman.

> I have been sick and I have been dreaming. In my dream I had
> been taken to the ancestor and cut into pieces on a black table.
> They chopped me up and then threw me into the kettle and I was
> boiled. There were some men there: two black and two fair ones.
> Their chieftain was there too. He issued the orders concerning
> me. I saw all this. While the pieces of my body were boiled, they
> found a bone around the ribs, which had a hole in the middle.
> This was the excess-bone. This brought about my becoming a
> shaman. Because, only those men can become shamans in whose
> body such a bone can be found. One looks across the hole of this
> bone and begins to see all, to know all and, that is when one be-
> comes a shaman. . . . When I came to from this state, I woke up.
> This meant that my soul had returned. Then the shamans de-
> clared: "You are the sort of man who may become a shaman. You
> should become a shaman, you must begin to shamanize!"[28]

Here the dismemberment, the dissolution of the profane self, is clearly experienced as a necessary preliminary to his receipt of shamanic
powers, and this is associated with the return to bone, which is
symbolic of a return to the source. The underlying schema is more
apparent in the initiatory dream of a Samoyed shaman reported by
A. A. Popov.[29] In this spontaneous experience the initiate encountered a naked smith working a bellows over a fire that was heating
a cauldron "as big as half the earth. . . . The man cut off his head,
chopped his body into bits and put everything in the cauldron.
There he boiled his body for three years." The naked smith then
forged the novice a new head on an anvil—"the one on which the
best shamans were forged"—gathered and rearticulated his bones,
and covered them again with flesh. In forging the shaman's new

head, he "taught him how to read the letters that are inside it. He changed his eyes; and that is why, when he shamanizes, he does not see with his bodily eyes but with these mystical eyes," that is, the inward or strong eye.

The experience of dismemberment is clearly prerequisite to the formation of the new self and to the development of the inward eye. Eliade cites repeated instances of this dismemberment symbolism related to the initiation of the future shaman in Siberia. And he notes that the structure has a much wider distribution. He finds a clear parallel among the Eskimos, where the postulant undergoes a long effort of physical privation and mental contemplation directed to gaining the ability to see himself as a skeleton and he quotes Knud Rasmussen, who interviewed the Iglulik Eskimos about this exercise:

> Though no shaman can explain to himself how and why, he can, by the power his brain derives from the supernatural, as it were by thought alone, divest his body of its flesh and blood, so that nothing remains but his bones. And he must then name all the parts of his body, mentioning every single bone by name; and in so doing, he must not use ordinary human speech, but only the special and sacred shaman's language which he has learned from his instructor. By thus seeing himself naked, altogether freed from the perishable and transient flesh and blood, he consecrates himself, in the sacred tongue of the shamans, to his great task, through that part of his body which will longest withstand the action of the sun, wind and weather, after he is dead.[30]

Eliade notes:

> In both regions alike [Siberia and Arctic America] the essential elements of this mystical vision are the being divested of flesh and the numbering and naming of the bones. The Eskimo shaman obtains the vision after a long, arduous preparation. The Siberian shamans are, in most instances, "chosen," and passively witness their dismemberment by mythical beings. But in all these cases reduction to the skeleton indicates a passing beyond the profane human condition and, hence, a deliverance from it.[31]

It is a long jump from the cold and snow of the Arctic to the hot, dry Australian bush, areas with cultures that, to our best knowledge, have been separated for thousands upon thousands of years. Yet, in his well-researched book *Aboriginal Men of High Degree*, written in 1947, Professor A. P. Elkin describes an uncannily similar phenomenon with regard to the Australian shaman:

> The description of the operation in the Mandjindja tribe, Warburon Ranges, Western Australia, adds the detail that two totemic spirits or heroes "kill" the postulant, cut him open from his neck to his groin, take out all his insides, and insert magical substances *(mabain)*.* They also take out his shoulder and thigh bones and insert mabain before drying and putting them back. They treat the frontal bone in the same way and also cut around the ankles and stuff mabain into those parts.
>
> In Central and North-central Australia, a similar experience must be endured. Spirits of the "eternal dreamtime" or spirits of the dead kill the postulant and through an abdominal incision remove his insides and substitute new ones together with some magical substances. If medicine men are the operators, the method is similar to that employed in the Wiradjeri and neighboring tribes of western New South Wales. Crystals, extracted from their own bodies, are pressed and scored and "jerked" into the postulant's body. He is also given crystals in his food and drink. In addition, a hole is pierced in his tongue.
>
> This ritual is interpreted by the members of the profession as a "death," during which the postulant is operated upon and receives additions to his insides, and after which he is restored to life.[32]

Campbell refers to the work of Baldwin Spencer and F. J. Gillen describing a similar event in the culture of the Aranda. The potential shaman leaves his camp and goes to sleep outside a cave. Here he is shot with a lance by a spirit being. The lance "pierces his neck from behind, passes through his tongue, and emerges from his mouth."

---

* Quartz crystals

The tongue remains throughout life perforated in the center with a hole large enough to admit the little finger; and, when all is over, this hole is the only visible and outward sign remaining of the treatment. A second lance then thrown by the spirit pierces his head from ear to ear, and the victim, falling dead, is immediately carried into the depths of the cave, within which the spirits live in perpetual sunshine, among streams of running water. The cave in question is supposed to extend far under the plain, terminating at a spot beneath what is called the Edith Range, ten miles away. The spirits there remove all of the man's internal organs and provide him with a completely new set, after which he presently returns to life, but in a condition of insanity.[33]

Soon the insanity resolves itself and the initiate can assume his shamanic vocation.

The phenomenon of being shot at or pierced with a lance or other projectile is a variation of the symbolism of initiatory death and parallels the dismemberment experience. This was the initial action in the events reported by Spencer and Gillen and is also noted by Elkin as typifying the inception of the initiation experience in Australia. And we recall the Tungus shaman's Siberian ordeal, when he tells us the deceased ancestors "stood me up like a block of wood and shot at me with their bows until I lost consciousness," which led to his further initiation. The symbolism also extends to the Americas. Rasmussen describes the initiation of a Caribou Eskimo shamaness who was hung up on tent poles in the intense arctic cold for five days and upon her release was shot by her shaman brother-in-law with a gun loaded with real powder but using a stone rather than a bullet. The shooting took place, we are told, so that she might "attain to intimacy with the supernatural by visions of death."[34] So it is in Siberia, the North American Arctic, and distant Australia.

And are we any longer surprised when we learn that Paul Radin, in 1908, interviewed members of the Winnebago Sioux tribe who described their initiation ceremonies, originally derived from their shamans, wherein the neophyte was shot by the ancestors with sacred shells, arrows, or other missiles until unconscious to begin the process of initiation?[35] Similar shamanic initiation ceremonies involving piercing or dismemberment were also to be found among the Pawnee and Ojibwa in North America. In fact, for the Winnebago this phenomenon is a practice that had its own archetypal precedent in the actions of the grizzly bear animal helper spirits, who, in Radin's account, initiated the shaman Thunder-Cloud, giving him their songs "as well as the power of beholding them, a holy sight." After his fasting and self-mortification, these spirit helpers revealed themselves in vision, bestowing their blessings and medicine upon Thunder-Cloud:

> Finally, these grizzly-bear spirits danced, exhibiting their powers when they danced. They would tear open their abdomens, then making themselves holy, heal themselves. Or, again, they would shoot bear-claws at each other and stand there choking with blood. Then, making themselves holy, they would cure themselves.[36]

The images of piercing or shooting again come together with images of dismemberment and evisceration. And these procedures are conducted by the inner forces of the spirit world and here imitated by the initiates, who similarly pierced or shot one another. Among the Pawnee, those shamans known as "bear shamans" also feigned disemboweling themselves in their ceremonies. However, this image of the grizzly bear spirit guides, tellingly, goes further. It reveals the larger initiatory purposiveness of those actions, for they are the necessary preliminaries to the spirits' ability to make themselves holy and to cure themselves. We shall say more about this later.

It is these spirits who appear during the shaman's fasting and torture. As part of the fasting and torture that produced this vision and consistent with the symbolism of dismemberment, Radin tells us, "in the early days, cutting off finger joints and offering them to the spirits was an accepted thing."[37] In fact, Campbell notes with regard to the vision quest that "such offerings were common among the Indians of the plains, on some of whose old hands there remained only fingers and joints enough to enable them to notch an arrow and draw the bow."[38] This, of course, uncannily recalls the images on the cave walls a full twenty-seven thousand years ago at Gargas Cave, at Cosquer, and at other Paleolithic sites, which depict similar images of digital dismemberment. We shall see in other traditions with a strong shamanic element similar images of digital dismemberment that are likewise depicted on cave walls. We further remember that hand stencils of entire hands were often found in the Paleolithic caves, perhaps as testimony to one's presence in shamanic initiations. In the caves at Gargas there are 231 hand images, at Cosquer a minimum of 46, and several at Chauvet. Such images are frequently found at American Indian rock art sites, both positive images and negative ones, made as they probably were in Paleolithic times by blowing or otherwise placing pigment around a hand held against a rock face.[39] At the Cave of 200 Hands in the American Southwest, there exist more than three hundred hand images painted in red, brown, and pink.[40] At many of these sites containing such hands, including that just mentioned, they accompany depictions indicating a shamanic context. In fact, American rock art is being recognized as recording the visions of shamans, as is much rock art in other parts of the world. And, interestingly, in the rock art of the Australian Aborigines, another culture with a strong shamanic tradition, the same hand images appear, sometimes evidencing apparent digital dismemberment in an Aboriginal art associated with the dreamtime, the reality that the shaman accesses in the trance state through the aid of his spirit helper.

Finally, with regard to the piercing motif, we recall that in Australia the ancestor pierces the tongue of the postulant to make him a shaman. This precipitates his vision and ascent to the dreamtime realm of the ancestors. In the world of the Classic Maya of Central America, the shamanic priest-king pierces his own tongue at the behest of the ancestors. He then enlarges the hole by pulling through it a knotted rope in order to reach, through visionary experience and the offering of his blood, the world of the ancestors. It is the ancestors who in vision instruct him in and orchestrate this process.

Eliade traces the theme of initiatory shamanic dismemberment, evisceration, shooting, or piercing into a number of other civilizations spanning the globe, including South America, Africa, and Indonesia. He further notes that this widespread practice bears a curious resemblance to other mythic and ritual patterns. The theme of the initiatory cutting up of shamans, he concludes, warrants extensive further investigation, for its resemblance to the myth and ritual of Osiris and the ritual dismemberment of the Hindu *meriah* (a sacrificial victim ceremonially cut to pieces) is "disconcerting" and has not yet been explained.[41]

We can see presentiments of a deeper significance and underlying purposiveness begin to emerge with regard to the symbols that we have been examining if we again take our key from Eliade, who tells us that "in the spiritual horizon of hunters and herdsmen bone represents the very source of life, both human and animal. To reduce oneself to the skeleton condition is equivalent to re-entering the womb of this primordial life, that is, to a complete renewal, a mystical rebirth."[42]

> We are here in the presence of a very ancient religious idea, which belongs to the hunter culture. Bone symbolizes the final root of animal life, the mold from which the flesh continually arises. It is from the bone that men and animals are reborn; for a time, they maintain themselves in an existence of the flesh; then they die, and their "life" is reduced to the essence concentrated in the skeleton, from which they will be born again. Reduced to skeletons, the future shamans undergo the mystical death that enables them to return to the inexhaustible fount of cosmic life.[43]

The symbolism of dismemberment and reduction to bone implies a return "of life to its ultimate and indestructible essence," "to the inexhaustible fount of cosmic life." It complements and fills out the general dynamic of initiation earlier recognized by Eliade that correlates symbolic "death" during the initiation experience with the shaman's mental crisis and recognizes both as a return to the cosmogonic source and rebirth. And, finally, it supplements the shaman's journey as a return to origin.

And while there may be different inflections in the manner in which the overall symbolism is expressed, the underlying morphology remains the same. For the Siberian and Eskimo shamans, this essential reality in relation to the dismemberment symbolism is expressed in the reduction to bone. And we may recall that the Australian shaman returns from his initiatory dismemberment as the literal embodiment of the world of essence, for this is precisely what the newly implanted quartz crystals represent, that is, the adamantine reality underlying creation or, as Campbell tells us, the "principle of permanence underlying the phenomenology of temporal change."[44] And just as was the case in Siberia, the same symbolism has a cosmogonic significance, for the enduring reality symbolized in the quartz, the new essence of the shaman, is the essential reality that underlies and supports the creation, referred to in Australia as the dreamtime. This world beyond time and change is the source of cosmogonic creation and the continuing source of the reality of our world. In returning to his "source," the Australian shaman returns to the one source, the cosmic fount where individual life experiences its roots in the life of the cosmos. We might also remember the Classic Mayan shaman and the painfully garnered blood of his self-mortification. This is likewise his vehicle of return to essence, for in the Mayan world blood is itself symbolic of essence; it is the source of the generation and regeneration of the cosmos, the very stuff of the cosmic fount. It leads the Mayan shaman in ecstatic vision to the realm of the ancestors, a parallel realm of essence that creates, supports, and sustains the Mayan cosmos. Thus, in each case, among culturally diverse peoples, the dismemberment symbolism has naturally appropriated to itself an element implying a return to the source of essential form. And, in each case, symbols implying initiatory death contain auguries of a larger design, suggesting illumination and rebirth upon a consecrated level.

Remembering that these are experienced realities for the shaman and not simply inherited creedal truths, perhaps we can gain an understanding of this overall direction of thought by examining a statement Jung made in the prologue to his autobiography:

Life has always seemed to me like a plant that lives on its rhizome. Its true life is invisible, hidden in the rhizome. The part that appears above ground lasts only a single summer. Then it withers away—an ephemeral apparition. When we think of the unending growth and decay of life and civilizations, we cannot escape the impression of absolute nullity. Yet, I have never lost a sense of something that lives and endures underneath the eternal flux. What we see is the blossom, which passes. The rhizome remains.

In the end the only events in my life worth telling are those when the imperishable world irrupted into this transitory one. That

is why I speak chiefly of inner experiences, amongst which I include my dreams and visions.[45]

It is this "something that lives and endures underneath the eternal
flux" that the shaman learns to experience in vision, the imperishable world that irrupts into this transitory one. And it is by virtue
of his inner experiences, visions, and dreams, reflecting the archetypal patterns at the root level of existence, that he does so, for
these serve as a bridge between the world of imperishable form
and that of time and change.

We can tie together much of what has been said in this chapter
and establish our path forward by reexamining an image from the
realm of vision and inner experience, which for the shaman traditionally mediates between the two worlds. This is the image of the
animal spirit helper. We have described the inward journey as a
trip backward into the mind. If we adopt Jung's psychological model,
it is a penetration of the rhizome level of consciousness, its deep
and abiding archetypal structures with their roots in nature. This
description found an echo in Michael Winkelman's determination
that the various techniques used in shamanic practice, which we
described earlier, trigger activities that rely on the hippocampal-
septal region of the mind—"part of the phylogenetically older part
of the brain," which includes "terminal projections from the somatic and autonomic nervous systems." Perhaps the two ideas can
be brought into relationship by returning to the observation made
by Lancelot Law Whyte that "in the unconscious mind lies the
contact of the individual with the universal powers of nature," a
contact that "is felt to be the source of power, the home of the élan
which moves us."

Interestingly, as we suggested in chapter 2, modern depth psychology indicates that the penetration of this deep layer of consciousness, where the mind reaches into its origins in the natural
world, tends to be autosymbolically imaged by liminal hybrids—
part human and part animal creatures, representing man's rapprochement with his nature and even nature in general and the cosmos.
Now the processes of sensory deprivation, fasting, self-mortification, and other techniques earlier described find their symbolic
equivalent in the "ego death" represented in the dismemberment

symbolism and the correlative opening of the inward eye. These are the very techniques that the shaman employs to lead to the vision of the animal spirit guide, for instance, the bear spirits of the Winnebago Indians appropriately found in therianthropic form, the form that symbolically articulates man's reconnection with the deep layers of consciousness and the significant archetypal forms that abide therein.

It is this world of archetypal form that invests the spirit guide with its significance. And this transpersonal aspect is ingeniously represented in the Winnebago dancing grizzly bear spirits that gnomically reenact the whole initiatory pattern; they are initiate and initiator, the curer and the cured. They pierce or eviscerate one another, yet it follows that this leads spontaneously not only to their own healing but also to their ability to cure others. Moreover, the tribulation of the ordeal of initiation gains the distance of a vision seen from the vantage point of the immortals. It becomes the patterned movement of the dance and assumes the shape of an eternally repeated archetypal pattern, as though the postulant's ordeal and ego death "were but a play," the eternal play, in fact, of the transpersonal realm of essential form, once again incarnated in human experience.

The return to the realm of essential form that autosymbolically images itself only indistinctly in these early stages of the shaman's inward journey will become a dominant motif as we proceed. At this stage it is only a vague presentiment of the inner lawfulness of the transpersonal realm that the shaman accesses, a flicker of light at the end of the shaman's disorienting and perilous journey. This is a journey that continues to repeat that taken thousands of years ago through the dark cave at Les Trois Frères and the other Paleolithic sites by initiates seeking the emergence of that same flicker of light that would herald their illumination. And it is thus entirely fitting that the "ego death" experienced by the Cro-Magnon initiate and the deeper reality he would discover there was also mediated by the sudden appearance of a similar half human, half animal dancing spirit guide with numinous, soul-piercing eyes known as the Sorcerer of Les Trois Frères (see Figure 22).

THE GUIDING SPIRIT

They and only they can acquire the philosophic imagination, the sacred power of self-intuition, who within themselves can interpret and understand the symbol, that the wings of the air-sylph are forming within the skin of the caterpillar. . . . They know and feel that the potential works in them, even as the actual works on them! In short, all the organs of sense are framed for a corresponding world of sense; and we have it. All the organs of spirit are framed for a correspondent world of spirit: though the latter organs are not developed in all alike.

Samuel Taylor Coleridge

We begin where we ended the previous section, with the arresting image of the therianthropic Sorcerer of Les Trois Frères. It remains difficult for the modern consciousness to raise this figure from the darkness that naturally shrouds it. Man, animal, animal spirit guide, costumed shaman, god of the cave—we grope for definition. We are torn between the completely alien nature of the creature and its strangely captivating numinous qualities, and we are reminded of a philosopher with the surest instinct for myth who examined Greek tragedy and its evolution from the chorus of satyrs. Man, goat, or god, Nietzsche asked himself with regard to the hybrid form of the satyr, or perhaps all; what was "this fantastic and at first embarrassing figure?" Such a "lowly" being was an affront to any modern conception of the divine realm, yet Greek tragedy was founded upon it. Gradually Nietzsche began to recognize the emissary of a different reality. "The satyr, as the Dionysiac chorist," he proclaimed in *The Birth of Tragedy*, "dwells in a reality sanctioned by myth and ritual," and as such he sensed that "before him cultured man dwindled to a false cartoon."

Nietzsche found his answer in the music, harmony, dance, and dynamics of the chorus, which he related to Schopenhauer's concept of music as the most direct expression of the World Will, the

formal principle investing the natural world. In this liminal creature—semidivine, animal and man combined—the formal creative
matrix of nature spoke directly to classical man. The chorus bespeaks "the eternal core of things," he declared, "the eternity of
the true being surviving every phenomenal change." The chorus
of goatlike satyrs represented to the Greek mind original wisdom,
which "proclaims a truth that issues from the heart of the world,"
and the satyr was for Nietzsche "a prophet of wisdom born out of
nature's womb," the gateway to the creative plenitude that informs
the world of individuated form.

Can we see the alien presence we have come to know as the
Sorcerer of Les Trois Frères as a "prophet of wisdom born out of
nature's womb," and did he play such a role in the shaman's universe? To answer this question, we must enter more deeply into
the world of the shaman's initiation and training. We remember
that the shaman experiences what we have termed an ego death, a
dissolution of his everyday consciousness and its typical orientation to reality. This "break with the universe of daily life" was fostered by various means, but it also took place spontaneously, making it clear that the initiatory pattern of experience was, in fact, a
process of reawakening, harnessing tendencies natural to the human mind. The overall schema initiated a transformation of consciousness, a death of the profane self with auguries of a rebirth on
a consecrated level of existence.

In Jungian terms this "ego death" constitutes a lowering of the
threshold of consciousness, which at first results in the onrush of a
flood of material from the unconscious mind. Under this onslaught
the novitiate shaman often experiences actual symptoms of possession by spirits or demons, illness, frenzy, hysteria, or madness. As
we have seen, at times the process expresses itself autosymbolically
in images of the ancestors or other creatures from the inner world
as agents of the dismemberment, evisceration, or piercing of the
shaman or as being responsible for the madness or frenzied possession that in some societies typifies this phase of the transformation. Often, in a telling symbolism, these spirit beings are actually
envisioned as swallowing or engorging the shaman—signalizing
his immersion in the anterior reality of the preconscious mind.
Thus, the Eskimo shaman is devoured by a bear from the spirit

world. In certain South American forms of shamanism, the shaman is devoured by a jaguarlike spirit being. His counterpart in Australia is swallowed by the great snake Wonambi, or Unggud, the creationtime serpent, and the Mayan shaman is engorged by the Vision Serpent, who literally leads the way to the Otherworld.

Whereas in other societies the aberrant symptoms triggered by the onslaught of preconscious contents would be repressed, many archaic societies, particularly those with shamanistic tendencies, took care to channel this behavior with rigorous training. As Roger Walsh informs us, in these circumstances, "The patient would be regarded as a shaman-to-be, and the symptoms would be regarded not as evidence of pathology but as evidence of a calling, not as an emergency to be suppressed but as an emergence to be guided."[46] As we have said, this guidance, or training, is both traditional and ecstatic. The traditional training takes the form of instructing the shaman in the local lore of the tribe and, particularly, its mythology. If the trainee is fit for the shamanic vocation, if he is one who experiences the sacred more intensely than others, then the local mythology speaks directly and intimately to the shaman. It is the peculiar sensibility of shamans to be able to "interiorize" it, to "experience" and use it as the itinerary for their ecstatic journeys. What for other members of the community is a traditional creedal truth, is for the shaman an experienced reality. Eliade explains this important point in detail.

> In the archaic cultures communication between sky and earth is ordinarily used to send offerings to the celestial gods and not for a concrete and personal ascent; the latter remains the prerogative of shamans. Only they know how to make an ascent through the "central opening"; only they transform a cosmo-theological concept into a *concrete mystical experience*. . . . In other words, what for the rest of the community remains a cosmological ideogram, for the shamans (and the heroes, etc.) becomes a mystical itinerary. For the former, the "Center of the World" is a site that permits them to send their prayers and offerings to the celestial gods, whereas for the latter it is the place for beginning a flight in the strictest sense of the word. Only for the latter is *real communication* among the three cosmic zones a possibility.[47]

As Campbell tells us, shamanism is the earliest example of "the serious use of myth hermetically, as *m-arga*, as a way to psychological metamorphosis."[48] We might use the Mayan ritual concept of "opening the portal" to describe these techniques, for they are meant progressively to alter the human consciousness and bring it closer and closer to its form-giving source.

This hermetic use of myth cannot be underestimated. Mythic symbols constitute one of the great keys unlocking the preconscious reservoir of the mind. "The reservoir is in the mind of mankind, but by no means all mankind draws from it," Oliver La Farge tells us. "Where the ideas are expressed in symbols, they serve one believer as doorways into the inner courts of understanding, another rather as doors at which thinking stops in favor of literal acceptance."[49] The symbols of traditional lore, themselves expressive of the preconscious creations of a culture distilled over generations by the ancestors, are deeply fascinating and activate the symbolic propensities of the preconscious. They open the doorways to the inner courts, or deep roots—what Jung called the psychoid level—of the human mind. This, in turn, fosters the creation of new symbols.

For the adept, the symbols become emissaries of an inner order; they provide directive signs to an emergent order of reality. According to Jung, the symbol represents or personifies "certain instinctive data of the dark, primitive psyche, the real but invisible roots of consciousness."[50] It effects a rapprochement with an inner reality precisely because it mediates between the unconscious substratum and the conscious mind. "It throws a bridge between present-day consciousness, always in danger of losing its roots, and the natural, unconscious, instinctive wholeness of primeval times."[51] The mythic lore to which he is exposed opens the shaman to the archetypal patterns of his larger transpersonal background and to the inner template of universal form that shapes our experience. It is for this reason that the shaman manifests what the Tukano refer to as "luminescence," an enlightened ability to discern the inner meaning and archetypal significance of myth and vision, an ability that, for the Tukano, symbolically emanates from the Sun Father, the source of all creation. Thus, this "instinctive wholeness" has a larger resonance, for, as we shall see, the shaman experiences these spontaneous productions of the unconscious as the expression of a generative force continuous with the cosmic creation, either of the creationtime itself or of the power that emanates from it, be it wakan, orenda, itz, n/um, or any of the other numerous expressions for the common formative force immanent in creation.

It is because the shaman has learned to "experience" myth and symbol, to become the vehicle or conduit of their deeply rooted expression, that he is typically the custodian and teller of the myths of his culture or tribe. For the same reason, it is he who interprets local myth as well as the visions, dreams, and trance experiences of his fellows. As he attains mastery of the power of the symbol, he finally becomes a conduit and molder of the unconscious psychic life of his culture, just as in the stages of his initiation, through his increased understanding of myth and vision, he gradually gained the ability to express and give shape to his own unconscious psychic life.

This hermetic use of myth complements the techniques of ecstatic training that we examined earlier. Both help overcome the dominance of the conscious mind, with its obsessive preoccupations, and effect a rapprochement with the preconscious. During this process the shaman learns to cultivate the wealth of mental images that access to these levels of consciousness has provided. In fact, according to Richard Noll, "Shamanism is an ecstatic healing tradition which at its core is concerned with techniques for inducing, maintaining and interpreting the experience of enhanced visual mental imagery."[52] He points out, as others have recognized, that a youth's spontaneous visions of "spirits" are frequently a preliminary sign of his shamanic calling.[53] The shaman is trained to increase first the vividness and then the control of his visions, for these are his vehicles to the sacred. In working with his visions, the shaman learns to gain a certain power over them while still respecting their spontaneous nature, which is what makes them significant. "Increasing control over mental imagery is mirrored in the developing shaman's increasing number of mastered spirits."[54]

It is not, however, simply the vividness of the visual imagery that is key to the shaman's training but the very nature of its creation and its "contents." Noll points out the autogenous nature of vision, which is experienced in a sense as spontaneous, self-generating form.

But like the demonic realm itself, of which it is representative, it has its roots in cosmic creation and the inwardly encountered formal power of a universe burgeoning with forms. It is experienced as both inward and transpersonal, a reflection of "the oneiric capacity of a race and of nature generally," as Nietzsche so well described this level of human visionary capacity.

Visionary and dream experience have traditionally had cosmogonic implications that we can detect in the numerous myths wherein Divinity dreams the world into being and, of course, in the dreamtime source of reality in Australian shamanism. Perhaps the best-known example is that of the god Vishnu asleep, floating on the cosmic sea, and dreaming world upon world innumerable into existence. Tellingly, a related archetypal representation of cosmic creation, itself at times regarded as the active reflex of the still-dreaming substratum represented by Vishnu, is Shiva, lord of dancers. With drum and dance, in one aspect, he represents the world's perpetual unfolding. These cosmogonic symbols are age-old; the drum in Hindu myth is an agency of cosmic creation, and, as Heinrich Zimmer tells us, "dancing is one of the many aspects of his [Shiva's] divine essence, one of the allegories in which his infinitude assumes perceptible form."[55] And, finally, from the time of Pythagoras, through Schopenhauer, Richard Wagner, and Nietzsche, music itself has always been a foremost symbol of the unimpeded immediate creation of form by the self-generating cosmic force. Interestingly, the cosmic formal power of the Huron and Iroquois, orenda, is derived from a root meaning "song."[56] For archaic man, human creativity is grounded in cosmic creativity and music and dance articulate a connection between the two. Archaic man's sense of continuity with this creative force is well expressed by the Aztec claim to have sung and danced their cities into creation.

These examples are not merely arbitrary. The shaman's training is multiform, enlisting powers addressed to all the senses. Dance, drum, vision, and song all symbolically suggest man's link with the cosmic creation. Simultaneously they also function psychophysiologically to bring the individual into harmony with the greater force of which he now experiences himself to be an expression. In dancing to the percussive beat and rhythm of drum, chant, and song, the shaman becomes one with the cosmic creation. At the same time, dance, hypermotility, percussive sound, physical exhaustion, and the other "techniques" that we examined previously actually effect on a psychophysiological level the experience of overcoming individuated form and attaining ecstasy. Each of the senses is harnessed to lead to a spontaneous regression to the ground of human experience, which is also experienced as the ground of the being of the world. The combined result is overwhelming, and to describe it in a language somewhat commensurate with its effect, we might again borrow from Nietzsche's description of Dionysiac exaltation in *The Birth of Tragedy*. Here we might say "man is incited to the greatest exaltation of all his symbolic faculties. . . . The essence of nature is now expressed symbolically. . . . and the entire symbolism of the body is called into play, not the mere symbolism of lips, face, and speech but the whole pantomime of dancing, forcing every member into rhythmic movement. Then the other symbolic powers suddenly press forward, particularly those of music, in rhythmics, dynamics and harmony." The result is ecstatic transpersonal experience, "oneness as the soul of the race and of nature itself."

As the shaman gains access to deeper levels of consciousness, the ecstatic and the mythic begin to coalesce, and the chaotic welter of images demonizing the shaman crystallizes into a mindscape with form and meaning. In this process, the shaman ultimately recognizes the forms that first threatened him with mental dissolution as the forms of his mind's self-revelation. They come to be recognized as "tools of the gods" and, finally, salvific forms by which the Divine imposes itself upon the human mind. And it is because he penetrates in ecstasy the level of consciousness that gives these images their meaning that the shaman is able to understand and to follow them in the direction in which they lead him. Cast against the template of the deep structures of the mind, they assume an archetypal form with its own universal lawfulness. And it is because he experiences the inner lawfulness, the inner teleology, spelled out by these images, that they can constitute, in Eliade's terms, a "mystical itinerary" or, in Campbell's, a "way to psychological metamorphosis." The images become guides to the reality the shaman is to experience.

Larry G. Peters, in an article discussing Tamang shamanism in Nepal, gives an illuminating example of this process. He notes that "the Tamang shaman's apprenticeship results in a mastery of altered states of consciousness involving voluntary entry into and exit from these states."[57]A dominant feature of the shaman's trance is possession. The Tamang "distinguish between individuals who are involuntarily possessed (interpreted as an illness) and the shaman who 'possesses spirits.'" The shamanic initiation consists of a movement from being possessed to possessing, a process consisting of four phases. "Tamang shamans are called to their profession through a crisis-type experience typical of many Asian shamans." The shaman "has a spontaneous vocation in which he is inflicted by spirits that possess him and drive him into solitude, demanding he become a shaman. This unsolicited altered state of consciousness that afflicts future Tamang shamans is called crazy possession *(lha khoiba mayba)*."[58] It is marked by convulsive shaking, incoherency, and chaotic visions. "The shaking becomes identified as the possession of an ancestor, and the visions and dreams are related to mythology and other aspects of the belief system." Trance states are deliberately induced. "The idea behind the training exercises is that the more one becomes entranced, the more control is gained over the trance state."[59] Through such mythic and ecstatic training, the shaman-to-be moves from one possessed to one who possesses the powers of possession.

One can possess the powers of possession because they emanate from the same source as do the deep structures of the human mind. The fact that they are in one sense forms of the mind's self-revelation, however, does not indicate that they are illusory; it rather establishes their credentials as spiritual entities. They embody the reflexivity characteristic of the mythic visionary world, which always leads back to the source of its own creation. In this way, they are guides, instructors with their own manifest intentionality. The problem for the initiate is to understand this intentionality, to follow its guidance until he realizes that it expresses something innate and necessary within his own preconscious mind. As the conscious mind, through ecstatic and traditional training, grows more accustomed to the reflexes of its preconscious source, an underlying identity begins to emerge.

We can discern this structure in the initiatory dream journey of Sereptie Djaruoskin, a Tavgi Samoyed shaman of Siberia.[60] The journey presents a rich and terrifying dreamscape portraying the dissolution of human consciousness, the descent into the spirit world where men "lose their minds." "Some just start singing, others losing their minds, go away and die; others again become shamans. . . . If you find the spirit of madness, you will begin to shamanize," Sereptie is told by his spirit guide. And, finally, he is told, "Shamanizing, you will find your way, by yourself." Although he is at first led by the "intentionality" of the spirit guide, the dynamic of the journey is progressively revealed to be autoinitiatory, the reflex of the initiate's own mind. Ultimately, Sereptie becomes his own spirit guide.

The dream begins with Sereptie cutting down a tree to construct a sledge to carry holy relics. "When the tree fell, a man sprung out of its roots with a loud shout." "Well, my friend," he tells Sereptie, "I am a man, who came out of the roots of the tree." The strange revelation continues:

> "The root is thick, it looks thin in your eyes only. Therefore I tell you that you must come down through the root if you wish to see me."—"What sort of a tree is that?" I asked. "I never could find it out." The man answered: "From times of old, it is of this tree that the kuojka sledges have been made and the shamans have been growing from. Rocked in the cradle, they become shamans—well that's what this tree is for."

The spirit, clad in a hide parka resembling "the wild reindeer's hide during moulting time," leads Sereptie's descent.

> As I looked round, I noticed a hole in the earth. My companion asked: "What hole is this? If your destiny is to make a drum of this tree, find it out!" I replied: "It is through this hole that the shaman receives the spirit of his voice." The hole became larger and larger. We descended through it and arrived at a river with two streams flowing in opposite directions. "Well, find out this one too!" said my companion, "one stream goes from the centre to the north, the other to the south—the sunny side. If you are destined to fall into a trance, find it out!" I replied: "The northern stream

originates from the water for bathing the dead, and the southern from that for the infants."—"Yes, indeed, you have guessed right," said he.

The guide leads Sereptie through various stages of initiation, but in each instance Sereptie innately knows their significance and successfully intuits their meaning. The spirit guide takes Sereptie into the first of a series of tents. "What is the meaning of the bars that hang horizontally above the fireplace of the tent?" the guide asks.

> Suddenly I found one of the bars in my hand and struck my companion with it. "These bars are the borderline between two daybreaks, the backbone of the firmament. The northern bar is the beginning of the polar light, the southern one—the beginning of the cycle of dawns." When I said this, my companion praised me. I got frightened. "And what is the tent tied round with a rope?" asked my companion. And I said: "When men go mad and become shamans, they are tied with this rope." (I was quite unconscious and was tied up too.)

On their journey they confront terrifying visions of "naked men and women who were singing all the time while tearing their bodies with their teeth" in an initiatory dismemberment and madness preliminary to becoming shamans. "If you find the spirit of madness, you will begin to shamanize, initiating (new) shamans," Sereptie is now told. At this point, images of an underwater journey emerge: "When I submerged, I arrived at these places, and it seemed as if I were swimming in the water," he informs us in a symbolism we shall find in other shamanic experiences. To receive the clothes and drum of his shamanic vocation, Sereptie must consult "the mother of the wild reindeer" and a special stag reindeer who is "the master spirit of the wild reindeer stags." Another tent he enters "not as a man but as a skeleton." Here he finds a woman who looks as if she were made of fire and a smith who forges molten metal from the heat of her body. His spirit guide again asks,

> "What do you think, what tent have we entered?" "I don't know," said I. "However, it must be here that the pendants of the shaman's

clothes are forged and it is probably these people I have to ask (for pendants), for my clothes. The man (= shaman) descends from many places, this is surely one of them."

The skeletal form, the reduction to bone, presages a return to origin, "the origins of the shamans," and, in a now familiar symbolism, becoming a shaman.

"When I entered as a skeleton and they forged, it meant that they forged me. The master of the earth, the spirit of the shamans, has become my origin. When a shin-bone or something else is hit and the sparks fly, there will be a shaman in your generation."

Now able to shamanize, the shaman's mystical itinerary will begin to crystallize and Sereptie will no longer need the spirit guide.

"Now that we have arrived here, I will leave you alone," said my companion. "If you return, you will be a man, if not—you will die. Henceforward I cannot lead you anymore. I have led you to all the origins and way of diseases. Shamanizing, you will find your way, by yourself."

From here Sereptie does find his own way to the source of his shamanizing ability, which is also the source of life itself inwardly encountered in the preconscious where, as Nietzsche recognized, "original wisdom speaks from the womb of nature." He ultimately encounters the archetypal "mistress of the earth," whose realm is that of the seven mountain peaks Sereptie has been forced to scale on his journey toward initiation.

Then I said to myself: "I am sure that I have reached the place whence every man descends" and, turning towards the woman, I said aloud: "You are surely the mistress of the earth who has created all life." "Yes, that is so," she said.

And, she reveals, "These seven peaks are the origin of every plant: the future shamans go around them. In these nests there are spirits—the master spirits of all the running and flying birds and game."

Through this vertiginous fall into madness, the inner resources of the mind lead Sereptie to a center of sanity. He experiences that the deep ground of his being encountered subjectively within himself, his psychophysical origin, reaches back into the plenitude of cosmic creation, the realm of "the master spirits of all the running and flying birds and game." He discovers, as Jung tells us, that "he is of the same essence as the universe, and that his own mid-point is its center," and it is from this experience that his power and curative ability arise. It is this process that rescues him from madness and death and allows him to return a shaman. He awakens from his trance state, still beneath the tree that "shamans have been growing from"—the place where the "shaman receives the spirit of his voice"—now consecrated with the shaman's powers.

In this visionary experience we witness how the "intentionality" of the spirit guide eventually merges with the "intentionality" of an inner schema within the mind of the initiate. The two are in fact one, and the initiation is less a learning of something new than a discovery of something innate. It is this inner purposiveness of the mind that initiates the shaman. If we take a step back, however, we realize that this was implicit from the beginning, for this is the *dream* of Sereptie, the visionary product of his own mind. It gives witness to Eliade's recognition that it is perfectly possible for the initiation to be performed in the candidate's dreams or ecstatic experiences precisely because it is innate. But what is quite remarkable is that in this spontaneous ecstatic experience of an individual in Siberia we find the lineaments of shamanic experience around the globe and, perhaps, over eons. Here we can only outline certain elements of this archetypal experience, but each will gain flesh and life as we progress.

Briefly, we recognize the trance experience, the shaman's tree, and the inward journey as a descent into a recess or hole representing an inner realm without dimension, which appears too "thin" to enter but grows larger and becomes accessible to the transformed consciousness. The initial stages of trance are experienced as a submersion in water. We are introduced to a traditional image for embarking into the unconditioned realm, that is, the passage through what we shall come to recognize as the Symplegades, the portal where opposites converge ("two streams flowing in opposite directions," between the realms of birth and death, "the borderline between the two daybreaks," "the backbone of the firmament"), followed by the perilous journey, madness, dismemberment, skeletalization, a descent that paradoxically becomes an ascent (that is, up the seven mountain peaks), and a return to origin. In association with this schema we encounter the theme of the mystical origin of the accoutrements of the shaman's profession; the spirit guide who leads to the realm of the master spirits, that is, the master stag reindeer of which the guide in his molting reindeer parka is a representative; the reconsecrated (forged) adamantine body of the shaman from which sparks will fly if it is struck; and, ultimately, the return to the cosmic fount, the nucleus of eternal form represented by the master spirits of the animal kingdom, and the cosmic origin as the source of the shaman's powers. It is this emergent relationship to the source that provides the "luminescence" that allows Sereptie to formulate and follow the mystical itinerary in the first place. It is also the source of the power that invests him with his charismatic and curative abilities. And at each stage of the initiation and acquisition of shamanic powers, Sereptie finds that he himself innately knows the lineaments of this shamanic universe. Eventually, through shamanizing, he guides himself through the visionary initiatory cosmos.

We shall see a structural pattern similar to that which we encountered in Sereptie's dream emerge in varying but still recognizable forms throughout our study. For now let us proceed to note one facet of its functional aspect, for the intentionality of the spirit guide and the inner lawfulness of the structure of this schema relate to the shaman's abilities to function as a healer. Jung's clinical work revealed a level of consciousness, often evoked in response to psychic crisis, where symbolic forms indeed act autonomously with their own "purposiveness." As we mentioned in chapter 1, he recognized these archetypal patterns of experience as being "evidently an *attempt at self-healing* on the part of Nature, which does not spring from conscious reflection but from an instinctive impulse," that is, from the a priori formal capacities of the human psyche groping for its own salvation. It is in part because he is able to enlist a similar inner dynamic that the shaman is recognized variously as a "wounded healer" or a "cured curer." Many commentators have emphasized that the shaman is a sick man who has healed himself. S. M.

Shirokogoroff notes, "The shaman may begin his life career with a psychosis but he cannot carry on his function if he cannot master himself."[61] Eliade also emphasizes this point and indicates that the pattern of initiation itself helps implement the cure.

> But the primitive magician, the medicine man, or the shaman is not only a sick man, he is, above all, a sick man who has been cured, who has succeeded in curing himself. Often when the shaman's or medicine man's vocation is revealed through an illness or an epileptoid attack, the initiation of the candidate is equivalent to a cure. The famous Yakut shaman Tüspüt (that is, "fallen from the sky") had been ill at the age of twenty; he began to sing, and felt better.[62]

We remember that the Tungus shaman, Semyonov Semyon, likewise resolved his initiatory illness by becoming a voice for the sacred. It is not the illness but rather the cure, which the depth of the crisis reveals to the shaman, that lies at the heart of shamanism. As Eliade tells us, the shaman's psychopathic experience has a theoretical content. "For if they have cured themselves and are able to cure others, it is, among other things, because they know the mechanism, or rather, the *theory* of illness."[63] The shaman is able to harness the *"attempt at self-healing* on the part of Nature" that Jung saw expressed in archetypal symbols. Employing the mind's native teleological capacity, he moves from crisis to cure in his own initiation and in other rites and ceremonies.

This movement from crisis to cure is appropriated to the symbolism of the spirit guide. On one level, in its terrifying and devouring aspect it represents the crisis evoked by the chaos of unleashed forces emanating from the preconscious mind. We remember that as symbolic of this process, the novitiate shaman is often envisioned as being engorged by therianthropic creatures of the preconscious emerging in vision. With a further deepening of inner experience, however, we can discern that we are approaching in these half-animal forms a telling symbolism for that which, as we mentioned earlier, Jung recognized as the mind's penetration of the psychoid realm, which in a very real sense unites man with nature and cosmos. As Ira Progoff explained earlier:

In Jung's scheme of thought, the *psychoid* level of the unconscious represents the point at which the psyche is so close to the animal world as not yet to be differentiated from it. It still is directly connected to the realm of nature in its mode of functioning, and it is thus the aspect of the human organism that can be most directly experienced as part of nature.

We remember that in his work with his patients, Jung found that images of hybrid human and animal forms were spontaneously produced as uniting symbols as the patient struggled to achieve a balanced relationship with the deep levels of the psyche. With this as our guide, several levels of meaning come to the surface. In reaching this level "directly connected to the realm of nature," we are enlisting that "*attempt at self-healing* on the part of Nature" that Jung recognized as an innate, but generally unconscious faculty of the innermost psyche. Just as the body has miraculous natural powers to heal itself in ways our conscious mind can only partly fathom, so does our mind receive salutary aid from the integration of the all-nourishing root levels of our psyche. It is, thus, an entirely appropriate autosymbolism that the emergence of the animal spirit guide marks the mind's encounter with nature's—that is, its own—instinctive healing powers. And if Jung was right that the archetype at its deepest levels is "an image of instinct," in the archetype of this liminal being from our animal ancestry we have this most aptly symbolized.[64]

On another intimately related plane, this level of consciousness does indeed involve, in Ira Progoff's terms, the "inner experience of the deep ground of the Self experienced subjectively within ourselves and also objectively as part of the whole realm of nature." In Jungian terms, and reminiscent of Sereptie's experience, the shaman here first approximates the seminal experience that "he is of the same essence as the universe and that his own mid-point is its center." He experiences himself as in some sense continuous with the creative plenitude and inner wisdom of nature and the cosmos. And in this process of transformation, forms that at first assailed the shaman are ultimately revealed to be emissaries of this inner wisdom, and the very forces that previously threatened to engorge the shaman become his guides. Thus, the bear that devoured and dismembered our Eskimo shaman becomes his totem guide, the jaguar becomes the spirit guide of the South American shaman, the serpent that engorged the Australian shaman becomes the vehicle of his ascent to the dreamtime, and the Mayan Vision Serpent becomes the conduit of the journey to the Otherworld. In this respect, we might also remember the dancing grizzly bear spirit guides who initiated the Winnebago shaman, Thunder-Cloud, for in the Winnebago medicine rite, the vapor-bath lodge that by virtue of the psychophysiological effects of the sweat bath prepares the mind for inner revelation is symbolically cast in the form of a great bear that engorges the initiate entering the bath.[65] Initiation is performed "within the belly of the beast," the same beast that is to become the shaman's mentor, for it is this very experience that leads to the revelation of the higher truth and power represented by the spirit guide. It is these strange creatures, part human, animal, and divine, who will teach the shaman the secrets of his calling. As in the case of Sereptie, the guide will initiate him into his vocation and evoke his true identity as a shaman, vesting him with the implements of the shamanic vocation and leading him to the very sources of life. As the rapprochement between life and its source continues, the shaman will learn to speak the language of his spirit guide, the guide will speak through the shaman, and, finally, the shaman may symbolically or in trance metamorphose into the form of the spirit guide.

Speaking of the meaning implicit in the ancient Chinese shaman's symbolic metamorphosis into the animal spirit, Eliade explains:

> Imitating the gait of an animal or putting on its skin was acquiring a superhuman mode of being. There was no question of a regression into pure "animal life"; the animal with which the shaman identified himself was already charged with a mythology, it was, in fact, a mythical animal, the Ancestor or the Demiurge. By becoming this mythical animal, man became something far greater and stronger than himself. We are justified in supposing that this projection into a mythical being, the center at once of the existence and renewal of the universe, induced the euphoric experience that, before ending in ecstasy, showed the shaman his power and brought him into communion with cosmic life.[66]

This statement very well captures the essence of the shaman's relationship to the spirit guide as a source of both power and communion with cosmic life. And we can see this "euphoric experience" well represented in the shamanism of the Huichol Indians, as expressed in the peyote hunt. We shall briefly examine this hunt to illustrate this important point and to capsulize much of what has been presented in this chapter in a still living and meaningful example.[67]

The Huichol Indians have their homeland in the Sierra Madre mountains of western Mexico. They describe the goal of the peyote hunt as being "to find our life," for peyote and the transformation of consciousness implicit in the quest are the portal to the immanent powers of creation. "Like so many American Indians, the Huichol understand the natural phenomena—including man—in terms of immanent and innate powers of creation through transformation," Peter T. Furst informs us.[68] All phenomena are imbued with an immanent force and power, and the goal of the quest "to find our life" is to become one with this power, in Eliade's terms, to be brought "into communion with cosmic life."

The "hunt" not only connotes a quest but also is symbolized in terms of an actual animal or, more precisely, deer hunt. This is a context that cannot help but draw our glance back to the Paleolithic caves and the scenes depicted on the cave walls in relation to the first forms of shamanism we know about and the transformation of consciousness evoked by these caves. This is, indeed, as Furst tells us, a story from "ancient, ancient times":

> The primary focus of this system is the "peyote hunt." It is a "hunt"
> in the literal sense, because to the Huichol, peyote and deer are
> synonymous. The first of the sacred plants to be seen by the leader
> of the hunting party contains the essence of Elder Brother
> *Wawatsári*, "master" of the deer species, and manifests itself as
> deer, which in turn explains why it is first "shot" with bow and
> arrow before being dug from the ground and ritually divided among
> the participants in the hunt.[69]

This hunt is an inward journey of the soul, in familiar terms, led by the shaman:

It goes without saying that the leader must know the minutest mythological detail of the itinerary, as well as the correct sequence and proper manner in which each ritual is to be carried out at the sacred places along the way and, above all, in the peyote country itself. And he must "see" with an inner eye, for only he will recognize the tracks of the Deer-Peyote and see the brilliant rainbow-soul of Elder Brother *Wawatsári*, the Principal Deer, rise from the peyote plant as it is "slain" by his arrows.[70]

We might note here the reliance on the "inner eye," which we have seen elsewhere. And it is the deer spirit guide, Káuyumarie, who serves as the shaman's "inner eye" and leads him on his mystical itinerary. "He is conceived both in deer form and as a person wearing antlers."[71] It is he who knows the way, who points out the major impediments to the quest, and who can lead beyond them. As such, he is, according to Barbara Myerhoff, "an intermediary who bridges the mundane and ideal."[72]

The quest takes the form of an actual journey from the Huichol homeland. Originally, it was undertaken entirely on foot and entailed the privation and physical exhaustion that we have seen as traditionally marking the shaman's journey. It still maintains many of the stages that we associate with the quest. The pilgrimage on which the spirit guide leads the shaman begins with a ritual of confession and purification. This represents the shedding of the profane self so that, as Ramón Medina Silva, the shaman friend and informant who escorted both Furst and Myerhoff on the quest, tells us, "you will be new." But it is a metamorphosis, or transformation, of consciousness—and not absolution—that is at the heart of the ceremony, and, as Myerhoff makes apparent, its symbols point simultaneously to a return to childhood (individual origin), mythic times (human origin), and to the creation itself (cosmic origin).[73] The *peyoteros* who follow Ramón on the quest have received through prior ceremonies both traditional and ecstatic training from early childhood to prepare them for the quest. In the earlier ceremonies the deer spirit guide symbolically led the young initiates into ecstasy and magical flight, for the skin of the deer forms the head of the ceremonial drum and the children transform into hummingbirds and fly eastward toward the source of life, carried on the vibration produced by the shaman's rhythmic beating of this instrument.

On the peyote quest the deerskin-covered drum of the earlier ceremony undergoes a tellingly symbolic transformation. As Furst tells us, it becomes identical with the bow carried on the hunt by the shaman. As they proceed on the hunt, the string of this bow is beaten with an arrow used as a drumstick:

> The bow serves as drum throughout the peyote pilgrimage. Its beat tells the supernaturals that the pilgrims are coming and guides them through the dangerous passage of the Clashing Clouds. It is also played to "make Elder Brother happy" in the ritual tracking and stalking of the Deer-Peyote in *Wirikúta* [the sacred land of the peyote].[74]

The baton or scepter is a traditional emblem of the shaman's vocation. In this instance, assuming the form of the *muviéri* or ceremonial arrow carried by the Huichol shaman, it frequently plays a significant role in the hunt. The arrow is topped with pendant hawk feathers. According to Joan Halifax, this prayer arrow is used for healing and seeing.[75] The shaman's scepter traditionally marks his connection with the archetypal world, and this function is repeatedly emphasized in the Huichol quest. Brushed with the ceremonial arrow, the initiates themselves become archetypes, and each is given a new name in the likeness of one of the mythical first seekers, that is, the followers of the first shaman, Tatewari, making them identical to the ancestors and heroes of the paradigmatic world. It is, likewise, this baton, topped with feathers indicative of the same transformation of consciousness symbolized by the children's avian metamorphosis and magic flight in the earlier ceremony, that is instrumental in effecting the crossing of the threshold to cosmic life and power. This threshold, which only Ramón and his spirit guide can see, is represented in the mystical landscape by the Huichol incarnation of the Symplegades symbolism in the form of incessantly opening and closing mythic "cloud gates" as the entrance to the realm of the ancestral gods.

To implement passage of the cosmic threshold, Ramón uses the ceremonial arrow to describe a mandala marking the four quarters and the sacred center that is the key to the passage. Symbolically, the pilgrims are penetrating the sacred center, the source of divinity, and breaking the plane along the cosmic axis that the feathered scepter archetypally represents.* After the shaman has marked the mandala pattern at the cosmic threshold, Furst describes his action in effecting the dangerous passage through the clashing cloud gates:

> Ramón stepped forward, lifted the bow, and, placing one end against his mouth while rhythmically beating the string with an arrow, walked straight ahead, stopped once more, gestured (to *Káuyumarie* [Ramón's deer spirit helper], we were told later, to thank him for holding back the cloud doors with his horns, at the place called "Where the Clouds Open"), and set out again at a more rapid pace, all the while beating his bow. The others followed close behind in their customary single file.[76]

It is Ramón, bow lifted with one end held in his mouth and beating a rhythm with an arrow, and the antlered Káuyumarie who penetrate the cosmic threshold. We remember that Káuyumarie is Ramón's spirit helper, a reality speaking through and in a sense identifiable with the shaman.[77] It is by virtue of his unity with the principle represented by the spirit guide that Ramón, and consequently the other initiates, can penetrate the threshold to cosmic life, for it is the spirit guide who symbolically unites our changing world of time and death with the eternal world of essential form.[78]

The symbolism surrounding the muviére now becomes sexual in nature, with a familiar dual aspect.† Sexuality indicates the creative

———

*This process of crossing the cosmic threshold is symbolically related to magical flight. In the earlier ceremony the hummingbird children fly through this clashing gate, and Ramón emphasizes the same symbolism here by making feather offerings to help implement safe passage "to the other side."
†It should be noted that this symbolism was implicit in the role played by the arrow in crossing the cosmic threshold, for upon crossing, the initiate enters the place called Vagina, a symbolic indication that this is, indeed, an inward journey; "the passage into the Land of Our Origins, the Place of Beginning" (Myerhoff, p. 139).

plenitude of the generative source, on the one hand, and, on the other, the coincidence of opposites signaling unity. Crossing the threshold, the pilgrims come to the Springs of Our Mothers, a cluster of water holes surrounded by a marsh, which they consider the wellsprings of the waters of life. Here, in a series of repeated acts, the scepter is ritually inserted into the cavities of the wellsprings of life. Other ritual applications of the scepter reinforce its phallic character and suggest the union of male and female principles on a cosmic plane. Furst elaborates, "However, despite such readily apparent sexual symbolism, it would be simplistic in the extreme to reduce this particular ritual at *Tatéi Matiniéri* to the level of symbolic coitus alone. . . . What the *mara'akáme* [shaman] simulates with his ceremonial arrow, therefore, is not coitus but unity—the life-producing union of the male and female principles in all nature."[79] As such, this symbolism is, as Myerhoff notes, directed toward evoking the experience of the unity and plenitude that lies beyond the *coincidentia oppositorum*, that point where opposites coalesce.[80]

Passing through the Springs of Our Mothers and the coincidence of opposites it implies, Ramón leads his pilgrims to the sacred mountains at the end of the world, the abode of the *Katauyarixi*, the "ancient, ancient ones," or "ancestral gods." It is here that the final portion of the drama is played out in the "deer hunt" in a manner that is on one level purely characteristic of the Huichol but at the same time transparently manifests continuity with mythic structures of an ancient pedigree.

The procedure takes the outward form of an actual hunt. The men test their bows, place their arrows, and search on the ground for the tracks of the mythical deer, which is, of course, the peyote cactus. Soon Ramón shouts, "There, there, the deer." He takes aim and slays Elder Brother, the mythical deer, in the form of a peyote plant:

> The companions formed a circle around the place where Elder Brother lay "dying." Many sobbed. All prayed loudly. The one called *Tatutsí*, Great-grandfather, unwrapped Ramón's basket of power objects, the *takwátsi*, from the red kerchief in which it was kept and laid it open for Ramón's use in the complex and lengthy rituals of propitiation of the dead deer and division of its flesh

among the communicants. Ramón explained how the *küpúri*, the life essence of the deer, which, as with humans, resides in the fontanelle, was "rising, rising, rising, like a brilliantly colored rainbow, seeking to escape to the top of the sacred mountains." Do not be angry, Elder Brother, Ramón implored, do not punish us for killing you, for you have not really died.[81]

Furst continues his description of the ritual, which proceeds to articulate the moments of death and eternal rebirth:

> To push the rainbow-*küpúri*, which only he could see, back into the Deer, Ramón lifted his *muviéri*, first to the sky and the world directions, and then pressed it slowly downward, as though with great force, until the hawk feathers touched the crown of the sacred plant. In his chant he described how all around the dead deer peyotes were springing up, growing from his horns, his back, his tail, his shins, his hooves. *Tamátsi Wawatsári* [the master of the deer species], he said, is giving us our life. He took his knife from the basket and began to cut away the earth around the cactus. Then, instead of taking it out whole, he cut it off at the base, leaving a bit of the root in the ground. This is done so that "Elder Brother can grow again from his bones."[82]

In a symbolism that marvelously combines the image implicit in Jung's description of the transpersonal plane of existence as the "rhizome" level of continuing life and the ancient image of bone as a return to essence and as a source of renewal and mystical rebirth, Ramón carefully removes the peyote plant from the ground. "Then instead of taking it out whole, he cut it off at the base, leaving a bit of root in the ground. This is done so that 'Elder Brother can grow again from his bones,'" we are told in an image that carefully preserves an extremely ancient mythological conception. In death, and by virtue of Tamátsi Wawatsári, the deer-peyote mystically becomes the source of plenitude and renewal. Symbolically, the shaman, the conduit of renewed power, describing a mandala with his ceremonial arrow, restores the source of plenitude to the earth and in chant describes how all around this dead deer peyotes are springing up, growing from his horns, his back, his tail, his shins, his hooves.

"*Tamátsi Wawatsári,*" he says, "is giving us our life." Finally, as the shared source of life, the deer-peyote becomes the sacramental meal and the source of ecstasy and vision.

It is again as though Elder Brother Deer's "death were but a play," but a very significant play. Elder Brother, we are told, "has not really died," for in essence it is Tamátsi Wawatsári, the Master Deer, the deer deity to whom the slain manifestation returns. And it is here that the therianthropic spirit guide, deer and human at the same time, in a symbolism both sophisticated and poetic, serves as a bridge between our world of individuated form and the world of essential form. Each realm is represented by a particular aspect of the deer itself—our world of time and change by its temporal manifestation, which dies and is reborn, and the realm of essential form by that representative of cosmic life, the Master Animal, the eternal form of the deer that transcends time, change, and mortality. And the deer is likewise the spirit guide who mediates these realities, leading the shaman on the inward journey. As such, the deer is specifically identified with the transformation of consciousness that the journey elicits, represented by the peyote itself. All is the play of the unitive life force in its various manifestations. The ritual is carefully constructed, and, as in the protodramas that preceded and gave rise to Attic tragedy, there is only one player-god, the shape-shifting Dionysian life force, wearing various masks at various times. Recalling the total structure, we note that Elder Brother Deer is both the sacrifice and the sacrificer; finally he is also the deity to which sacrifice is offered. He is the slain animal, he is the spirit guide that is the agency leading Ramón to the kill, and he is, in essence, the Eternal Deer Deity himself. He is also the peyote that aids the transformation of consciousness that evokes this unifying experience. Thus, in Huichol visionary experience, we can see a living example of Eliade's earlier observation, for the spirit guide becomes "the center at once of the existence and renewal of the universe." He is specifically identified with the shaman's "euphoric experience" and has indeed "showed the shaman his power and brought him into communion with cosmic life."

As a result of such experience, the shaman traditionally understands himself as expressing the cosmos. This is often symbolized on his costume, for not only does he have the various mementos from his integration with the world of the animal guide—pendants, skins, bear claws, feathers, serpentine embellishments, as the case may be—but he also establishes his greater relationship with the cosmos by adorning himself with various symbols indicating that he is nothing less than the medium of cosmic power. Thus, the animal guide is both the threshold guardian and the porter at the door to the creative plenitude that the cosmos expresses; he is an emissary of the potential present in the human mind where it contacts its own creative wellsprings, that, as Schelling recognized, emanate from the common formative force man shares with the cosmos.

It is thus that the shaman becomes a conduit of divine power through his association with his spirit guide, for the animal guide is everywhere associated with the access to the cosmic power and plenitude that fires the fecundity of creation. As Michael Harner points out, "The guardian spirit is sometimes referred to by native North Americans as the *power animal*, as among the Coast Salish and the Okanagon of Washington. This is a particularly apt term, for it emphasizes the power-giving aspect of the guardian spirit as well as the frequency with which it is perceived as an animal."[83]

And while the power represented everywhere has its own particular characteristics, it is traditionally associated with the power of the Creation, the exemplary first creation that, to the archaic mind, fosters all creation, and the enduring or paradigmatic reality of a time still grounded in the flow of primordial plenitude. As the forms of mythical or durative time, these creatures represent not the actual animals incarnate in everyday existence, but rather the essential forms of the animal world. They are the archetypal pattern of everlasting creation, the mystery of permanence in change. As we shall see, they are frequently represented as surrounding or emanating eternally from the source or fount of creation as the ever generated forms in which eternity becomes manifest in time. This is the womb of creation, an example of which we have seen represented by the mistress of the earth in Sereptie's vision and her realm inhabited by "the master spirits of all the running and flying birds and game." As such, these creatures are not bears, wolves, or eagles, but Bear, Wolf, and Eagle. They are the soul, spirit, or essence of entire species, beyond the corrosive effects of time and in their immortal forms translucent to their enduring source. To quote

Campbell describing the mythical bull buffalo of the Blackfoot Indians of Montana:

> Or again, using a philosophical term not as remote from primitive thought as it may seem, we might say that the great bull represents the Platonic Idea of the species. He is a figure of one more dimension than the others of his herd: timeless and indestructible, whereas they are mere shadows (like ourselves), subject to the laws of time and space. They fell and were killed, whereas he was unharmed. He is a manifestation of that point, principle or aspect of the realm of essence from which the creatures of his species spring.[84]

Here Campbell detects a continuity of the expressions of the spirit over thousands of years, for this he recognizes to be the same vision as that enduringly inscribed or painted in the great caves of the Upper Paleolithic period. These caves, he tells us, represent "the timeless abyss of the night," and their paintings "are the prototypes, Platonic Ideas, or master forms of the temporal herds of the earth."[85] With this recognition in mind, we can return to the half-human, half-animal, semidivine figure represented in the Sorcerer of Les Trois Frères, for it is he who mediates the perilous journey through the narrow confines of the cave's entrance to the timeless forms of the transpersonal inner world represented in the cave's interior. Here, within the intrauterine cave sanctuary burgeoning with its exquisite animal forms, "the herds of eternity," we can now answer the question posed earlier and understand that this strangely provocative figure from that level of consciousness "still directly connected to nature in its mode of functioning" conveys to the transformed mind of the initiate an original wisdom that "proclaims a truth that issues from the heart of the world" and, in a very real sense, is "a prophet of wisdom born from nature's womb."

Chapter 4

THE LUMINOUS CAVE: THE GREAT DREAM OF THE MUNDUS ARCHETYPUS

Mythology comes into being through a necessary process (necessary in respect to consciousness), the origin of which loses itself in a suprahistorical realm. Consciousness may resist the process in certain particulars, but cannot impede, much less reverse, it as a whole. . . . Mythological ideas are neither invented nor voluntarily accepted.—Products of a process independent of thought and will, they were unequivocally and undeniably real for the consciousness subjected to them. Peoples and individuals are only instruments of this process, which they do not perceive as a whole, which they serve without understanding it. It is not in their power to cast off these ideas, to accept them or not to accept them: for these ideas do not come from outside but are within the mind and men never know how they arise: for they come from the innermost consciousness, on which they imprint themselves with a necessity that permits no doubt as to their truth.

F. W. J. Schelling

If the archetype is, in Jung's terms, "an image of instinct," that is, of the a priori form-producing principles deep within the psyche that act with the autonomy, necessity, and spontaneous pattern-generating propensities that we associate with the world of instinct, then the Sorcerer of Les Trois Frères, the half-human, half-animal spirit guide, is its perfect autosymbolic representation. And the realm into which he guides us is the deep inner sanctum containing the seeds of our conscious experience, the unconscious regulators and stimulators that operate to form and order our reality. For the interior cave is not simply the womb or fount of cosmic creation. It also represents the creative source within the human mind, where the human creator momentarily experiences himself as expressing something beyond himself. It is the objectification of the transformation of consciousness evoked by the perilous journey and heralded by the appearance of the spirit guide, the transpersonal archetypal reality of "the 2,000,000 year old man who is in all of us."

Here form emerges from the stony void of the cave walls just as the first dark urgings to form issue from the human unconscious and as cosmic form emanates from the pregnant silence of the Godhead. And miraculously, in a manner that must have impressed archaic man as to their shared source, each, cosmic and human creativity alike, manifests itself in beauty of form, the beauty with which these images of eternity appearing from the blank cave wall so impresses us. Erich Neumann expresses this well:

> The creative function of the unconscious . . . produces its forms spontaneously, in a manner analogous to nature, which—from atom and crystal through organic life to the world of the stars and planets—spontaneously creates forms susceptible of impressing man as beautiful. Because this substratum and background of the psychophysical world is forever bringing forth forms, we call it creative. And to the unknown in nature which engenders its forms of the external world there corresponds another unknown, the collective unconscious, which is the source of all psychic creation: religion and rite, social organization, consciousness, and finally art.[1]

"For nature itself in its deeper sense is not the sum total of created things but the creative power from which the form and order of the universe are derived," Ernst Cassirer informs us, and these forms within the cave are not imitations of nature but the expression of humanity's inward encounter with this "psychophysical substratum," the deep, unconscious urge to form and order that is the nuclear force of all we experience or create.[2] It is here that, in Schelling's terms, the formal powers of cosmic creation invest the dream of mythology with a "profundity, permanence and universality . . . comparable only with Nature herself," a process that is at once spontaneous and deeply necessary. Here, as Nietzsche tells us, human creation merges with and expresses "the Genius of the Universe" and itself becomes the expression of cosmos.

The fount of cosmic creation likewise speaks to the shaman—and it speaks from within, in the reality of vision, dream, and ecstasy. He turns the eye inward in both his ecstatic and mythic training and reaches the "magical space of God," as Campbell has aptly termed the inner grottoes of the Paleolithic caves.[3] We have traced the inward journey of the shaman into the depths of the mind symbolized by the interior cave. We shall now examine several examples of shamanism from diverse parts of the globe and unrelated cultures, often nearly as different from one another as they are from the Ice Age people who first saw in these caves the fitting projection for the inner templates of their minds and the universal dream of mythology. In each we shall discover important features that will further our understanding of shamanism. Moreover, in each we can discern striking structural and functional similarities despite differences of time, distance, and cultural orientation. And in each, the cave, or its equivalent symbol, is the initiatory entrance to the dreamtime ecstatic realm of visionary experience.

THE "CLEVER MAN" OF AUSTRALIA

The Aboriginal inhabitants of Australia are, as far as we can tell, an extremely ancient race whose way of life, some argue, "has not substantially changed for perhaps about 35,000 years."[4] Given this conservatism and the continent's natural isolation, the universal nature of certain of the characteristics of its shamanism is, as Eliade states, "disconcerting to the scholar." We have previously discussed some of these characteristic features, particularly in relation to Siberian shamanism, but here we seek to view them in a larger context. Fortunately, Professor A. P. Elkin, in the first half of this century, was able to gather and discuss many of the characteristics of Aboriginal shamanism in a book he first published in 1945, *Aboriginal Men of High Degree: Initiation and Sorcery in the World's Oldest Tradition.*

The details of shamanism as a worldwide phenomenon with its own peculiar structure were not nearly as well-known at the time when Elkin wrote as they are today. One of the first things that impressed Professor Elkin, however, was the uncanny universality revealed in the forms of shamanism across the continent of Australia, even in many minor details. He tells us:

> At first sight, there is nothing stranger in anthropological literature and in fieldwork than the descriptions given by Aboriginal medicine men of the way in which they received their power. These seem so impossible and fantastic that we could be pardoned for dismissing them as mere inventions or as the results of nightmare. But a study of the distribution of these experiences and an examination of their patterns give pause for thought. For the striking fact is not so much the weirdness of the details as their similarity over wide regions of the continent and even in apparently widely separated regions. In other words, we are confronted by a prescribed pattern of ritual experience through which medicine men are made.[5]

And as we look at this "prescribed pattern of ritual experience," we can recognize an even greater resonance beyond Australia, a distinct similarity to what we have discussed so far and to what remains to be presented—shamanism as a form of the universal dream of mythology. For the dream of mythology is a particularly apposite expression with respect to Aboriginal Australia, where all reality depends upon a psychophysical substratum they refer to as the "dreamtime," and the shaman is its primary emissary.

The foreword to the 1976 edition of Elkin's work summarizes some of its important parts and can serve as a point of entry for our discussion of the Australian shaman, or "clever man":

> The "clever man," as some English speakers call him, has acquired wonderful powers through direct contact with the beings of the

dreamtime: the rainbow serpent, the sky gods, the spirits of the dead. He has come to this state through a long and rigorous apprenticeship and an initiation of terrors and ordeals beyond those that ordinary men undergo. He is what Elkin calls a man of high degree; his experiences have changed him utterly. He has died and come alive again; his entrails have been taken out and replaced; he has been swallowed by the rainbow serpent and regurgitated; magic crystals have been put in his body; he has acquired an animal familiar that dwells within him.[6]

We immediately recognize familiar themes: the ordeals of initiation, dismemberment, ego death, being swallowed and regurgitated (or excreted), the rebirth motif, the adamantine substance (in this case quartz), the acquisition of an animal guide, and the role of the ancestors or "spirits of the dead," beings from a world beyond, in this case the dreamtime.

We can proceed to examine these initial steps in the "prescribed pattern" of Australian shamanism and add those that complete the schema as well. The Australian shaman-to-be, as is frequently the case in other cultures as well, "must have shown from his earliest years a leaning toward the profession."[7] He may receive a special calling in dream. The initial experience often ecstatically initiates the postulant, leading him spontaneously along his mystical itinerary. We shall see examples of this "autoinitiation" as we proceed. As in other cultures, the shaman's training typically is both ecstatic and traditional. The Aborigine's world is likewise filled with myths and symbols that are employed to awaken the interior reality of the dreamtime. Myth and traditional lore are sanctified as the expressions of the formal power of the dreamtime, the same "psychophysical substratum" penetrated in ecstasy. And the perceived relationship between the tribe's mythic heritage and its source in the dreamtime is made absolutely clear, for the mythic lore is generally referred to in the various languages of the different tribes by the very same word that signifies the eternal dreamtime.[8]

In ecstatic training, drums, dancing, and inhalation of smoke from sacred herbs may be used in order to induce a profound trance condition that is also called the dreamtime.[9] Elkin, however, emphasizes the meditative aspect of the shaman's communication with the dreamtime world. In either case, the end result to be sought is the same—a transformation of consciousness. An informant tells Elkin:

> In all his dream or trance experience, the trainee's mind is being "conditioned." He is being shown in his mind what to do. And by his total experience and training he is set aside, ordained as we might say; he becomes an expert.[10]

Elkin describes an initiation with many typical features that took place in northern Kimberley, Western Australia.

> During his initiation a young man would get the idea of being a *banman* or *bainman* (doctor-man), and if he had dreams or visions of water, pandanus, and bark when near a water place, he was said to be chosen by Unggud [the creationtime serpent] to be a banman. A vision of his dream-totem's visit to heaven would have the same significance. After his initiation into manhood, he went with a medicine man to the water place where he felt that "Unggud had killed him." He sees the same Unggud rise out of the ground or the water, but in its "very essence," which is visible only to medicine men. He sees the giant "snake" with its arms, hands, and a feather "crown." He faints and is led by Unggud to a cool and dry part of a subterranean cave, where his transformation into a banman takes place. Unggud gives him a new brain, puts in his body white quartz crystals, which give secret strength, and reveals to him his future duties. He may remain unconscious for some time, but when he wakes he has a great feeling of inner light. He is certain of being equal to Unggud. Instruction, guidance, and experience follow for many months, even years.

This experience is the source of the shaman's powers:

> The newly made doctor learns to see and understand hidden things. He will be able to see before his inner eye past and future events and "happenings in other worlds." He learns to read other people's thoughts and recognize their secret worries, to cure illnesses with the "medicine" stones, to put himself in a trance, and to send his

ya-yari (his dream familiar) from his body to gather information.

The psychic element in these talents is clearly all-pervasive. It is termed *miriru* and comes from Unggud. Fundamentally it is the capacity bestowed on the medicine man to go into a dream state or trance with its possibilities. Indeed, miriru makes him like a Wandjina, having the same abilities as the heroes of "creation times."[11]

What initially stands out is the role played by and the description of the dreamtime animal spirit guide, Unggud. Unggud chooses the postulant in vision or dream. After his initiation, he feels that Unggud has "killed" him. Unggud leads him to a cave, where his transformation into a shaman takes place through the dismemberment symbolism with which we are now familiar. The snake gives him a "new brain," symbolic of his new psychic powers, and puts quartz crystals in his body, emblematic of his relationship to the unchanging realm of essence, of which the dreamtime serpent is representative.

For Unggud is, himself, a creature of "essence." The future doctor is able to see the "very essence" of the snake, which others cannot see. This is because he is becoming invested with the "inner eye" or, in Aboriginal terms, the "strong eye," which turning inward sees the realities of the dreamtime, the ontological ground supporting existence. And thus envisioned, the dreamtime snake is not an ordinary serpent but has arms, hands, and a feathered crown. He assumes the therianthropic form of the spirit guide with all the implications of this form that we have previously explored. He has the power to enlighten the *banman* as to the forces latent in his own soul, and when the doctor awakens he has a great feeling of inner light; he is illuminated from within by the constant creative forces of the dreamtime. He becomes equal to Unggud, a creature invested with the power that infuses creation, and identical with the heroes of the dreamtime, who created and still create the world.

A whole universe of shamanic themes with global distribution is contained in this short description, which we can touch on only briefly. We note that upon encountering Unggud, the postulant "faints and is led by Unggud to a cool and dry part of a subterranean cave, where his transformation into a *banman* takes place."

Eliade emphasizes the importance of the cave in the initiation of the Australian medicine man. The cave, he remarks, is a common symbol of passage into another world, and he notes its use in shamanic initiations in other parts of the world.[12] Elkin also points out that in some areas, after the act of piercing the tongue of the shaman, which we discussed earlier, "the victim falls dead and is carried into the depths of the cave," where the ancestral spirits of the dreamtime complete his initiation into their reality.[13]

Here the cave symbolizes the process of initiation itself, the trainee's "conditioning," which leads back into the preconscious and, indeed, into "another world," that is, the dreamtime. Appropriately, as the place of the shaman's illumination, rather than remaining a place of darkness the cave becomes luminescent. It paradoxically acquires a celestial aspect. Among the Kurnai, Eliade tells us, "its [the cave's] celestial character is clearly emphasized by the luminosity of the initiation cave. . . . The cave is bright because it is covered with quartz crystals, that is, it ultimately partakes of the mystical nature of the sky."[14] Andreas Lommel likewise cites similar examples of the luminous cave spontaneously produced in the initiatory dreams of the Australian shaman:

> Such dreams of being called are described as follows: The soul of the man who is becoming a shaman leaves him. His body lies asleep. It is a deep sleep and no one dares to wake the sleeper, even if this sleep lasts for days. During the sleep the soul goes to the water-hole from which it originally came. It does not remain in this water-hole, however, but dives down from there into the innermost part of the earth. There, after a long journey through dark water, it suddenly comes to a brightly lit cave in which two snakes, a male and a female, are mating. From the union of these two snakes there continually spring "child-seeds"—many of which enter into the shaman's soul, so that henceforth he bears more soul-strength than an ordinary person.[15]

The conjunction of the initiatory descent, the luminous cave, and male and female polarity symbolizing the creative power infusing the shaman's soul strikes a now familiar chord. Lommel cites another example:

Another account of the experience of being called in northwestern Australia runs: "Perhaps a man is lying asleep, he is an ordinary man, but in his sleep he suddenly thinks: 'Why am I not a shaman? I could become a shaman.'"

He lies down at the edge of a water hole and falls asleep.

In his dream his soul dives deep down into the water to the place where it becomes black and dark, and in his dream the shaman feels himself die. But the dead soul dives on until it comes to a cave in which it is dry and bright and in which the sun is shining. In the hole there is a great snake. The soul sits down and the snake speaks to it and gives it "medicine." Thereupon the soul rises to the surface of the water again and comes back. The man wakes and feels that he is alive again.[16]

Among the Aranda, Eliade tells us, the spirits who pierce the tongue of the candidate and then tear out his inner organs live in the initiatory cave in perpetual light near cool springs. In fact, he informs us, the cave represents the Aranda Paradise.[17] Thus, the cave becomes the portal to the Otherworld. And it also implies a return to origin, both the origin of the cosmos and the point in the mind that reaches back into cosmic creative plenitude by virtue of illumination and trance, penetrating the dreamtime matrix of creation. In fact, in the Australian visionary cosmos, the "dreamtime" is also the "creationtime," the form-generating source of the "Origin" as a reality always accessible to the shaman.

The chasm or hole in the ground play roles that parallel the cave symbolism. The *rai*, the spirits of the dead, initiate the shaman in their home, a chasm in the ground. It is here that the shaman learns to travel to other worlds in a trance. Likewise, in mandala-like ground paintings consisting of concentric circles around a central aperture, the Northern Aranda depict the sacred water hole, or soak, that was the center of creation and the birthplace of the primal ancestor, Karora, the place from which all life and the sun itself emanated. In Figure 24, the central figure, with a striped and feathered pole above his head, represents Karora. It is believed that "in the beginning," Karora lay asleep under this holy ground and that above his head arose a sacred decorated pole reaching the sky. Awakening, Karora burst from beneath the ground, creating the hole that became the Ilbalintja Soak. "The shaman," we are told, "enters this place in the process of his initiation."[18] Once again we have the cave or hole in the ground associated with both initiation and a return to the origin of creation.

As part of this cave initiation, we recognize the familiar symbolism of ego death, the symbolic correlative of the conditioning of the trainee's mind of which we were earlier informed. In the example from northern Kimberley quoted at length earlier, Unggud, a creature of the preconscious mind, has killed the initiate. In this instance, the novice's brain is removed and replaced, and quartz is inserted within his body. In other areas of Australia, the process is more detailed and graphically depicted. The initiate is cut up, or his flesh is scraped away; his insides (intestines, heart, lungs, liver, kidneys) are removed; and his bones are disarticulated, cleansed, and reunited along with a new viscera, often accompanied by such agents

FIGURE 24. *Northern Aranda tribesmen and sacred ground painting representing Ilbalintja Soak, Central Australia.*

as quartz, pearl shell, spirits, snakes, or other familiars. In many areas, as it was in the example given previously, this process of dismemberment or initiatory death is envisioned as being performed by a creationtime serpent, but in others, in a manner entirely consistent with what we have previously encountered, it is carried out by the ancestors, the spirits of the dead, shamans, or the dreamtime heroes. We may also remember that in a symbolism analogous to these visions of radical dismemberment, the Australian shaman is pierced through the back of the neck and outwardly through the tongue. Not only is the hole in the tongue indicative of the shamanic vocation but, moreover, the vocation somehow depends upon it, for if it heals, the shaman's powers will disappear.

In the description of the banman's initiation quoted earlier, he feels as if he is killed by the dreamtime serpent. In many other instances the novitiate is said to be initially swallowed by the serpent. "The Wirangu (at the head of the Great Australian Bight)," Elkin tells us, "say that a postulant is swallowed by Djidara, a large snake whose tracks are Lakes Gardiner, Torrens, and others . . . and after having been passed through this creature's insides, becomes a medicine man,"[19] and, "In western South Australia, the postulant is put in a waterhole, where a mythical snake [Wonambi] swallows him but later ejects him in the form of a baby onto a supposedly unknown place. After a long search, he is found by the doctors and is restored to man's size by being sung to in the midst of a circle of fires."[20] At this point he announces that he knows Wonambi, having been inside his stomach. "He and Wonambi are friends."[21] Thereafter he endures a period of seclusion and further ordeals that complete his initiation into the powers of his trade. Wonambi is a creature of the creationtime "who is alive today, even though his mythical exploits belong to the ancestral dreamtime."[22]

It is important that the therianthrophic spirit guide is the mediator between the shaman and the reality he accesses. As we remember in our previous example, it was from the snake, Unggud, that the postulant received his calling. In numerous mythologies as well as in our dream experiences, as Jung and others have recognized, therianthrophic, serpentine, or saurian forms symbolize the unconscious deep structures of the mind, and their appearance heralds our encounter with these structures. These forms, at first frightening, eventually reveal themselves to be the very emissaries of the altered state of consciousness that will enlighten and empower the shaman and lead him to the realm of vision. They signal a "turning of consciousness," the opening of the inward eye, and the symbols by which this altered form of consciousness expresses itself likewise "turn." Because this transformation entails a transcendence of our normal modes of thought, it employs a series of images relying on paradox or a coincidence of opposites to tease us beyond our logical categories of thought and to suggest a reality not to be grasped by the intellect. The reality the shaman seeks is not the reality of the intellect per se, but that of inner experience, and it is precisely the inward relocation of the real at the expense of our everyday consciousness that the swallowing by—or death by means of—the dreamtime snake symbolizes. But the death is paradoxically a rebirth on a consecrated level, as we have seen, and it is interpreted generally not as an actual death but as a trance state opening the portal of our world to its essential reality. Thus, the dark cave paradoxically becomes luminescent, and the shaman devoured by the Wonambi serpent learns that "he and Wonambi are friends." Symbols of descent into the interior give way to symbols of transcendence. The cave or chasm leading to the Otherworld becomes associated with symbols of ascent to a "higher" reality along an astral (aerial) rope or cord that only the "strong eye" of the shaman can see and by which he can travel to the sky world.

The serpent itself, and the unconscious schema of illumination it represents, also becomes a paradoxical symbol and literal vehicle of ascent. As we noticed earlier, the Unggud serpent had a feathered crown, and by virtue of this feature, we are told, this typically chthonic creature can fly. Indeed, in some areas of Australia the postulant and the initiating shaman are said to fly through the air astride this snake. In some areas, the symbolisms of the cord and the serpent as a vehicle of ascent are combined. For example, in the Forrest River district of northern Kimberley, where the shaman receives his powers from the rainbow snake, Brimurer or Ungur, Elkin tells of his ascent led by an older shaman. The method "is for the older man to take the form of a skeleton, sit astride the rainbow snake and pull himself up with an arm-over-arm action on a rope."[23] Having reached the sky, the doctor inserts into the young man some little rainbow snakes and some quartz crystals, making him a shaman.

These often unconsciously produced associations begin to coalesce into a cluster of images sharing a similar paradoxical nature with a poetry of their own. Together they imply a *coincidentia oppositorum*, suggesting an underlying totality, as Eliade observes. "Indeed, Unggud, the master and protector of waters, being the Rainbow Serpent, also extends to the sky. From a certain point of view, one might say that Unggud represents the mythological expression of the effort to unite the opposites, to articulate polarities into a paradoxical unity."[24] In this respect, we might also point out that Unggud is bisexual, combining masculine and feminine in a creative complementarity indicative of the inexhaustible source. The rainbow image paradoxically lifts the earthbound iridescent serpent to a celestial venue. The snake's home is represented as being in the water, but the rainbow combines fleeting particles of water with solar permanence to intimate in its iridescent form the principle of permanence in change, also symbolized in quartz and bone. As noted, the serpent itself is feathered and can fly, and the chthonic cave of initiation becomes luminescent and opens to the Otherworld, the dreamtime. It leads to an ascent through trance up the astral cord produced from the shaman's own body or up a tree associated with the cord. Apparent death becomes rebirth, a world of essence. The shaman ascends in skeletal form both on the visionary serpent and, varying the symbolism, in the rites of dismemberment that reduce him to essence. Quartz is the primary symbol of the principle of permanence underlying change, and, as we shall see, doused in "liquefied quartz" the shaman himself becomes feathered and winged. The symbols weave and intertwine to everywhere lift the world of our changeable earth to the durative dreamtime reality that permanently informs it.

In the Unggud serpent and its variations we can recognize a symbolism occurring with striking frequency among the world's various forms of shamanism. As spirit guide, Unggud unites the three cosmic realms. It is a denizen of the depths, both in the waters below the earth's surface and in its home beneath the earth; a creature intimately associated with the earth's surface, which it scuds across on its belly; and, in this case, as the flying plumed serpent, it becomes celestial. It symbolically establishes a vertical axis that unites the shaman's cosmos. Eliade sets the cornerstone for understanding the shaman's universe:

> The pre-eminently shamanic technique is the passage from one cosmic region to another—from earth to the sky or from earth to the underworld. The shaman knows the mystery of the breakthrough in plane. This communication among the cosmic zones is made possible by the very structure of the universe. . . . The universe in general is conceived as having three levels—sky, earth, underworld—connected by a central axis.[25]

It is a recurrent feature of shamanism throughout the world that the shaman's experience symbolically establishes this central axis of "vertical" communication uniting the three realms.

The cave itself repeats the same uniting function. It leads from the earth to the underworld but at the same time becomes a passage through trance to the dreamtime celestial world, again bringing together the three realms. In this way, it appropriates the entire process of ecstatic and mythic or traditional training as a "trip backward into the mind," where the conditioning techniques related to ecstasy and its inducement and the symbols of the native mythic tradition function in the manner examined in the previous chapter to reintegrate the mind with its inward source. The immersion in the cave is symbolically doubled by the postulant's being engulfed by the serpent guide, and both signal the relocation inward of the focal point of what is considered to be real. Here, as elsewhere, the therianthropic spirit guide serves as a mediator between man and the deep roots of his consciousness, which the shaman experiences as uniting him with the plenitude of creation. So initiated, the shaman realizes "he is equal to Unggud" or that "he and Wonambi are friends." Symbolically, the spirit guide serves as a focal point for a *coincidentia oppositorum*, uniting the many into one and transcending the conditioned world of opposition to become a symbol of ascent to a "higher" reality accessible to the shaman.

Thus, the unifying vertical axis uniting the three realms has another important aspect. For everyday consciousness, reality tends to assume the form of what we may classify under the paradigm of "horizontal" causation—linear cause and effect in time eventually leading back to a temporally remote act of creation whether by the "big bang" or in a garden in Eden. The shaman's transformation of consciousness leads him to experience reality differently. It is experienced as the continual unfolding of an ontologically prior source of plenitude immanent within the creation. Creation is a perpetual unfolding of essence, and the origin is an accessible reality ever present through trance ascent. Uniting the three realms reveals that all is a reflex of this higher reality—in Australia the dreamtime—and that in essence we are the dreamtime heroes.

As we may remember, the serpent, Unggud, originally appears to our banman not as an ordinary snake but as the snake's "very essence," which is visible only to medicine men. It is only thus that it appears in the form of the spirit guide with its "arms, hands and a feather 'crown'" and leads to the cave of vision. It is the emissary of the generative matrix of essential form inwardly encountered. For in the shamanic mythology of this area, the shaman, the "clever man," can gain contact with an individual assistant spirit guide, bird or animal, by going in trance to the bird or animal's "clever place," the place from which it derives its essential form. This is its sacred mythological center, or its "dreaming," to use a widespread northern and central Australian term.[26] Here the creature is born as a coinage of eternal form, "born from his own eternity" as the Aborigines poetically say. It is precisely, as Campbell described the totem animal in other shamanisms, the representative of "the realm of essence from which the creatures of his species spring," the cosmic fount of eternal form encountered in dream, trance, and vision, and thus appropriately termed by the Aborigines the "dreamtime."

The clever place, the totem animal's sacred mythological center or "its dreaming," is represented in the cave and rock paintings of various Australian tribes. Andreas Lommel tells us:

The Australian aborigines describe the time of Creation as the dream time. The first beings dreamed the animals and plants; they painted the dream images on the rocks, filled them with a soul-force, and from the rock-paintings the souls of the beings represented spread over the world in a physical shape.[27]

According to Lommel, among the Unumbal, for whom the cosmic serpents Wallanganda and Unggud dream the world (the two may well be celestial and chthonic aspects of each other, suggesting a coincidence of opposites), the dream forms of creation were shaped into images by Wallanganda, and these images, painted red, white, and black, were projected onto the rocks and caves where they exist today.[28] "The paintings," he tells us, "are the spiritual centers of those beings [that is, of the first dream forms of creation]. They are the Fathers; and the living beings of each kind are Brothers."[29] They are the essential forms or prototypes of all animal and plant life emanating from their cosmic source, and it was only after their creation that their living representatives were created. Alongside these master spirits of the animal and plant world are depicted the Wondjina, anthropomorphic images without mouths who live in caves and are the dreamtime heroes and lawgivers. Among certain tribes, they are aspects of Unggud and continue the serpent's world creation at sacred sites.

According to Eliade, the paintings of the caves and rock shelters of northern Kimberley depict the mythology of the tribe and in so doing simultaneously function to reanimate contact with the dreamtime. Each gallery includes a depiction of at least one anthropomorphic being—a Wondjina—and representations of different species of animal forms.[30] The images are a reservoir of dreamtime plenitude. "In northern Kimberley, if a rock painting is touched by a man from the proper totemic clan, rain will fall and the spirit children will become available for incarnation. Likewise, repainting the animal and vegetal images is said to increase the respective species."[31]

This act of touching may be memorialized in numerous hand images found on the cave walls. These images are both positive and negative, the negative apparently made by the familiar process of blowing pigments around the hand placed on the cave wall. In some areas finger joints are missing, perhaps suggestive of a dismemberment symbolism, a symbolism that we have seen repeatedly in conjunction with the cave of initiation. Perhaps a similar symbolism is implied by the fact that some of these prints are made with an ochre mixed with human blood. The caves seem to have been of ceremonial usage, and some of their embellishments are of great antiquity—they are presently thought by some to date back to 40,000 B.P.

or, according to very recent discoveries, perhaps far longer.

The clever man, the shaman, through his initiatory experience likewise becomes grounded in his own clever place, for his "sacred mythological center" reaches back into and expresses the dreamtime. The soul, Plato tells us, is a first movement, the immediate expression of self-generating form and the oldest of all things. And so it is also with the Aborigines, for part of the soul is actually descended from a Wondjina or, in different tribes, is "a particle of the ancestor's 'life'" and ultimately stems from Unggud as the embodiment of the dreamtime. In essence, each man is a Wondjina, ancestor, or dreamtime hero, and his soul innately carries the features of a paradigmatic reality. In periodically repainting the Wondjina images, the participant actually recreates himself, that is, his dreamtime self, which shares the same source as do the plant and animal essences. "His most secret self is a part of that sacred world he is periodically trying to recontact," Eliade points out. "But he does not know his own real identity: this must be revealed to him through initiation rites. Thus, one may say that the initiation reinstates the young Australian in his original spiritual mode of being."[32] Myth and ritual progressively thin the distance between life and an understanding of the creationtime archetypes that inform it. The process is an anamnesis, an unforgetting of what is innately known; a "going back" in both mind and time to what "has been and is and will be in all time." Not only are a person's acts the same acts as the ancestor *ab origine*, but he actually is the ancestor and shares his "glorious preexistence." In Jung's terms he, indeed, incarnates "the 2,000,000 year old man who is in all of us."

If the term *religion* originally was derived from *religare*, in the sense of "binding back" (*re*=back + *ligare*=to bind)—relinking or reconnecting with a sacred reality—this process of Australian "remembering" is its epitome. Eliade finds this idea implied in very old Aboriginal images of ascent by tree, ladder, cord, or mountain, representing a vertical axis that originally connected heaven and earth but later became severed, resulting in a profane world. Symbolic of this axis is a sacred pole literally central to the process of initiation. Mythically, this pole was planted by the cultural hero of the Achilpa—Numbakulla, whose name denotes "always existing" or "out of nothing"—in the middle of a sacred ground. Anointing

it with blood, he climbed up it and instructed the first Achilpa ancestor to follow him. The blood-stained pole, however, proved too
slippery, and the man fell to the ground. "Numbakulla went on alone,
drew up the pole after him and was never seen again."[33]

In Aranda initiation ceremonies a similar sacred pole relinking
man with the ancestors is planted. It is banded with alternate rings
of red and white bird down and topped with a tuft of feathers. It is
around this sacred pole that the previously circumcised initiate is
subincised, suggesting the union of sexual opposites in the person
of the initiate, an approximation of the dreamtime totality that the
central sacred pole reconnecting man with the eternal ancestors
reiterates.[34]

The dreamtime is the time of exemplary creation; the time when
the ancestors or dreamtime heroes gave form to the present creation. These theriomorphic creatures, themselves uncreated or
"born from their own eternity," variously share human and animal
forms and are "commonly designated totemic ancestors." As representatives of primordial creative plenitude, they are also cultural
heroes who "taught men how to make tools and fire and to cook
food, and they also revealed social and religious institutions to
them. . . . Such happenings," Eliade tells us,

> are supremely significant; that is to say, in our terminology they
> have a religious value. Indeed, the events that took place in the
> mythical times, in the "Dream Time," are religious in the sense
> that they constitute a paradigmatic history* which man has to fol-
> low and repeat in order to assure the continuity of the world, of
> life and society.[35]

---

*This paradigmatic worldview, so typical of archaic people, is not as
naive as it appears to be when judged by our modern preconceptions. In
The Birth of Tragedy Nietzsche well captures the effect on a culture of
such an archetypal orientation when he tells us, "It may be claimed that
a nation, like an individual, is valuable only insofar as it is able to give to
quotidian existence the stamp of the eternal. Only by so doing can it
express its profound, if unconscious, conviction of the relativity of time
and the metaphysical meaning of life."

For the Aborigines the creative plenitude of the dreamtime remains a continuous force, and its archetypal reality ever incarnates itself in the world. As Elkin states, "The 'dreamtime' and its heroes are the source of life in man and nature. Therefore, to be brought into full realization of the *Altjiringa* (dreamtime) is to share actively in that stream of life and power that is not hampered by the limitations of space and time."[36]

The dreamtime is an enduring reality, paradigmatic and essential, the source and support of our own temporal forms. At the same time, it is accessible, an "ever present Origin" characterized by inexhaustible creativity. And its realization is the goal of the shaman's visionary quest, for it is perceived by the strong eye, the eye that turns inward to become one with the primal architect of the universe, the cosmic fount of creative plenitude. For dreamtime is precisely the manifestation in the human mind of that common formative force in nature and in the human preconscious that Schelling saw expressing itself in universal forms in the dream of mythology. It is the expression of man's inward experience of the all-creative "psychophysical substratum," the primordial formal power of human creation and the Creation. As "dream" it is autogenous—"born from its own eternity"—spontaneous and at the same time necessary and universal. In a certain sense, in its relationship to the world of the ancestors it significantly parallels Jung's description of the collective unconscious, which he encountered in his psychological research. "[It] comprises in itself the psychic life of our ancestors right back to the earliest beginnings," and "contains the whole spiritual heritage of mankind's evolution, born anew in the brain structure of every individual." But it is important also to realize that here ontogeny and ontology overlap, for it is "born anew" in each of us precisely because this innate spiritual heritage is itself the expression of the formative force that constantly becomes incarnate in the creation. It is representative of what Jung ultimately referred to as the durative reality of the "continuous creation," the same inwardly encountered and synchronistic ever present origin that the shaman himself expresses in vision.

In this sense, the shaman expresses cosmos. In Elkin's terms, he partakes of an "unbroken channel" of power that emanates from the inexhaustible reality of the dreamtime.[37] And it is because he is invested with this formal cosmic power that he can understand and express the inner meaning of myth and vision, which are themselves the productions of the dreamtime. He is, thus, keeper of myths, poet, artist, singer, and ritual leader with a deep knowledge of the traditional and religious life of the tribe. As he progressively, in trance, vision, or ritual reenactment of the creationtime myths, recovers his own "clever place," his ground in the dreamtime, his psychic capacity makes him like a Wondjina, having the same abilities as the heroes of creationtime. The initiated shaman experiences a reawakening; he discovers that he is the reincarnation of the creators from the dreamtime. "This dramatic revelation of the identity between the eternal ancestor and the individual in which he is reincarnated can be compared with the *tat tvam asi* [that thou art] of the Upanishads," Eliade tells us.[38] And we remember that the postulant, called by the creationtime snake, Unggud, to his vocation in our earlier example, awakens from trance to experience "a great feeling of inner light. He is certain of being equal to Unggud." In fact, according to a tradition recorded by Elkin, the shaman, rather than dying a normal death, "would go into the earth one day and change himself into an Unggud snake."[39] In this tradition the shaman finally becomes the feathered serpent of creationtime.

Henri Bergson, himself trying to awaken man to the creative force, the *élan vital*, that the human mind shares with the world around it, poetically observed, "The matter and life which fill the world are equally within us; the forces which work in all things we feel within ourselves; whatever may be the inner essence of what is and what is done, we are of that essence. Let us then go down into our inner selves; the deeper the point we touch, the stronger will be the thrust which sends us back to the surface."[40] This very well expresses, at least in part, the role played by the shaman in human life. He delves deep into the mind and returns with revivifying creative power and plenitude. We can see this poignantly expressed in a tale related by Andreas Lommel of his own encounter with a leprous old Aboriginal shaman, Allan Balbungu, and it is fitting that we end our discussion of Australian shamanism on this more human note.

Allan, though old and infirm, still carried the reputation of being a big shaman, as well as an artist and a poet. Lommel encountered Allan at the corroboree ground, the place where several tribes gathered in shared celebrations. Hesitantly, Allan discussed his role as shaman and poet and how he received the inspiration that informed the songs and dances he passed on to the tribes assembled there. He described how he was able to separate his soul from his body, how, with the aid of a spirit helper, his soul entered the Otherworld, the world of the ancestors, to "find" the songs and dances he brought back. Lommel relates Allan's experience:

> When the shaman wakes his experiences with the spirits seem to him like a dream. From now on he thinks of nothing but the dances which he has seen and his soul keeps on going back to the spirits to learn more and more about the dances. His wife may then notice that his soul has been leaving his body every night, and she will say: Why do you always leave me? But the shaman will tell her that he goes to the spirits to learn dances. Then he will explain the dances to his wife and sing them to her, and after that he will teach them to everyone else. That is how the magnificent pantomimic dances of the Aborigines come into being.[41]

Sometimes the gift of visiting the spirits appears to be lost, and the journey becomes difficult. "He suddenly becomes incapable of making contact with the spirits and his poetic gift for creating songs and dances vanishes. In such cases all the men gather together to re-establish the broken link with the dead forefathers." The men sing and rub the shaman for hours until he finally is able to fall into a trance, where he receives the promise of help from the spirit world:

> After a time—it is perhaps one evening when the people are sitting quietly and talking—the shaman suddenly hears a distant call. It is a helping spirit calling him. He goes off by himself and converses for a while with the spirit. But a few days later his soul leaves his body. His body lies quietly sleeping. But under the leadership of the helping spirit others now come up from the underworld and take possession of the shaman's spirit, which they want to see among them again. They tear the soul to pieces and each spirit carries a piece into the underworld. There, deep under the earth, they put the shaman's soul together again. They show him the dances again and sing songs to him.[42]

Allan translates his visionary experience onto the corroboree ground. The poet has delved deeply into the creative source, the world of the spirit, and touched its deepest point. He is thrust back to the surface inspired. This art not only represents his reception of the songs and dances he has experienced in the Otherworld but also the very structure of the creative visionary experience itself. It is performed against a backdrop of dancers painted with white stripes, who represent in skeletal form the spirits of the dead ancestors, the very source from which the poet receives his inspiration. Allan himself, accompanied by an ecstatic chorus, sings of his visionary encounters with this matrix of plenitude from which they draw their reality. "It was a beautiful scene," Lommel relates, "the dancers with their vivid painting, the ecstatic chorus led by Allan himself and the high dark trees vaulting over everything." The people sing and dance until morning. "With mounting ecstasy, the song became louder and people fell into trance."[43] The poet's world becomes complete, and the audience is transported to the visionary realm, touching that deepest point man shares with the creative source. We cannot help but see here in what Elkin refers to as "the world's oldest tradition" an image strikingly kindred to one that also lies at the very base of our most inspired Western art, in which another ecstatic visitant to the Otherworld, a god of ecstasy and intoxication, torn to pieces by the spirits, sang and danced likewise accompanied by a chorus of liminal creatures from whom he symbolically received the formal powers of his inspiration. This is, of course, the god Dionysus, from whom we received the world of Greek tragedy, perhaps the West's greatest poetic accomplishment.

"The matter and life which fill the world are equally within us; the forces which work in all things we feel within ourselves; whatever may be the inner essence of what is and what is done, we are of that essence." It is this sense of vital connection between the creative forces in man, nature, and the cosmos that we find expressed in the Greek satyr chorus and in the dancing spirits from the Otherworld conjured into artistic existence by Allan, the shamanic ecstatic dream artist. The substance of the vision was well described by David Mowaljarlai, an Aboriginal Australian, in 1993, in a transcribed conversation discussing Lommel's article. He tells about Allan's ecstatic flights in which he rides to the Otherworld on a

"Wunggud" snake, a snake invisible to all but the shaman. He explains that while Allan's body lies still, his spirit is traveling to the source of his inspiration:

> You see him breathing but he gone. He travelling. And that how uh they compose corroboree there. . . . When they get all the story belong to every *Wunggud*, snake story, Wondjina story, any animal. We dance now. They teach us now. That how he go. It's all round the nature power. Power all belong nature. We all get the power from land. That's why it's important.[44]

THE MAYA AND THE OLMEC

Let us now focus our attention on another localization of the "great dream of the *mundus archetypus*," that of the Classic Mayan civilization of Central America, half a globe away from our previous venue of attention. Several things draw us to this locale. Perhaps the first is the exciting freshness of the information being disinterred in this region of the world. While certain aspects of Mayan civilization have long been known, much of its essential substance remained a mystery because the system of writing employed by the Maya could not be fathomed for centuries. Within the past two decades, however, rapid progress has been made in this area, resulting in many entirely new and surprising revelations.

This area is also interesting because it is so different from the cultures we have so far examined. It was an agriculturally based system of considerable sophistication. The Classic Mayan world flourished for a period of more than a thousand years (200 B.C. to A.D. 900). At its apogee, it consisted of fifty or more independent states and encompassed more than one hundred thousand square miles of forest and plain. The divine *ahauob* (kings) ruled cities characterized by pyramids, temples, palaces, and vast open plazas with urban populations numbering in the tens of thousands.[45] It was, in short, a developed and complex civilization.

Yet, as newly discovered information about the Maya grew, a definite shamanic structure began to crystallize within the Mayan cultural system.[46] As noted in *Maya Cosmos: Three Thousand Years on the Shaman's Path*, this structure displays a remarkable durative power, particularly when viewed in the temporal framework we associate with the New World. To establish this three-thousand-year-old pedigree, the authors of *Maya Cosmos* direct our attention to a consistency of form and meaning underlying Mayan ritual and cosmology that has survived for at least two millennia. They trace the surviving elements of this view into present day Mayan culture. They believe, however, that its origins predate Mayan civilization and that in some instances these structures of belief have descended from the earlier Olmec civilization, having roots that are three thousand years old or perhaps even older.[47] It was the ancient Olmec, who began building cities at places like San Lorenzo and La Venta between 1200 B.C. and 900 B.C. who first established the worldview that the Maya inherited a thousand years later, and, on the basis of the recent evidence indicative of a cultural continuity between the Maya and the Olmec, these authors suggest that the seeds of the shamanic elements of Mayan culture date back to Olmec civilization. Furthermore, in *The Olmec World: Ritual and Rulership*, these authors and others have offered detailed and convincing proof of shamanism in the Olmec civilization. This work illustrates the manner in which strikingly beautiful objects in Olmec art portray an entire array of shamanic ritual techniques, practices, and symbols—from trance inducement to spirit guide transformation, magical flight, and ecstasy—and serve to establish elements of continuity with later cultures, including the contemporary Maya.

Before we begin our examination of shamanism among the Classic Maya and the Olmec, let us briefly say a few words about its survival in contemporary Mayan culture. Barbara Tedlock has done interesting work with the contemporary Maya of Momostenango, in Guatemala, and it may be useful briefly to summarize some of her findings, particularly because they provide hints with regard to aspects of shamanism absent from the older archaeological record. She finds that most of the classic elements of shamanism still exist in varying degrees among the contemporary Mayan communities that she studied (although she notes they are combined with elements many commentators may regard as "priestly"). "Clearly, shamanism—defined . . . as necessarily involving direct communication between spirits and the diviner through dreams, visions, or spirit possession—exists in many Mayan communities," she tells us. "Mayan diviners are shamanic in their recruitment, initiation, and practice. Recruitment is both by hereditary transmission of the shamanic profession and the spontaneous 'call' or 'divine election,' just as it is in Asia."[48] She notes examples of ecstatic initiatory dreams and visions, initiatory illnesses, and "callings" received by the postulant from supernaturals. "Further, an examination of the recruitment of Mayan diviners reveals the presence of all of the classic ways of becoming a shaman: through sickness, dreams, and ecstasies, as well as inheritance."[49] As an example, she cites a first-person account, collected by Sister Blanche M. Leonard from a Yucatec shaman, of what she regards as "a classic narration" of shamanic recruitment:

> When I was starting out I had a strange experience. Unknown to my father, I set out for the sacred hill and cenote, Tetzik. I fell asleep and had a long dream. Many spirits beat me and punished me. When I woke up I found the divining stone (a crystal) and a special stone, a sacred stone which the Lord of the Field left for me. When I returned home I was sick for nine days and could not speak.[50]

She notes that in certain instances refusal of the call will mean death, but successful acceptance can lead to direct communication with the spirits, gods, and ancestors and the ability to divine and to heal and to interpret dreams and myth.

The association of the receipt of the shamanic vocation with crystal or quartz is important. The Mayan shaman uses quartz crystals in conjunction with seeds and the 260-day Mayan calendar to divine the future. For the Maya, the calendar is not a mere linear progression of time but the unfolding of an essential order implicit in reality itself. Symbolically, time is "spatialized" through ritual and other associations, while "space is temporalized" simultaneously. The result suggests that it is not merely time but "reality" itself, time and space, that reveals itself in the unfolding calendrical round. Divining with crystals, the shaman mediates this unfolding reality. And in an interesting conjunction of ideas, while the diviner is manipulating the quartz crystals, Tedlock tells us, "it is at this time that gifted diviners often have the experience described as 'his blood speaks,'" providing the shaman with important insights during the divinatory process.[51] Thus, the quartz and blood both give access to the essential world, and in his divination the contemporary shaman can summon the ancestors from this realm and, like the other shamans we have examined, becomes a conduit of the regenerative power of creation.

The institution of shamanism probably existed among the common folk in the ancient Mayan civilization much as it does among the Maya today. However, we can know little about such peasant practices with regard to the Classic Maya because our basic surviving information comes from a different level of society. It is the myth and ritual surrounding Mayan kingship that have been most revealing and have survived in the inscriptions and the rich stone iconography of the Mayan temple structures. As a conduit of power and the focal point of the basic force investing the cosmos, the Mayan kingship employed the shaman's symbols and techniques to validate its right to rule this society. The king, the divine *ahau*, was himself a specialist in ecstasy, in the attainment of altered states of consciousness that in vision allowed him to deal with gods, demons, ancestors, and other unseen but powerful beings and to gain access to the world of Xibalba, "the parallel unseen Otherworld into which the Mayan kings and other shamans could pass in ecstatic trance."[52]

To access the world of vision, the Mayan ahau used familiar methods: exhausting dance, rhythmic drumbeat, perhaps drugs or intoxicants, and, most of all, ritual bloodletting.[53] "Before and during rituals," Michael Coe informs us, "food taboos and sexual abstinence were rigidly observed, and self-mutilation was carried out by jabbing needles and sting-ray spines through ears, cheeks, lips, tongue and penis, the blood being spattered on paper or used to anoint the idols."[54] Bloodletting not only lowered the threshold of consciousness and may have increased the flow of trance-inducing endorphins into the mind but also was symbolic in several senses. Such piercing, which Mary Miller and Karl Taube recognize as a form of "autosacrifice,"[55] has the same symbolic value as dismemberment and suggests the annihilation of the "old self" and the undertaking of the ordeals preparatory to altered consciousness. Blood in Mayan iconography and symbolism is associated with the "soul force" of the universe, its essence and continuing vitality, and its letting in this phase of Mayan ritual plays a role similar to that of bone or quartz crystal as symbols of reduction to essence in other forms of shamanism.[56] Dismemberment and sacrifice play major parts in Mayan ritual. They represent a return to origin, for they symbolically repeat the first sacrifice, the creation, and the spilled blood provides sustenance for the gods. The symbolism of bone and that of blood may have played similar roles, each representing a return to essence, for the words for "bone" and "essence" or "seed," implying rebirth, are homophones, and the Maya often employed homophones to suggest symbolic parallels between ideas.[57] We thus have familiar structural and functional elements. Hypermotility, physical exhaustion exacerbated by bloodletting, and drug induction are all techniques conducive to a transformation of consciousness and the cultivation of vision. They are accompanied by symbols heralding a return to essence and cosmogonic origin. Such techniques and symbols helped impel the shaman-king on the vision quest to the Otherworld, for in his bloodletting the ahau was able to open a portal to the supernatural realm.

The piercing technique employed by the Maya often involved perforating the middle of the tongue. Then the hole was enlarged by pulling a thorn-intersected cord through it. Often, with male shamans, the penis was the locus for such bloodletting exercises.

> Blood could be drawn from any part of the body, but the most sacred sources were the tongue for males and females, and the penis for males. Representations of the act carved on stelae depict participants drawing finger-thick ropes through the wounds to guide the flow of blood down onto paper. Men with perforated genitals would whirl in a kind of dervish dance that drew the blood out onto long paper and cloth streamers tied to their wounded members. The aim of these great cathartic rituals was the vision quest, the opening of a portal into the Otherworld through which gods and the ancestors could be enticed so that the beings of this world could commune with them. The Maya thought of this process as giving "birth" to the god or ancestor,

enabling it to take physical form in this plane of existence. The vision quest was the central act of the Maya world.[58]

Just as it was in the forms of shamanism previously discussed, where the ancestors or spirits pierce or dismember the shaman, so it is here. Mayan iconography reveals that it is symbolically the spirits or ancestors who pierce the shaman, for the ancestors are depicted as participants in this very ceremony that gives birth to them. The symbolisms, piercing and giving birth to the gods, are parallel, and the ancestors themselves play an integral part in the shaman's trance journey to the Otherworld.

In classic period imagery, the Vision Serpent was invoked during the ritual of communication between this world and the Otherworld. In fact, the letting of blood was often the vehicle through which its presence was conjured.[59] Interestingly, this serpent-formed spirit guide plays an essential role in Mayan ritual and iconography. It is the Vision Serpent that symbolizes the path of communication between the two worlds, and ancestral figures were often shown leaning out of its open jaws. Conversely, the serpent becomes the vehicle of the shaman's journey to the Otherworld. In fact, this symbolism seems to have survived into contemporary Mayan shamanism in a way that may enhance our understanding of the serpent's role in Classic Mayan times. J. Eric Thompson records the following incident from his research among the Maya of Belize, describing the final initiation of a shaman in the village of San Antonio:

> The instructor and the initiate retire to a hut in the bush for a month or so, so that there may be no eavesdropping. During this period the initiate is taught by his master all the different prayers and practices used in causing and curing sickness. At the end of the period the initiate is sent to meet Kisin. Kisin takes the form of a large snake called Ochcan (*och-kan*), which is described as being very big, not poisonous and having a large shiny eye. When the initiate and the ochcan meet face to face, the latter rears up on his tail and, approaching the initiate till their faces are almost touching, puts his tongue in the initiate's mouth. In this manner, he communicates the final mysteries of sorcery.[60]

Here the snake assumes the role of spirit guide and instructor with which we are familiar. A more telling incident was recorded from the village of Sokotz, Belize, involving a snake and an ant's nest:

> Each ant's nest is presided over by a master, who is inevitably an expert in brujeriá [shamanism]. The grandfather of an informant made this trip in the company of a *Hmen* [shaman], who was teaching him. The master knocked three times on the nest, and a serpent issued forth. The master had previously removed all his clothes and was standing nude. The snake came up to him and after licking him all over, proceeded to swallow him whole. A few moments later he passed him out of his body with excrement. The master didn't appear to be much the worse for his adventure.[61]

Interestingly, in some versions of this incident, this initiatory swallowing takes place inside a cave.[62] We have the familiar conjunction of the spirit guide swallowing the shaman and cave initiation. In fact, the cave is a recurrent location for initiation and shamanic ceremony in contemporary Mayan shamanism. And the cave similarly played a central role in Classic Mayan symbolism in conjunction with the Vision Serpent, the "World Tree," and the mountain. Karen Bassie-Sweet notes that "the most venerated ritual location was the cave."[63] Moreover, the cave was frequently portrayed as being located at the base of the World Tree, marking entry into a mythical mountain, tree and mountain both associated with an axis mundi symbolism.[64] The serpent and cave, she further notes, are also mythically assimilated.[65]

"To the Classic Maya," the authors of *Maya Cosmos* tell us, "all natural openings into the earth, whether caves or cenotes (sunken waterholes), were portals to the Otherworld. Their architecture echoes this belief."[66] The pyramids and temples, for which we so admire the Mayan civilization, were decorated with symbols that identified them as sacred mountains. The mountain symbolism clearly harks back to the "First True Mountain," the place of the creation. "The mouth of the mountain is, of course, the cave, and Maya mythology identifies the road to Xibalba [the Otherworld] as going through a cave. The Maya not only used natural caves as the locations of bloodletting and vision ritual . . . but the inside of

their temple was understood to be the cave pathway to the Otherworld."[67] "The royal mountain thus contained the cave that formed
part of the path that led to the supernatural world."[68] Moreover,
the mouth of the "cave" was at times depicted as an engorging serpentine or saurian form. The path, of course, was traversed in trance,
and the Vision Serpent, as we know, was the embodiment of the
path to and from the Otherworld. Thus, entering the cave was symbolically equivalent to being swallowed by the serpent.

Here a number of familiar symbolisms begin to coalesce. The
cave as the place of bloodletting and vision marks interiority, the
relocation of reality inward that we have seen in a number of
shamanic symbols. In some caves the familiar hand images are found,
and in some instances they appear to show evidence of mutilation.
This symbolism is reinforced by the swallowing motif as a loss of
everyday orientation and individuation and further by the serpent
and saurian associations, which are archetypal symbols of the preconscious. The cave, however, is within a mountain, a symbol of
ascent to a higher plane. The journey inward is paradoxically an
ascent and a return to origin. The mountain temple is the "First
True Mountain," the "ever present Origin," where the formal powers of the creation are encountered within, in trance and vision.
Once again the cave establishes the symbolic axis that unites the
three realms.

With this in mind, several features of the Vision Serpent now
arrest our attention. We have noted its chthonic association with
the cave initiation, swallowing and dismemberment; that is, with
initiatory death. Yet it also implies the turning of consciousness
implicit in illumination, the shamanic trance, and the trip to the
Otherworld. The symbol for Personified (or "Holy") Blood, an emblem of the world of essence parallel to quartz and bone, is usually
attached to the serpent's tail as a representation of the substance
that materializes it.[69] In certain depictions the serpent arises from
the burning papers saturated with the blood let from the shaman-
king and becomes the very embodiment of trance vision and ascent.[70] Moreover, as a symbol of ascent, it is often portrayed as a
feathered serpent and has marked celestial connotations. It thus
implies a coincidence of opposites as the gateway to illumination in
a now familiar symbolism. The portal to the Otherworld is through

the clashing jaws of the serpent, that is, through the Symplegades, also identified with the cave. The words for "sky" and "snake" are homophones in the Mayan languages,[71] and, in the form of the Double Serpent Bar held by the king, the Vision Serpent becomes identified with the sky. The feathered serpent is, of course, a well-known Central American figure in art and myth. In Mayan symbolism the serpent and ornithological representations combine in a *coincidentia oppositorum* to form the Celestial Bird, "also known as the Serpent Bird,"[72] which sits atop the World Tree, the Mayan symbol of the cosmic creation and illumination.

The essential elements of this symbolism are very old and can also be found far earlier in surviving Olmec art. The Olmec devoted much of their great artistic sensibility to depicting the shaman's visionary itinerary, and both the cave and the feathered serpent played essential and hallowed roles. Caves, we are informed by Richard Diehl and Michael Coe, "were believed to be portals to the underworld, transition zones between the 'real' world of the flesh and the world of the mind and spirit."[73] Andrea Stone surmises that the sanctity of the cave derives from earlier populations because the major Olmec sites are located in a swampy coastal plain, not near caves.[74] Representations of the cave, however, frequently are to be found on Olmec shrines and in mobiliary art. In addition, caves such as those at Juxtlahuaca and Oxtotitlan, both a significant distance from what is believed to be the Olmec heartland, are embellished in Olmec style and share a symbolism common to other Olmec art forms.

Juxtlahuaca is a deep cave possessing nearly a full mile of passages, with its paintings found 3,400 to 4,000 feet from the entrance in a lower-level passage. "Their remote setting is unquestionably deliberate and strongly suggests a ritual motivation," according to Andrea Stone.[75] Several of the authors of *The Olmec World* have identified this ritual motivation as shamanic. Stone informs us that "Juxtlahuaca's Gallery of Drawings contains a work known as Painting 1, in brilliant red, yellow and black. It features a standing anthropomorphic jaguar who towers over a small seated figure sporting a beard"[76] (Figure 25). The seated figure shows evidence of high rank in his costume. The anthropomorphic jaguar form is a very common embodiment of the spirit guide in Mesoamerican shamanism and in other examples of Olmec art. The depiction strongly implies a version of shamanic initiation or vision quest materializing the half-human, half-jaguar form, which traditionally mediates the shaman's visionary experience.

Two other paintings exist within the cave. One underscores the role of the theriomorphic spirit guide, perhaps in its terrifying aspect, which complements the autosymbolism of the cave as a swallowing of the initiate. It is a jaguar with a "lolling tongue." More significant, perhaps, is the epiphany of a serpent with a feathered crown, a bifurcated tongue, and crossed-bands set into the eye.[77] The symbol seems to imply that, mediated through the spirit guide,

FIGURE 25. *Massive standing anthropomorphic jaguar and small seated figure with beard, at Juxtlahuaca, Guerrero, Mexico.*

the journey inward becomes an ascent epitomized by the chthonic serpent, which becomes feathered. Avian transformation is a familiar metaphor for the shaman's trance ascent, and Olmec statuary contains numerous examples of the shaman's similar metamorphosis. Thus, deep within the cave we find symbolism implying that it is the trance portal to the Otherworld.

All these elements of symbolism seem to coalesce in the cave at Oxtotitlan. Here, one important painting shows a feline standing next to an ithyphallic man who holds one arm raised (Figure 26). Some have viewed this as a scene depicting copulation. Stone calls this view into question and notes the stylistic differences between the man and the feline, suggesting that the figures do not form a coherent composition and that "the jaguar represents later repainting."[78] The fluid calligraphy and ornate style of the jaguar, however, seem to suggest not so much a different hand in its creation as a different world. It clearly appears to be the materialization of a creature from the visionary realm heralded by the raised arm of the

FIGURE 26. *Cave painting from Oxtotitlan depicting a visionary jaguar and ithyphallic man, Guerrero, Mexico.*

solidly conceived and executed noble figure who has conjured it. The pronounced penis may indicate by a sort of symbolic short-hand that it is the vehicle of visionary bloodletting, for which ample evidence exists among the Olmec. On the other hand, the ithyphallic shaman's sexual relationship with an animal spirit has a long history and wide dissemination among the world's shamanic traditions, and some researchers see this as another avatar of this symbolism.

Not surprisingly, the feathered serpent forms a dominant and recurrent motif within the cave itself. Stone points out that it is depicted three times, in varying degrees of abstraction (Figure 27).[79] Again we seem to have the theriomorphic spirit guide (see Figure 26) heralding the visionary experience represented by the feathered serpent and avian transformation. In a painting on a grotto wall above the cave entrance all these elements are articulated with an artistic fluency seldom found in cave art since the Upper Paleolithic period. This mural is large (3.8 meters in width, 2.5 meters in height) and remarkably well preserved considering it has survived the elements

FIGURE 27. *Plumed serpents portrayed in varying degrees of abstraction, Oxtotitlan.*

for a period of time dating from seven hundred years before the birth of Christ (Figure 28). It depicts a costumed man seated on what appears to be a thronelike structure. Kent Reilly tells us, "The enthroned figure's most striking article of costume is his complex bird helmet or mask, which was once physically connected to a feather cape and backrack." The mask is cut away to reveal the human face beneath. Reilly describes the figure's costume in a manner that leaves no doubt as to the avian symbolism.

> The rest of the costume reiterates the avian theme. A feathered cape suspended from the arms replicates the wings of a bird. Both the down-pointing right hand and arm and the uplifted left arm are hung with what are almost certainly jade bracelets, with bands to which the feathered cape is attached. When the arms

FIGURE 28. *Drawing of the mural above the grotto at Oxtotitlan Cave.*

are outstretched, these allow the cape to spread like the wings of a bird. Behind the seated individual is a backrack with an intricate feathered-tail assemblage. Around his waist is an apron or loin-cloth hanging over a brown, possibly hide, skirt, which is painted with two hand-paw-wing motifs, each containing an inturning spiral. The association between the hand-paw-wing motif and the inturning spiral and avian themes serves to identify this figure as a cosmic flier, which is further supported by the crossed-bands pectoral on the chest.

Reilly concludes, "The elaborate clothing . . . identifies the painting's subject: a specific moment in a shamanic flight or cosmic travel ceremony," and "the figure at Oxtotitlan is depicted at the precise moment before he will lift off and fly through the thin membrane of the cosmic portal to another reality."[80]

The iconography and natural setting associated with this figure support Reilly's interpretation. Although it is, in part, badly damaged, the throne upon which the cosmic flier sits depicts a tricephallic zoomorph. The middle face appears to be a form of the plumed serpent, with eyes marked with familiar crossed-bands indicating that it is represented in its celestial aspect. Apparently similar serpent forms hang down on either side of the throne to form its legs. In other words, the shaman rides the tricephallic plumed serpent in ecstatic vision through the sky. But the symbolism is even more ingeniously conceived, for as Stone points out, the placement of the zoomorphic mask over the cave entrance was purposeful: the cave forms the zoomorph's mouth.[81] Viewing the work as a whole, we can discern that the feathered serpent swallows the initiate entering the cave. Here the initiate encounters the theriomorphic spirit guide depicted in Figure 26 who mediates between this world and the next. In the interior of the cave, images of the feathered serpent indicate that the cave journey has itself become the vehicle of ascent, that is, of the entry into the reality that evokes the experience of ecstatic flight represented in the literally overarching symbol of the bird-shaman above the cave entrance. Thus, this shaman's vehicle of flight, the plumed serpent that first engorged the initiate, incorporates the entire symbolism of cave initiation and of the cave and the feathered serpent as the entrance to a visionary reality. This same iconography is found in all its essential elements in other sculptured Olmec representations.

The feathered serpent and cave, thus, once again unite the three realms—the earthly world from which we enter the cave, the interior underground world, and the world of trance ascent and flight, or the celestial world. Uniting the three realms, they establish the paradigm of verticality as an ontological principle and all that this implies, as we examined in the last section, including the "ever present Origin" of creation as a reality open to the shaman. This unitive vision is reinforced by another symbol literally central to the Olmec and Mayan visionary cosmos, a symbol with which the feathered serpent is often interchangeable and that, among the Maya, is itself to be found within the visionary cave. This is the World Tree. This symbolism begins with the Olmec. For the Olmec, the tree grows from the place of creation, the axis mundi (or cosmic center), and is associated with a sacred quaterion or fourfold orientation in the cosmic directions. Its top is feathered, representative of the bird-topped tree. This central tree traditionally unites the three realms and is symbolically the place where the shaman undergoes transformation into the avian spirit guide and embarks on his celestial flight. The principal elements of this symbolism survived into the time of the Maya and were further developed by their culture.

The Classic Maya also envisioned the world as a mandala-like structure. "The four cardinal directions provided the fundamental grid for the Maya community and for the surface of the world."

> Each direction of the compass had a special tree, a bird, a color, gods associated with its domain, and rituals associated with those gods. East was red and the most important direction since it was where the sun was born. North, sometimes called the "side of heaven," was white and the direction from which the cooling rains of winter came. . . . West, the leaving or dying place of the sun, was black. South was yellow and was considered to be the right-hand or great side of the sun.[82]

At the center of this quarternary structure lies the *Wacah Chan* axis, the World Tree, which ran through the center of existence.

The name of the tree literally meant "raised-up sky." The Classic texts at Palenque tell us that the central axis of the cosmos was called the "raised-up sky" because First Father had raised it at the beginning of creation in order to separate the sky from the earth. Each World Tree was, therefore, a representation of the axis of creation.[83]

The World Tree intersected the four cardinal directions at the center and symbolized the axis connecting vertically the lower, middle, and upper realms.[84] Atop the World Tree was seated the Celestial Bird or, combining the serpent and ornithological symbolisms, the Serpent Bird. In some representations the trunk of the World Tree splits to become the Vision Serpent, whose gullet is the path taken by the ancestral dead and the gods of the Otherworld as they travel between this world and the next, an appropriate symbolic accretion because the Tree is also "the path of communication between the natural and supernatural worlds as it is defined at the center of the cosmos."[85] Thus, "this axis was not located in any one earthly place, but could be materialized through ritual at any point in the natural and human-made landscape,"[86] that is, any place where the plane to the Otherworld was penetrated in trance.

In a manner that exemplifies the Mayan obsession with uniting diverse symbols into a single pattern everywhere translucent to its source, the World Tree is recurrently associated with the symbolism of the cave. Within the temple cave of the pyramid, as Schele and Freidel point out, the ritual of bloodletting was meant to make manifest the World Tree as the path to the supernatural world.[87] "In the rapture of bloodletting rituals, the king brought the great World Tree into existence through the middle of the temple and opened the awesome doorway into the Otherworld."[88] Thus, "within this cave grew the Tree of the World marking the center, the place of the portal,"[89] which becomes the ultimate representation of ascent and communication with the powers of creation. This is, of course, consistent with the Olmec iconography, in which the cave journey also led to symbols of ascent and magical flight to the Otherworld.

Interestingly, we also find the image of the celestial cord, rope, or umbilicus as a symbol of ascent both in Classic and later Mayan shamanism. According to Peter Dunham, a living rope passes through the World Tree at the center of creation.[90] Moreover, it appears from the evidence of past and contemporary Yucatek shamanic practice that this cord can be rejoined through ritual, relinking this world and the Otherworld.[91] "The Precolumbian Maya represented this conduit between the supernatural and human worlds as a snake-headed cord that emerged from the belly of the Maize God and the sacred place they called Na-Ho-Chan. Classic Kings carried it in their arms in the form of the Double-headed Serpent Bar,"[92] which was itself a form of the shaman's scepter. Again tree, mountain, feathered serpent, and astral cord coalesce at several points as paths of ascent to a higher plane of reality.

As mentioned, the Vision Serpent is often depicted as emerging from the World Tree as a symbol of the creation itself. This is entirely appropriate, for the Vision Serpent is the emissary of the creationtime. It is a creationtime serpent from the world encountered in vision, dream, and trance. For this reason, it is often iconographically depicted in conjunction with the birth of First Father from a cleft in the earth at the time of the creation, when he raised the World Tree at the sacred "center" to create the cosmos. First Father and the twin heroes of the Popol Vuh, the Quiché Mayan creation myth, are denizens of the Otherworld and are responsible for the creation of the Mayan world in its present form. All significant Mayan activity reincarnates the paradigmatic acts of the creationtime, and any materialization of the ancestors or supernaturals reenacts the original resurrection of First Father and the creationtime reality.

The Vision Serpent of trance is the guide to this reality. It is, in a sense, an example of the traditional totem, or animal spirit guide, of shamanism. The Serpent is a form of the *way*, or animal spirit guide of the Mayan shaman, and the *way* leads to the Otherworld. "The *wayob* [plural of *way*] of Classic Maya imagery appeared in many guises, including humanlike forms, animals of all sorts, and grotesque combinations of human and animal bodies."[93] Mayan iconography depicts rulers with feathered headdresses and "personified wings" dancing with living snakes, and in one such depiction, Pakal, the King of Palenque, performs the snake dance dressed as First Father.[94] Dancing as wayob, people become gods and gods become people:

Both gods and humans danced, and through the dance the one became the other. For the Maya, the ambiguity was as it should be. Sorcerers, kings, and nobles transformed into their *wayob* and journeyed into the Otherworld before the transfixed gaze of their people.[95]

The glyph that reads *way*, or animal companion spirit, derives from the words "to sleep" and "to dream" as well as "to transform."[96] Thus, the Vision Serpent is appropriately both a creation and dreamtime creature and a symbol of the transformation of consciousness that penetrates the threshold between the world of men and the creationtime reality of the gods, heroes, and ancestors.

All these symbols were centered upon the divine ahau as the focus of the shamanic symbolism of Mayan ritual, for he became the very path of ascent, the bird-topped World Tree itself, center of universal creation:

> The king upheld his part in this divine covenant through his en-actment of many rituals of power performed for his people. In-deed, he *was* power, power made material, its primary instrument. On public monuments, the oldest and most frequent manner in which the king was displayed was in the guise of the World Tree. Its trunk and branches were depicted on the apron covering his loins, and the Double-headed Serpent Bar that entwined in its branches was held in his arms. The Principal Bird Deity . . . at its summit was rendered as his headdress. This Tree was the conduit of communication between the supernatural world and the human world: The souls of the dead fell into Xibalba along its path; the daily journeys of the sun, moon, planets, and stars followed its trunk. The Vision Serpent symbolizing communion with the world of the ancestors and the gods emerged into our world along it. The king was this axis and pivot made flesh. He was the Tree of Life.[97]

The shaman-king is himself the medium connecting this world and the life force of the creationtime. As such, he becomes a reflex of cosmic power, the power represented in the term *itz*. Itz is the formal power of the cosmos, energy on the cosmic scale, which is equated with the sap of the World Tree itself. "In antiquity *Itzam* generally meant 'shaman,' a person who works with *itz*, the cosmic sap of the World Tree." In the imagery of the classic period, itz has two personified forms, *Itzamna*, who was the first shaman, and *Itzam-Yeh*, the great cosmic bird. This bird, whose name means "Itzam Revealed," may actually be the *way* (animal spirit) of Itzamna, pointing to a symbolism implying avian transformation.[98] The shaman, Itzam, is literally "one who does the action of *itz*," or an *itzer*, one who manipulates the power of the cosmos.[99] Thus, Itzamna represents the very formal power at the heart of the cosmos, and the shaman-king in ritual becomes the focal point of this cosmic force, activating it inwardly. In his temple cave, in trance at the world center, raising the cosmic World Tree in mimesis of First Father and surmounted by the ornithological symbolism of *Itzam-Yeh*, he, as does the Australian clever man, becomes an "unbroken channel" of cosmic creative power.

SHARED VISIONARY WORLDS

"The deeper 'layers' of the psyche lose their individual uniqueness as they retreat farther and farther into darkness," Jung declared in a manner reminding us of the cave journey itself. Here "they become increasingly collective until they are universalized," merging with the body's instinctual and biological functions and eventually with nature itself. "Hence, 'at bottom,'" he continues, "the psyche is simply 'world.'" "In this sense I hold Kerényi to be absolutely right when he says that in the symbol the *world itself* is speaking. The more archaic and 'deeper,' that is the more *physiological*, the symbol is, the more collective and universal, the more 'material' it is."[100] J. J. Clarke, commenting on this passage, notes, "The archetypes, therefore, represent the uniquely human means whereby instinctual, biological energy is transformed into the meaningful symbolic life of the human psyche."[101] "Meaning and purposefulness are not the prerogatives of the mind; they operate in the whole of living nature," Jung explains. "There is no difference in principle between organic and psychic growth. As the plant produces its flower, so the psyche creates its symbols. Every dream is evidence of this process."[102] And just as nature, body, and instinct express themselves in universal patterns, so does the human psyche. The archetypes of the preconscious are a priori form-generating propensities in the human mind, causing it to organize experience into certain patterns that may vary without losing their essential configuration and underlying identity. Moreover, though largely products of the preconscious mind, such symbolic patterns are, in fact, "meaningful"—when not concerned with coping with the exigencies of daily life, these form-giving principles of the mind spell out the features of an inner world with its own significance and reality, a topos of the soul connecting the mind inwardly with its source and allowing it to experience the larger transpersonal world that creates and sustains it.

In our examination of Australian and Mayan shamanism we have attempted to place some of the general features of shamanism, which we have examined in the previous chapters, into the cultural matrix of a particular society where they could be seen in a more nearly integral setting. Viewed as a whole, however, the examination seems to imply more. We have examined two very different societies whose cultural contacts or common sources, if they existed at all, must have been in the most remote times. Yet, in each, a visionary world, a pattern of inner experience, endures, with many of the same essential structural and functional features, a shared grammar of symbols employed to both effect and reflect the experience, in Eliade's terms, "of deeply meaningful altered states of consciousness." And in each society these states themselves purport to unite man with a durative form-generative source that is itself characterized by enduring paradigmatic and universal patterns of experience. I do not want to repeat all of the similarities between these two shamanic traditions, but I would like to summarize features surrounding the symbolisms of dismemberment, the cave, the spirit guide, and ascent or magical flight in each. Later, other related similarities will come into focus.

Each culture shares the same initial stages of call and initiation, often in autoiniatory dream experiences and ecstasy. Each employs traditional ecstatic training methods, including ordeals of self-mortification designed to effect the erasure of existing patterns of thought and behavior and elicit a transformation of consciousness. In each tradition dance, rhythmic drumbeat, and, perhaps, narcotic stimulation complement this process. These techniques help effect the dissolution of the "old self." Graphic images of dismemberment and piercing characterize this stage of transformation in each society. The Mayan ahau, standing in the pyramid niche that symbolizes the initiatory cave, conjures the ancestors, who join in a painful ceremony centered around the piercing of the vision-seeker's tongue in a ritual that opens the cave portal to the Otherworld. In certain instances, the Australian shaman is led to the initiatory cave by the ancestors, who likewise pierce his tongue. The hole in the tongue symbolizes the successful quest, which opens the cave portal to the Otherworld—for the shaman's power depends upon it. If the hole heals, he loses his ability to shamanize. And in each society the participant's presence is symbolized on the cave walls by hand images, and these hands are sometimes "mutilated," implying ritual dismemberment.

In Australian shamanism, after his "death" or dismemberment at the hands of the spirits, quartz crystals are said to be inserted into the shamanic postulant. The crystal symbolizes the shaman's new relationship to the dreamtime world of essence, and after this procedure the shaman has new psychic powers that allow him to see into the future and to be a mediator of the dreamtime world of unfolding essential form. In fact, the Australian shaman uses quartz crystals to divine the future. We noted that in the Mayan autoinitiatory dream presented by Barbara Tedlock, immediately after his initiatory ordeal in which he is beaten and punished by the spirits, the postulant awakens to find a divining stone, a crystal, emblematic of his new shamanic powers. Crystal in Mayan society likewise allows the Mayan diviner to look into the future and to mediate the unfolding reality represented by the Mayan calendrical round.

We have previously noted the role played in the Americas by the jaguar as spirit guide. Joan Halifax draws our attention to late Classic period Mayan statues of the jaguar initiator in *Shaman: The Wounded Healer*. "The neophyte-shaman is here being dismembered and devoured by a supernatural jaguar-initiator," she notes.[103] Peter Furst cites the role played by the jaguar initiator in Olmec shamanism and compares it to the jaguar spirit guide in parts of South America. In ecstatic trance, the initiator meets Omaókóhe, master of all felines:

The candidate asks Omaókóhe to strip him of his human flesh. The jaguar does so, without injuring his bones. The neophyte then requests the jaguar to reclothe his skeleton, and the giant feline replaces his flesh with the flesh of a bat. The jaguar also supplants the candidate's vital organs and innards with magical ones made of shiny rock crystal. The initiate's new organs will enable him to sing powerful curing songs and understand the language of animals. He is now a Bat Man.[104]

This living tradition may provide a missing element with regard to the spirit guide initiator that the ages have erased from the archaeological record in Classic Mayan and Olmec shamanism. If so, it brings us uncannily close to the role played by our Australian spirit guide initiators and to their forms of initiatory dismemberment, the importance attributed by them to bone, as well as the transubstantiation represented by crystal insertion and the restoration of the flesh. It also implies a variant of the familiar symbol of avian transformation in the form of the Bat Man, avian transformation being represented in Olmec art and in Aboriginal lore.

We previously noted Eliade's observation with regard to the symbolism of dismemberment and reduction to bone in relationship to Australian shamanism. It not only implied an initiatory death but also a reduction to essence, particularly in its association with the quartz inserted into the body of the dismembered initiate. At the earliest stages of the novitiate's experience this foreshadowed the larger process of initiation as a crisis, the death of the profane man, a return to the creative source, and a rebirth with enhanced power. The same process of implying the larger pattern of initiation—return to origin and consequent regeneration—seems to survive in the Mayan world. Reduction to bone is likewise a return to essence, for here "bone" and "seed" or "essence" are homophones that the Maya often used to suggest a relationship between concepts. The bloodletting sacrifice has a similar symbolic value. The Maya closely associated blood with "the soul stuff of the cosmos"; the gods create the universe with their own blood, and human blood opens the path to the Otherworld in vision quest and sacrifice. The mutual exchange effects regeneration on both an individual and a cosmic level. And, finally, when using quartz to divine, the blood of the contemporary Mayan shaman speaks to him, that is, it is the conduit of knowledge from the world of the ancestors.

In each form of shamanism, the cave or its iconographic representation plays a central role and represents the transformation of consciousness implied in the inward journey. This same role is sometimes symbolically assumed by the hole in the ground, the chasm or water hole or, among the Maya, the cenote. In each society the cave's initial penetration is associated with self-mortification, piercing, or dismemberment and with the encounter with the spirit guide, the vision serpent, or, among the Olmec and Maya, the jaguar as well. It becomes autosymbolic of opening inwardly, through trance, man's innate relationship with the source both of his own experience and of the cosmos. In this sense, the dark cave is paradoxically a source of illumination, in Australia symbolized by the actual luminosity of the cave and in Central America by the fact that the World Tree grows in trance ritual within the cave itself. In fact, in each society the cave journey becomes associated with the same symbols of ascent: tree, astral cord, cosmic umbilicus, magical flight, and avian transformation. Finally, the cave is seen as the portal to the Otherworld in each culture. It fulfills the essential cosmological function of uniting the three realms, a role doubled by the feathered serpent and the cosmic tree or pole in each society. The cave becomes a conduit of cosmogonic power, for symbolically the essential forms of creation emanate from the cave in each shamanism, as does the power, political or otherwise, of the shaman himself.

In each society the role of the cave is complemented and, to a certain extent, duplicated by the serpent-form spirit guide. In each, this creature of the preconscious mind is revealed in trance, and it is, in its initial revelation, a terrifying being, that is, the monstrous devouring maw leading to the Otherworld in Mayan shamanism and the instrument of the killing and dismembering of the initiate in Australia. In both cultures, the serpent is represented as swallowing the initiate and excreting or vomiting him out with the enhanced powers of his vocation. As a variant of this symbolism, the snake imparts secret shamanic knowledge, or "medicine," to the postulant to complete his initiation. In both shamanic traditions the snake signals a turning of consciousness, and its initially fierce aspect gives ways to its role as spirit guide. The Australian shaman realizes that "I and Wonambi are friends," and the Mayan shaman dances in ecstasy with his serpent spirit guide, crossing the threshold to the Otherworld. Thus, in each, as a symbol of the way to higher consciousness, the serpent paradoxically becomes feathered, can fly, becomes associated with the sky, and is the very vehicle the shaman rides on his celestial ascent. The spirit guide, like the cave, becomes the mythological expression of the *coincidentia oppositorum*, uniting the three realms and joining the cosmos with itself.

Just as the subterranean cave becomes luminous and, in Eliade's terms, assumes a "celestial" character, and just as the chthonic serpent spirit guide becomes feathered, each symbolizing the ecstatic goal of the inward journey, so in each form of shamanism is the postulant frequently represented as undergoing an avian transformation as the result of his initiation. In Australia the initiates were sprinkled with "liquefied quartz," at which time it was said that "feathers emerged from the latter's arms, which grew into wings in the course of two days."[105] In the Olmec world artifacts recurrently represent the shaman in various stages of transformation into a birdlike being, as does the mural at Oxtotitlan, and the Mayan king's ceremonial dress incorporates a similar iconography. In each culture other emblems of ascent, such as the ritual pole or the World Tree, are also associated with ornithological symbolism.

The symbols relating to the cave, spirit guide, and avian transformation are intricately interwoven. In Australia the feathered serpent leads to the cave of initiation, doubles as the cave by swallowing the shaman, symbolically articulates the *coincidentia oppositorum*, and later becomes the vehicle of the shaman's ascent as he rides it in magical flight to the sky. In Mayan and Olmec iconography, the spirit guide serpent also represents the cave, its maw being the initiatory portal to the Otherworld as well as the path along which the shaman makes his ascent. In the Olmec caves of Juxtlahuaca and Oxtotitlan, the feathered serpent is also the epiphany of the cave's depths, where the inward journey becomes a trance ascent. And here the symbols coalesce with those of avian transformation and shamanic flight. As we remember, the cave that reveals the feathered serpent at Oxtotitlan as well as the feathered serpent itself, whose mouth is formed by the actual cave entrance, and the journey of initiation it implies, are the vehicles for the magical flight of the shaman depicted over the cave grotto. And the shaman wears a bird mask and other elaborate ornithological garb symbolic of the trance journey. Cave, spirit guide, coincidence of opposites, and representations of ascent or avian transformation thus form a grammar of symbols with different nuances of expression but a single and recurrent underlying form.

Moreover, and very significantly, in each society these structural similarities are bent to the same functional end, marking the visionary itinerary that the shaman follows in his realization of an altered form of consciousness and serving as psychopomps symbolically effecting and reflecting the shaman's ability to experience the source of life and power shared by man and the cosmos. Thus, each culture uses similar symbols of ascent to articulate a larger worldview, a vision that everywhere reinforces the paradigm of verticality discussed earlier, that is, that our world is the expression of an enfolded order, an ever present origin or source of essential form that creates and sustains reality and is simultaneously accessible to the shaman in vision or trance. Creation is not an event distant in time but a constant source of plenitude inwardly encountered in the mind of man as well as the form-generating support of the world around him.

In the Mayan and Olmec worlds, the great unifying expression of this experience is the World Tree. We recall that the luminous cave, the feathered serpent, and the descent that becomes a magical flight all implied a mythological expression of the coincidence of opposites, and the tree symbol follows this same pattern. It is the center of the world, the point that unifies opposition. It is known in later Mayan mythology as the Father-Mother Tree, combining sexual opposites. The tree can be raised anywhere, for the center of the world exists at any place that the vertical paradigm establishes the relationship between the relative world and the "absolute" reality that informs it and gives it being. The axial tree thus unites the three realms and becomes a symbol of ascent. At its top sits the feathered celestial bird, sometimes assimilated to the *way* of the first shaman, symbol of shamanic enlightenment. In Olmec and Mayan ritual the central axis symbolized by the tree is the place of sacrifice, initiation, and vision quest. In fact, the shaman becomes the very embodiment of the tree in elaborate ritual identification.

A similar though less well-defined role is played by the ritual pole in Australian shamanism. Eliade sees it as embodying the archetype of the central axis that unites the three realms.[106] In its association with Numbakulla, "born from his own eternity," it once united man with the celestial realm. It again can be ritually raised anywhere, for Eliade tells us:

> During their wanderings, the Achilpa always carry the sacred pole with them and choose the direction to follow by its slant. While continually moving about, the Achilpa are never allowed to be far from the "Center of the World"; they are always "centered" and in communication with the Heavens where Numbakulla had disappeared. When the pole is broken, this is a catastrophe; in a way, it is the "end of the world," a regression into chaos.[107]

Thus, the central pole mythologically reestablishes the relationship with an absolute reality capable of giving the tribe its bearings in a relative world, an axis that also gives the world its being, that is, prevents the reversion into chaos. As the sacred pole used in Aranda initiation ceremonies, it is likewise associated with initiation and vision quest. It is also bird-topped, having feathers affixed to its apex. It is associated with the same union of sexual opposites we saw implicit in the Father-Mother Tree, for it is here that the male initiate is subincised, symbolically combining the sexes. And while the Mayan ahau establishes the vertical axis and becomes a conduit of power through ritual identification with the central bird-topped tree, the Australian actually performs the same function by climbing this central feathered pole during initiation.

In the Mayan cosmos the place of creation is formed in the shape of a mandala. At the center the primal ancestor, First Father, created the world by raising the bird-topped World Tree into the sky. Symbolically, it is here that First Father arose from a cleft in the earth and the cosmos was created. In Australia the point of creation is also envisioned in the form of a circular mandala, the Ilbalintja Soak. It is here, at the center, that the primal ancestor, Karora, lay asleep under the soak and raised a pole that reached the sky. And here he burst from the central cleft of the soak, as did the sun and the cosmos. Karora is ritually assimilated to the feather-topped pole (see Figure 24) at the world center, just as First Father is identified with the central World Tree with the celestial bird at its apex. In both cultures this center and origin become associated with the shaman's initiation and trance flight.

Each society employs its shamanic techniques to articulate an identification between the creationtime heroes and the shaman. This is possible because in each society the shaman is able to access a "parallel world" in trance, the dreamtime in Australia or the Otherworld among the Maya, and this reality is associated with the creation itself. It is also the continuing source of the paradigmatic form that is fundamental to the existence of the world and its cultural institutions. The shaman who can tap this source of cosmic plenitude becomes, in Elkin's terms, an unbroken channel of power and in the Mayan world an itz-er, one who manipulates the power of the cosmos.

We remember that the Australian clever man obtains his animal spirit guide by tracing it to its clever place, its sacred mythological center or, as the Aborigines call this place of creative origin, its "dreaming." It is here that it receives its essential form from the dreamtime psychophysical substratum that informs creation. The shaman can transform himself into this animal form. And it is this creature that, in turn, can lead the shaman to the dreamtime world of the ancestors. For the Classic Maya the term *way* shares a very similar significance. It means both animal spirit guide and "to dream" as well as "to transform." Thus, the Mayan shaman can likewise transform into the animal spirit. It is also related to the later Mayan term *nawal* or *nagual*, which carries the meaning of an enduring inner essential form or "spiritual essence," often expressing itself in the form of an animal spirit.[108] Again in Mayan thought the *way* guides the shaman across the cosmic threshold to the creationtime world of the ancestors.

It is not surprising that in each society the part-human, part-animal spirit guide is associated with dreaming and leads to the revelation of the dreamtime or creationtime source. The spirit guide represents the continuum between the formal powers of man's mind and those of nature and cosmos, the very powers that Schelling and Jung see at work in all artistic and mythic creation. We are reminded of the words of Jung:

> Meaning and purposefulness are not the prerogatives of the mind; they operate in the whole of living nature. There is no difference in principle between organic and psychic growth. As a plant produces its flower, so the psyche creates its symbols. Every dream is evidence of this process.

It is dream, vision, and trance that open this realm to the human mind. And it is thus understandable, then, that if we examine a visionary experience reported by A. W. Howitt marking the initiation of a Wiradjuri medicine man of Australia, we recognize all the elements of the grammar of symbols examined in this chapter, gnomically capsulized and with different inflections but with the same underlying pattern of experience and symbolic representation.

According to Howitt's account, when the initiate was about ten years old he was taken to tribal initiation ceremonies. There, in his visionary experience, the initiate's body was first rubbed with quartz crystals, which were then put in water for him to drink. After this he was taken into a grave, where he saw a dead man; the latter rubbed him all over to make him "clever" and gave him some quartz crystals. His father pointed to a *Gunr*, a tiger-snake. "That is your *budjan* [secret personal totem]; it is mine also," his father told him. To the tail of the snake a string was tied such as "the doctors bring up out of themselves." The account continues as follows:

> He took hold of it [the cord], saying, "Let us follow him." The tiger-snake went through several tree trunks, and led us through. Then we came to a great Currajong tree, and went through it, and after that to a tree with a great swelling round its roots. It is in such places that *Daramulun* lives. Here the *Gunr* went down into the ground, and we followed him, and came up inside the tree, which was hollow. There I saw a lot of little *Daramuluns*, the sons of *Baiame* [the High God]. After we came out again the snake took us into a great hole in the ground in which were a number of snakes, which rubbed themselves against me, but did not hurt me, being my *Budjan*. They did this to make me a clever man, and to

make me a *Wulla-mullung*. My father then said to me, "We will go up to *Baiame's* camp." He got astride of a *Mauir* (thread) and put me on another, and we held by each other's arms. At the end of the thread was *Wombu*, the bird of *Baiame*. We went through the clouds, and on the other side was the sky. We went through the place where the Doctors go through, and it kept opening and shutting very quickly. My father said that, if it touched a Doctor when he was going through, it would hurt his spirit, and when he returned home he would sicken and die. On the other side we saw *Baiame* sitting in his camp. He was a very great old man with a long beard. He sat with his legs under him and from his shoulders extended two great quartz crystals to the sky above him. There were also numbers of the boys of *Baiame* and of his people, who are birds and beasts.[109]

According to Elkin, the shaman receives his power by transforming into these birds and beasts, who are essential forms of the animal kingdom.

We are now in a position to understand this visionary symbolism. First the Wiradjuri initiate undergoes a symbolic death but is then rubbed with quartz crystals, presaging the larger pattern of initiation and return to origin. He is introduced to a serpent spirit guide, who—like the feathered serpent—is paradoxically a symbol of ascent, for to his tail is tied an astral cord. Taking hold of the cord, he is led to a hollow tree. Here he enters a hole in the ground, the hole being a recognized variation of the cave symbol in Australian shamanism. We may also recall the initiatory cave at the base of the Mayan World Tree, which was itself a symbol of ascent. Confronting more snakes within the initiatory hole, snakes associated with this spirit guide, he becomes "clever," or enlightened. His descent now becomes an ascent up the astral cord. He passes through the opening where Doctors go, "which kept opening and shutting very quickly," an instance of the Symplegades symbolism and the *coincidentia oppositorum*. Wombu, the bird of Baiame, crowns the axis of his ascent up the astral cord in a symbolism reminiscent of the axial bird-topped World Tree and the feathered pole of the Aranda initiation ceremony. Here he finds himself at the very cosmic fount of animal forms, where Baiame is surrounded by "his people, who are birds and beasts," creatures of essence from whom the shaman receives his power. In the same tradition, as a preliminary to gaining their full powers, including magical flight, the initiates are sprinkled with liquefied quartz by Baiame, at which time it is said that feathers emerge from their arms, which later grow into wings. Thus, finally, the shaman's ascent and empowerment are associated with avian transformation.

If we think back to chapter 3 and to the initiatory dream of Sereptie Djaruoskin, the Samoyed shaman of Siberia, we shall recollect a similar pattern of experience. Sereptie is confronted by a theriomorphic spirit guide associated with a tree and a hole at the root of the tree from which the spirit guide emerges. The tree is the tree "the shamans have been growing from." The hole is the entry to the shaman's initiation: "It is through this hole that the shaman receives the spirit of his voice." As a symbol of the entrance that the "old self," the profane man who must suffer a symbolic death, cannot enter, this hole beneath the tree is at first too small. As Sereptie intuits its meaning, that is, becomes "clever," it opens to him. On his inward journey the process of initiatory death is further emphasized in Sereptie's madness and skeletalization. (Here we may recall the skeletal form of the Australian shaman astride the feathered serpent in some variants of the Aboriginal experience.) In the process, his initial descent becomes an ascent up seven mountains. He likewise passes through the Symplegades in several variations: the hole that is too small, the central point between the rivers of life and death, and "the borderline between two daybreaks, the backbone of the firmament," implying the *coincidentia oppositorum*. Reduced to bone, he is forged an adamantine body in a symbolism that recalls that of dismemberment, bone, essence, and the role played by quartz in Mayan and Australian shamanism. Finally able to shamanize, he reaches on these peaks the mistress of the earth, "who has created all life" and upon whom the shaman's power depends. Sereptie, likewise, has reached the cosmic fount, the realm of the creatures of essence—"the master spirits of all the running and flying birds and game"—just as the Mayan shaman penetrates the parallel world of "essential forms" represented in the animal form of the *nagual* or *way* or as our Australian initiate finally encounters Baiame surrounded by "his people, who are birds and beasts," in each case essential forms from whom the shaman receives his power.

The tree "the shamans have been growing from" has a widespread tradition in Siberian shamanism. It is associated with the World Tree, the tree at the center of the earth that, as Eliade has so many times pointed out, is recognized in the local traditions as uniting the three realms.[110] And like Karora's sacred pole and the Mayan World Tree, it is also associated with the mandala symbolism, here a quaternity with intercardinal points. As Uno Holmberg notes, "On the yellow navel [the center] of the eight-edged earth . . . there is a dense, eight-branched tree," an example, as Eliade recognizes, of the World or Cosmic Tree.[111] Among the Buryat shamans of Siberia this tree is referred to as the "porter god" or the "guardian of the door," for it marks the way to the Otherworld.[112] At its top is an eagle held to be the father of the first shaman.[113] (Compare this bird with Wombu, the bird of Baiame at the top of the astral cord, or with Itzam-Yeh at the top of the Mayan World Tree.) During initiation the Siberian shaman makes sacrifice at this tree and climbs it or, in initiatory dream, flies to the top of the bird-topped tree. Siberian shamans wear bird costumes to this day. Andreas Lommel tells us that when the bird costume is employed, "the appropriate head is a bird's head, while the shoes are made to look like bird claws. Numerous appendages symbolize the bird's wings and feathers."[114] Eliade observes with regard to this phenomenon in Siberia that feathers are mentioned more or less everywhere in the descriptions of the shaman's costume and that the very structure of the costumes attempts to imitate the form of a bird.[115] The shaman's ascent and empowerment are once again symbolized by his avian transformation.

Marguerite Biesele presents a closely analogous account related to her by an old !Kung Bushman from the Kalahari regions of southern Africa when she was a Harvard doctoral candidate in anthropology. A continent away from our previous examples, this visionary experience combines many of the motifs and symbols with which we are familiar. Pertinent parts of the account are as follows:

Just yesterday, friend, the giraffe came and took me again. Kauha (God) came and took me and said, "Why is that people are singing, yet you're not dancing?" When he had spoken, he took me with him and we left this place. We traveled until we came to a wide body of water. It was a river. He took me to the river. The two halves of the river lay to either side of us, one to the left and one to the right.[116]

Old K"xau has entered a well and this river is symbolically "underground." We are reminded of the initial stages of Sereptie's journey, where he enters the hole in the earth, also led by his spirit guide. "We descended through it and arrived at a river with two streams flowing in opposite directions," Sereptie relates of the beginning of his journey, repeating an experience quite close to that of this !Kung visionary traveler.

As Old K"xau travels in trance, carried by the river's flow, he tells us, "My sides were pressed by pieces of metal. Metal things fastened my sides."[117] J. D. Lewis-Williams tells us that for the Bushmen to enter the water is metaphorically equivalent to entry into trance, the ecstatic state the !Kung shaman accesses through exhaustive dancing. And the entry into both water and a trance state are ritually assimilated to an initiatory death.[118] As Old K"xau informs us:

> I am a big dancer. Yes, I am a big dancer. I teach other people to dance. When people sing, I go into a trance. I trance and put *n/um* into people, and I carry on my back those who want to learn *n/um*. Then I go! I go right up and give them to God![119]

N/um for the !Kung is shamanic power or energy, which links the shaman to the cosmic source and is activated by dance. The shaman, *n/um k"xau*, is the "owner" of *n/um*,[120] and we are reminded of the Australian shaman, who, in Elkin's words, becomes a "channel of power" and, more precisely, his Mayan analogue, who is literally an itz-er, one who manipulates the cosmic force known as itz. In each case the informing power is revealed after an initiatory death, in the trance experience. And this experience is again initially represented as an actual entry into a hole in the earth. K"xau describes this pattern of experience as follows:

> My friend, that's the way of this *n/um*. When people sing, I dance. I enter the earth. I go in at a place like a place where people drink water. [In Australia the soak or water hole is a close analogue; in

the Mayan world it is the cenote.] I travel in a long way, very far. When I emerge, I am already climbing.[121]

Here initiatory death and the initial descent into the earth again paradoxically become an ascent, this time by the now familiar astral cord. K"xau continues the description of his visionary journey:

> I'm climbing threads, the threads that lie over there in the South . . . I take them and climb them. I climb one and leave it, then I go climb another one. I come to another one and climb, then I come to another one. Then I leave it and climb on another. Then I follow the thread of the wells, the one I am going to go enter! The thread of the wells of metal. When you get to the wells, you duck beneath the pieces of metal. (K"xau wove his fingers together and put them over the back of his head.) And you pass between them. . . . It hurts. When you lift up a little, the metal pieces grab your neck. You lie down so that they don't grab you.[122]

We remember the initial description of the trance experience, where as he traveled his "sides were pressed by the pieces of metal." Passing between these pieces of metal in the underground wells that he has entered we now recognize is passing through the Symplegades, symbolic of the coincidence of opposites and of entering the dimensionless realm of the spirit. As he tells us of his journey to God, "When you arrive at God's place, you make yourself small," just as Sereptie must do to enter the unconditioned realm of inner experience:

> When you go there, friend, you make yourself small like this. Friend, when you go there, you don't go standing up straight. You make yourself small so that you are a mamba. . . . When you go there, where God is, you are a mamba. That's how you go to him.[123]

A "mamba" is a snake, symbolically capable of slithering through the narrow aperture to the realm beyond spatial dimensionality.

After further perils, the trance experience leads to God's house, the cosmic generative source depicted in now familiar archetypes. Here he encounters the eternal source of the creation:

People say there are leopards there. People say there are zebras. They say locusts. They say lions. They say jackals. . . . They're in his house, right in his very house. . . . And pythons, they say, come and go in that house. . . . Elands are there. Giraffes are there. Gemsboks are there. Kudu are there. . . . These things don't kill each other. They are God's possessions.[124]

These are, in fact, the animals of eternity, master spirits of the animal species, for they "don't kill each other. They are God's possessions." And through shamanic power, n/um, they are also the shaman's possessions after he reaches this equivalent of their clever place. "Friend, that's how it is with this *n/um* that I do! Its possessions! They're many! Gemsboks, leopards, lions, things like that. When people sing, his possessions come, the great, great God's possessions!"[125] These animals incarnate the power of the source, the source of the shaman's power.

Chief among these power animals for the Bushmen is the eland. While the !Kung Bushman's environment does not provide the resources for rock art, the southern San Bushmen, who, as J. D. Lewis-Williams recognizes, shared a common "cognitive culture" with the !Kung, portrayed these animal forms in their rock art. In addition, the San artists also portrayed the trance dance of their shamans as well as the hallucinatory transformation undergone by the shaman in his visionary ascent to the source of power, the power that allowed him to heal, prophesy, and create the very art that is a reflex of this power. And in the portrayals of the shaman's transformation, he is shown in a series of stages as he becomes a feathered therianthrophic creature called an *ales*, a winged being apparently part antelope or eland and part human, who represents the shaman's magic flight to the source of power. In a related symbolism, Thomas A. Dowson recognizes that the shamans of this region "liken trance experience to flying. Some shamans say that they 'took on feathers and flew,' when in fact they are referring to entering a trance." He regards the curious ithyphallic creature portrayed in the rock engraving presented in Figure 29 as "a graphic representation of this flight metaphor."[126]

Again a certain basic form emerges. Trance; initiatory death; the theriomorphic spirit guide who leads a descent into a hole in the earth, a descent that paradoxically becomes an ascent, this time by astral cord; the perilous journey through the Symplegades; and a transformation of consciousness epitomized by magical flight and avian transformation. These familiar stages lead the shaman to the generative source of creation represented by its animal essences, which is the source of shamanic power, the shaman being a conduit of this power, an owner of n/um. The central features of this experience of these remote inhabitants of southern Africa are essentially parallel to those we found in Australia, Central America,

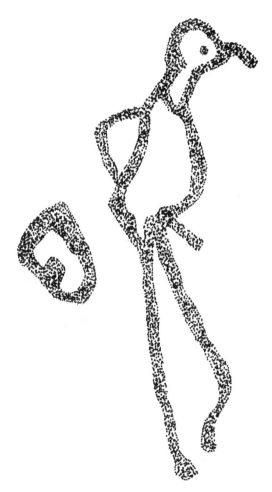

FIGURE 29. *Rock engraving implying shaman's avian transformation and magical flight, southern Africa.*

and Siberia. And if we shift the focus of our examination to the American Southwest, we discover the features of the same visionary world.

We can clearly see this structural similarity in an account given to Morris Opler by the son of a prominent Apache bear shaman.[127] The shaman's son recounts that his father lay asleep near a place called the White Sands:

> While he was sleeping at this place, something came to him. This happened toward morning, and he was sound asleep. Something touched him and told him to awake for it had good things to tell him. He pushed the cover off his head, and there beside him sat a silver-tip bear. It spoke in a human way to him and told him it was time for him to get up, that it was here he would get something to know and to travel by.
>
> He got up. He knew that a door was open to him. He just walked right in, into the rocks. He was led into a room, and the grizzly bear changed itself into the form of a man and told him to follow wherever it went.
>
> He showed my father through a gate where striking rocks were hitting against each other all the time. Then they came to a place where four points of rock went back and forth. They also walked through that. They came to another rock that was rolling and was in the form of a round ball, just like a hill. It hit the bank on the other side all the time. But they walked over it and didn't even notice it strike the bank. Then they came to a swinging rock door and passed through it safely.

Here we encounter once more the initiatory dream experience; the therianthropic spirit guide; the opening in the earth, which will become a "cave"; and the traversing of the opposites, both in the form of the Symplegades symbolism and, as we shall see, as animal pairs within the cave. The shaman has entered a door in the rock, which mystically opens to him much like the "hole too small" that Sereptie enters. And he finds himself within the type of the "holy caves shamans describe." More tellingly, the cave journey is through paired members of supernatural animal species, each characterized by opposition (in this instance black and white):

> They now saw two big bears, one black and one white, at a gate.
> The leader said to continue, and they went between them. Fur-
> ther on they came to two big snakes, a black one and a white one,
> but they went between these also without trouble. This time some-
> thing that was never seen before [in accounts of the acquisition of
> supernatural power known to the narrator] was present in the cave.
> It was the wolf, the big timber wolf. There was a black one and a
> white one. In all the holy caves the shamans describe, they never
> speak of seeing a wolf at all. They tell of coyotes, skunks, and
> other animals, but not wolves. The wolf spoke to my father, but
> still he went on. Now they came to the geese. There were a black
> one and a white one there. When they saw my father they tried to
> fly but came to the ground all the time, because they felt so good.
> They said, "We know you. We have known you all the time."

The last pair of animal essences recognizes a latent kinship with
the shaman initiate: "We know you. We have know you all the
time," they tell him, with a foreknowledge suggesting that his journey of initiation is somehow preordained. Led by the theriomorphic
spirit guide, he travels across "a spider thread that acted as a bridge"
into a paradisiacal realm, the source of power:

> Next they crossed a place where two moving logs were used for a
> bridge. Beyond this bridge they reached another more beautiful
> place. My father asked the guide what this place was and was told
> this was Summer's home. They left it, crossing a spider thread
> that acted as a bridge. They came to an even more beautiful coun-
> try with many flowers growing. All these spoke to them. My fa-
> ther asked what this place was, and the bear told him this was the
> home of the flowers and the herbs for curing men all over the
> world. "This is Medicine's home."

Once more the cave opens to the Otherworld in trance, it becomes
luminous as "Summer's home" and "Medicine's home." It is a portal to the Otherworld marked by symbols of ascent paradoxically
within the cave. The inward journey becomes an ascent to the four
Mountain Spirits. "They are the leading ones," he is told, "stronger than any you saw *in* any other *caves*" [emphasis added]. After

further encounters with various forms of the power he seeks, the shaman in ecstasy reaches the source of power. "He bowed down four times, and the fourth time he was before a man in a big white chair who had a white staff in his right hand. . . . The man handed my father a staff. 'You'll always have this. It will speak itself. It must never be lost.'" With regard to this staff, Opler informs us, "A shaman usually wears or carries something which acts as a link between himself and his source of power." With this he received the power of the Bear as well as the Goose, Wolf, Lightning, and Horse and became a Bear shaman. From the descent into the cave to the accessing of power marked by animal essences, this describes the same ecstatic experience in basically the same stages and symbols as our previous examples. The cave containing the Symplegades leads to the realm of paired animal essences and, harboring symbols of ascent within its depths, becomes a portal to the Otherworld and the shaman's ascent to power.

In the next section we shall examine another example that employs these same structural and functional forms. This additional example is fruitful and necessary because, more than the examples we have previously offered, it presents these forms in a manner that is still transparent to the inner meaning, rejuvenative force, and beauty that potentially informs the shaman's experience. In their subtle and sophisticated symbolism, the Navaho strive to unify rite, art, and myth into a visionary world that not only leads the mind back to the origin and source of power but also, in the words of the poet Rainer Maria Rilke, depicts a sacred reality that, in essence, "is origin still":

But to us existence is still enchanted; at a hundred
points it is origin still. A playing of pure
forces that no one touches who does not kneel and marvel.

Words still gently fade before the unsayable . . .[128]

Where "words turn back," however, the translucence of the visionary symbol is capable of establishing the perennial path to enlightenment and beauty, as it has in the shaman's world for millennia and as it still does for the Navaho.

THE HEROES OF THE SOUL

The entire visionary itinerary that we have been examining is set forth with an extraordinary economy in a Navaho legend, "Where the Two Came to Their Father." The heroes of the legend become the shaman's surrogates for the archetypal journey, and the mythical geography portrayed in Navaho sand paintings becomes its locus. The Navaho have a strong shamanic heritage, and, as Donald Sandner points out, though some might question whether the Navaho medicine man is a true shaman in the strictest sense of the term, "the scenario which the true shaman acts out in his person is projected by the Navaho medicine man into the contents of his myths and rituals, into the symbols of the chant." Navaho ceremonial is what he refers to as "symbolic shamanism."[129]

In the legend the mythical twin heroes, who venture to the Source of Power in the shaman's stead and who will be sent by the Navaho medicine man in his ceremonies to retrieve the lost souls of the suffering, are born when Changing Woman is impregnated by the Sun. They are born upon the central mountain, Mountain Around Which Moving Was Done, and begin their quest from there. We immediately see, gnomically portrayed, a mythical universe. Changing Woman is Mother Earth, with her patterns of birth, death, and regeneration; Sun is the principle of permanence informing the patterns of change; and Mountain Around Which Moving Was Done is the axis mundi, the still point in the turning world that connects permanence and change. These features are set within the backdrop of the Navaho cosmos, which describes a mandala with mountains at the four cardinal points. The four mountains are both the actual mountains of the Navaho landscape and, at the same time and without contradiction, mountains of a mythical landscape that constitutes a world of essence within the material world, an inner dimension of enfolded order that supports and orders the visible universe. Reality is seen as an unfolding of inner or essential form. As in other forms of shamanism, life opens flowerlike from inside outward, and the mystical journey is simultaneously a penetration of its source and a reassertion of what we have referred to as the principle of verticality, which the central axis represents.

The journey is thus a journey inward, wherein the heroes encounter the archetypal inner forces with which we are now well familiar. They encounter the hag, Old Age, in whose hands they suffer a death and rebirth, thus bursting the confines of ordinary mortal existence. And beyond the bourne of this existence they encounter the mythical force that silently spins it forth at the axis of creation, "the Fate-Mother of both the individual and the cosmos, wise with the wisdom of Fate," as Joseph Campbell describes her.[130] This is Spider Woman, a traditional spirit guide of tribes sharing the Navaho heritage. The twins first discover Spider Woman's domain when they notice a thread of smoke emanating from a hole in the ground.* In a symbolism precisely parallel to the story of Sereptie, the Siberian shaman, the hole of the spirit guide at the axis of creation at first appears too small to enter. The twins soon find, however, that they have transcended the ordinary laws of dimensionality, a traditional sign of the penetration of the visionary cosmos, and following the thread of fate they enter the inner dimension, the enfolded order wherein lies, in Campbell's terms, "the zone of Fate's supramundane secret."[131]

This secret is the very point of our present offering. It is embodied in a pair of living eagle feathers that Fate has stolen from the Sun and which she gives to each of the heroes to guard him on his journey to the Father. The feathers of the Sun represent the essential identity between the quester and the source, the sons and their father, individual soul and world soul. In a manner that neatly epitomizes the role of shamanic ornithological symbolism everywhere, the feathers become the vehicles of ascent and protection as the twins encounter the remaining perils of the soul's journey to its source.

Let us view the myth in a larger perspective. The story of the twin heroes of the soul is part of a ceremony performed by the Navaho medicine man and used traditionally both to empower

---

*That the descent into the enfolded order of Spider Woman's spinning place is a paradoxical ascent to the Sun is made clear in Navaho mythology, for Spider Woman, in fact, inhabits a very high spire in Canyon de Chelly.

Indian braves embarking upon warfare and to protect the body and cure illness. The version given here was told to Maud Oakes in 1942 by the aged medicine man, Jeff King, who in sorrow, passed it to a worthy white woman to save it from oblivion. It is believed to mark a resurgence in Navaho consciousness of traditions from their ancient Athapascan shamanic heritage. The ceremony does indeed exemplify what we have previously described as man's enlistment of his total symbolic propensities to draw the mind back to its preconscious sources, though this is done by the Navaho with measure and control rather than by anything suggesting Dionysian mania. Drum, dance, rattle, monotonous and lengthy chant, song, and prayer all contribute. Most interestingly, the Navaho employ art, the art of sand painting, to reconnect man with the plenitude of the creative source. In these sand paintings the various stages of the journey are recreated and placed in a meaningful mythic universe that the patient is himself expected to traverse under the medicine man's ritual guidance. It is within this framework that the heroes lead the soul to its source; that human consciousness finds its origin in the divine.

Let us now return to the Spider Woman. This arachnid equivalent of the therianthropic spirit guide, who unfolds the thread of life from the axis of creation, is a marvelous figure. The spider spins her own world from within herself just as we do, unconsciously creating the exterior world of our outward representations. As Nietzsche reminds us, "We produce these representations in and from ourselves with the same necessity with which the spider spins." As a consequence, he further informs us, we are normally able to "catch," or conceive, only what the web of our outward system of representation is woven to entrap. To penetrate the hole occupied by the Spider Woman, from which she unfolds reality, is to enter the enfolded order, to catch "God's foot upon the treadle of the loom" of creation.

The veil of material creation is a familiar mythic conception. It survives in the Indian concept of Maya. Weavers of man's fate live on in our Western tradition in the Norns of Norse mythology and the Fates of Greek myth. In Plato's *Republic*, the Fates weave man's destiny at the cosmic axis; it is here that the soul returns to the source and receives its true form and fortune, and all life and true knowledge are a reflex and anamnesis of this investiture by the Fates at the spindle of creation. In Norse mythology, likewise, the Norns, weavers of man's fate, do so from the root of the bird-topped World Tree, Yggdrasill, itself the axis of cosmic creation. It is here that Odin, the shaman-god, through sacrificing himself finds himself:

> *I ween that I hung / on the windy tree,*
> *Hung there for nights full nine;*
> *With the spear I was wounded, / and offered I was*
> *To Odin, myself to myself.*[132]

And it is here at the axis of creation that the true, or inner, form of the self is to be found by the twins. Through anamnesis—death of the profane structures of consciousness followed by the rediscovery of the mind's preconscious inner resources—they, like the shaman, return to the source of creation itself. And it is within the hole of Spider Woman that the twins first find auguries of the plenitude of the origin, for there they eat from a basket that, although apparently containing very little food, miraculously keeps refilling as they eat to gain strength for their journey.

But the true boon of the hero journey to this point is Spider Woman's gift of the living feathers that she has stolen from the Sun. They are emblematic of the "inner form" of the heroes and their shared essence with the Source, for they are sons of the Sun. The feathers and the identity with the Sun that they symbolize further represent the process of reawakening the deep structures of consciousness retrieved by entry into the world of the enfolded order. Derived from the Sun, the feathers become natural vehicles for the return to the Sun. For here the inner resources of the mind innately produce as a reflex of the Source the archetypal grammar of symbols that leads back to it. Our reawakened symbolic capacity effects a transformation of consciousness that reveals an identity with the form-producing deep structures of the psyche experienced as being continuous with the cosmic creation.

The feathers, representing this latent drive to identity, appositely become the vehicles of return to the Creator, and the stages of the journey crystallize, as we would expect, into a familiar archetypal configuration: death and rebirth; the encounter with the therianthropic spirit guide; the entry into the hole or cave of the spirit guide, which is at first too small but opens to the luminous Otherworld, the realm of Sun; a descent that becomes an ascent up the world axis; a perilous journey through the Symplegades, uniting opposites; and a return to origin, symbolized by animal essences, as the source of power and life.

Let us follow the remainder of the twins' journey after their encounter with the crone, Old Age, and entry into the inner domain of Spider Woman:

> The next morning, they went on their way. And they passed through a white passage and came to the Cutting Reeds. They told the reeds they wanted to pass through, and why, and the reeds said, "Go ahead, and we will let you pass." So they started, but the reeds closed in and tried to kill the twins. This happened four times. Then they thought of the feather . . . so they stood on the feather and blew their breath on the reeds, and the reeds parted and they passed through safely on the feather, tip first.[133]

The twins went on, and came to the Rock That Claps Together. "This rock would open, and when people entered, he would crush them." Again mounting the feather, they reached the other side unharmed. They similarly traverse the realm of the feared Cat Tail people, "who stabbed people to death." These creatures acted in the same way as the Cutting Reed People and closed in on them four times. They are able to pass through, however, "standing on the feather."[134]

It is precisely because they share their being with the essence of the cosmos that the clash of contraries cannot touch the twins and they can reach the unity that underlies all opposition. And it is this shared essence that continues to guide their journey with a sure-handed inner purpose as they continue. Thus, nearing their journey's end they sense a loss of direction. "The twins did not know where to go. So they stood on the feather, and the feather and rainbow carried them, and they thought, 'We shall know where we are going, when we get there.'"[135] And so, with a preordained certainty, they arrive carried upon the feather at the house of the Sun, the essential form lying behind the woven shapes of their spirit guide, Spider Woman, and the world of phenomenal forms symbolized by their earthly mother, Changing Woman.

The House of the Sun, as inner form of the cosmos, is itself in the shape of a mandala, characterized by redundant images of quaternity, fecundity, and creative power. "The house is guarded by four big bears, four big snakes, four big winds, and four big thunders."[136] It has four rooms. The east room "was full of black clouds of all shapes, lightning bolts, and all kinds of flowers growing." The south room has "all kinds of game, deer, mountain sheep, elk, antelope, and so on," all bunched together and anxious to get out. The west is "a vast country with all kinds of tame animals useful to man, all kinds of grain and growing things, and flowers."[137] This is the cosmic fount par excellence and bears an archetypal identity with visions of the shamanic origin we have experienced earlier, the world of the master forms of the animal spirits, their clever place, the origin and everlasting source of the animals of eternity. It is fitting that here at the source of cosmic plenitude in the north room the heroes will find their "medicine" and the strength to overcome the obstacles of the phenomenal world.

After further tests the Sun recognizes the heroes as his true sons, sons of his essence. As such they are each given a small image of a man to swallow, which represents their newly found "inner" or essential form. Having become invested with their true identity, the twins grow in size and power. The Sun also gives them a special feather representing their kinship with the creative origin, which symbolically crowns the axis of their ascent from the world of change and strife to that of essential form. And on their return to earth, Talking God, in a symbolism uniting the axis with the feathers, provides them with a feathered prayer stick. This recalls the staff given to the Apache shaman to mark his successful quest, which we were told served as "a link between himself and his source of power." It is this symbol of the knowledge and power gained from their successful journey to the Source that, in the form of a similar baton, will "open a way" for the heroes' soul retrieval journeys at the behest of the Navaho medicine men.

And now we can recognize the unifying significance of the central axis of the world, which, like the hero quest and the feathered wand that marks its success, likewise links the worlds of permanence and change. This is, of course, the "Mountain Around Which Moving Was Done." According to Joseph Campbell, this is the axis mundi of the Navaho universe, located at the center of the four mountains that mark the cardinal points of the Navaho natural landscape and define its configuration as a mandala.[138] Here at the cosmic center the twins' journey beyond death and into the dimensionless realm of the Spider Woman commences, and here they find the path of ascent that leads to the Father. As the "'point' upon which contraries turn" it naturally gives rise to the Symplegades symbolism, the clashing contraries that bar the entrance of the profane intelligence shackled to the polarities of a conditioned world but admit the intelligence that intuits its unity with the greater whole of the cosmos. It marks precisely that central point that exists everywhere that illumination occurs "and that is, in the last analysis, not any where or when, but within you," as Ananda Coomaraswamy tells us.[139] It is thus that the axis of ascent, the way "to break out of the universe"[140] is found within, here symbolically within the hole from which Spider Woman spins forth the warp and woof of the world of contraries.

According to Jung, the mandala is an image of unity and totality existing a priori and *in potentia* within the human mind. It represents the inner orderedness of the cosmic source, the foundation of beauty and harmony in a sacral cosmos, divinity unfolding in cosmos, nature, and mind. In reaching the source, the heroes experience this realm of inner order immanent in the creation. Understanding this experience is essential to understanding the Navaho visionary cosmos. For the initiated intelligence the "real" world, shorn of the husk created by a sensibility wedded only to material reality, is everywhere translucent to its origin and source. It is not too much to say that this sacred world basks in the auroral glow of the "Beginning." And here we might again quote Rilke: ". . . at a hundred / points it is origin still. A playing of pure / forces that no one touches who does not kneel and marvel."

In a manner consonant with this symbolism, the creationtime plays an important role in Navaho thought. Because a relationship to the origin makes sacred all creation, human and natural, from the time of ancient Sumer and perhaps earlier, men have introduced and sanctified their great myths by a repetition of their creation myths. This is precisely the case with the Navaho, for the prelude to the legend of the twins' ascent to the Sun Father is the Navaho myth of creation, which relates how the world was vested with the formal inner orderedness that transforms chaos into cosmos. And this is recognized to be the very cosmic formal power that, also investing human creation, gives man's mythic products their enduring archetypal form, the genesis of which is, therefore, the necessary preamble to the legend itself.

In Navaho mythology creation takes place at the Place of Emergence, which is also often depicted at the center of the mandala-form Navaho sand paintings. According to Gladys Reichard, the Place of Emergence is also "called 'Center-of-the-earth,' its location in this world is so much disputed that it should not be considered fixed."[141] It represents the archetypal image of the center that is potentially everywhere, that is, anywhere the sacred erupts into the relative world. Thus, as is characteristic of a large number of myths worldwide, the symbols of the center and the beginning are archetypally assimilated to each other. And it is typical of this center-beginning symbolism traditionally that here the "truly real" emerges, the first human couple is born, and the cultural paradigms and archetypes of all creation first come into being.

The Navaho visionary cosmos incarnates this archetypal pattern quite precisely. As Donald Sandner explains:

> In the first ceremony at the Place of Emergence, First Man created what is thought to be the earth's form and the inner forms of all things. These became the Holy People. "When he had covered them four times as described, a young man and woman first arose from there."[142]

All things, properly envisioned, manifest this "inner form," which reflects the harmonious order of the sacred creation. When this is realized, the natural world of the Navaho reveals itself to be a huge sacred mandala around the sacred cosmic axis. This mythical geography is marked by cardinal points represented by mountains inhabited by the Holy People as their inner forms. Each cardinal point is associated with a color, direction, precious stone, bird symbol, sound, plant, and various other elements. This configuration poetically displays the effulgent vision of diversity radiating from a central unity—a unity that subsumes diversity and returns it to its source, a source that, in fact, it never really leaves. As in the other cultures we have examined in this chapter, the creationtime is not a time past, but a continuing reality that gives form and order to creation here and now; it is the formal force that dwells within and sustains the manifest world. God and the creation are not sundered realities, and the final revelation is that the mandala-form source and the mandala-form creation are united; properly envisioned they are in essence the same. Finally, "The House of the Sun," Jeff King informed Maud Oakes, "is the same as Changing Woman's house,"[143] but this visionary equivalence is articulated only by virtue of the cosmic axis that represents the twins' journey and that, uniting the two mandalas, stands at the center of the visionary cosmos.

It is here that Navaho mythic sensibility displays its most subtle sophistication in the assimilation of ancient shamanic traditions. We remember that the vehicles of the journey to the Sun, the ascent to the source, were the miraculous feathers given to the twins by Spider Woman. This is a subtle transformation of the theme of avian metamorphosis we have seen marking the shaman's magical flight in so many cultures. The symbols of the completed journey were likewise feathers given to the heroes by their father, Sun, in recognition of their true patrimony as sons of cosmic power. The feather is thus the symbol of ascent to the top of the cosmic axis, to the solar principle itself—archetypally associated with flight and feathers. We noted that the symbols of the axis and feather are brought together in the feathered staff or prayer stick given to the twins by Talking God on their return journey. This holy object is known as the *kethawn*, which "probably means 'place-where-it-is-feathered.'"[144] The staff is a small-scale version of the feather-topped cosmic axis and represents the wisdom and power of the completed ecstatic journey. As such, as we noted, it "opens a way" for the twin heroes, as the shamanic surrogates of the medicine man, into the mythic world and, further, into the Place of Emergence to galvanize an inner power, which is equivalent to rescuing the lost soul of the ailing patient.

The Navaho medicine men adroitly employ the powerful symbols that are the legacy of their shamanic heritage to effect a transformation of consciousness in their patient. The transformation is, of course, similar to that evoked by the symbols in the hero legend, for the healer employs the very power the twins received from the sacred source as the basis of his healing technique. He will attempt to evoke an awareness of the inner form and order of the cosmos, the same inner form and order that the twins encountered at the cosmic center. For the Navaho the ordering of the mind and the cosmos are deeply kindred. This sense of cosmic and human harmony is beautifully portrayed in a song from the Navajo chant Mountaintop Way, wherein a dying brother bids farewell to his younger sibling when the gods summon him to their realm.

> *Farewell, my younger brother.*
> *From the high, holy places*
> *The Gods have come for me.*
> *You will never see me again.*
> *But when the showers pass over you,*
> *And the thunder sounds,*
> *You will think:*
> *There is the voice of my elder brother.*
> *And when the harvests ripen,*
> *And you hear the voices of small birds of many kinds,*
> *And the chirping of the grasshoppers,*
> *You will think:*
> *There is the ordering of my elder brother.*
> *There is the trail of his mind.*[145]

The initial stages in the evocation of this transformation are familiar, for they, like the journeys of initiation that we have studied, lead the patient away from the ordinary structures of consciousness back to his deeper mental resources. Prolonged song, prayer, dance, rattle, and drum work their effect, an effect that may be heightened by the sweat bath, fasting, and other methods of loosening the grip of everyday consciousness. As Sandner informs us:

> To unaccustomed ears the songs sound repetitious and monotonous, especially as they drone on through a long night. But the monotony itself, by lowering the threshold of consciousness, allows the constantly repeated images to register on the deeper subconscious layers. Though no one takes any notice of it, everyone is in an altered state of consciousness, and no one is allowed to sleep. At this time the symbolic imagery may have its greatest effect.[146]

Sand paintings are used to recreate the visionary cosmos and project the patient into it and song, prayer, and chant guide him along the way. The wand, symbolic of the axis connecting us back to the source and of the shaman's ecstatic journey, "opens a way" into the mythic realm for the heroes and for the medicine man and his patient.[147] The medicine man recites the prayer, and the patient repeats it line for line. Just as the sand painting elicits an awareness of the patient's inner affinity with the visionary cosmos, so does the larger ceremony evoke a recognition of identity between the patient and the creationtime "Holy People," who represent the inner or essential form of the creation. According to Reichard, "The chanter's ultimate goal is to identify the patient with the supernaturals being invoked."[148] Or as Sandner informs us, "Methods of diagnosis, myth-telling, impersonation, dramatic performance, singing, praying, dancing, sand painting, and even herbal medication are all ways of bringing about identification. Finally, with the identification comes the moment of psychic union through the medicine man with the god, supernatural animal, or tutelary hero, bringing the hoped-for healing influence."[149] The process is the familiar one of recognizing one's true identity as the creationtime hero, such as we encountered in Australia, or of "opening the portal" between this world and the next, which we met among the Maya. The sand painting becomes an altar through which "the gods come and go."[150]

Underlying this entire symbolism of identification is the mythic concept of the return to origins, to the creationtime, for the healing effect comes from rearticulating the connection to the source of power and plenitude. In *Myth and Reality*, Eliade makes an observation on archaic thought in general that, as Sandner recognizes, is crucial to understanding Navaho shamanism:

> Now, all the medical rituals we have been examining aim at a return to origins. We get the impression that for archaic societies life cannot be *repaired*, it can only be *re-created* by a return to sources. And the "source of sources" is the prodigious outpouring of energy, life, and fecundity that occurred at the Creation of the World.[151]

Of course, in the language of myth the creationtime is a presently accessible reality, and its recovery allows the patient to recreate himself in a state of health and wholeness. For health and wholeness accompany each other in Navaho thought, and the regeneration implied is spiritual as well as physical. Just as the artistic form of the symbols and sand paintings is used to lift the patient's mind to the formal source of all beauty, so this source, "the Beauty supreme," according to ancient wisdom, "fashions Its lovers to Beauty" as an integral part of the regenerative experience.[152] Thus, the prayer intoned over the patients, who symbolically become identified with the twin heroes and ultimately with the "inner forms" of the cosmos, ends with a stanza that beautifully reflects the depths of this regenerative experience:

> *The World before me is restored in beauty,*
> *The World behind me is restored in beauty,*
> *The World below me is restored in beauty,*
> *The World above me is restored in beauty,*
> *All things around me are restored in beauty,*
> *My voice is restored in beauty,*
> *It is restored in beauty,*
> *It is restored in beauty,*
> *It is restored in beauty,*
> *It is restored in beauty.*[153]

It is the perception of inner or ideal form that awakens man to beauty, an accord between the formal principles aroused in the mind grounded in the fountainhead of all form and the cosmos itself. It is this that makes the shaman the world's first artist, according to Andreas Lommel and others, and explains why art has been a necessary concomitant experience in most shamanic cultures from the Paleolithic times onward. Art and beauty join the shaman as psychopomps that lead to and express the formal source of human experience and are part and parcel of the transformation of consciousness implicit in the shaman's journey as a return to origins.

The Navaho seem to wrap this entire complex of associations into one phrase, *Sa'ah naaghái bik'eh hozhóón*, a phrase that has proved elusive to Western conceptualization.[154] Gladys Reichard feels that it is best translated as "according-to-the-ideal-may-restoration-be-achieved."[155] Viewed in this way, it brings together various ideas we have been exploring. Restoration is the result of a return to inner form, the very return to origins Eliade has stressed and particularly the inner or ideal form vested in the creation at the Place of Emergence. According to Sandner, one well-informed Navaho medicine man said that "*Sa'ah naaghái* meant 'you observe things, you look at them, you open your eyes,' and that *hozhóón* meant 'holiness,' so that the whole concept would mean something like 'to see holiness' or 'to see according to holiness,' which could be the ultimate teaching of symbolic healing."[156] And, finally, we might add that "to see holiness" and "to see according to holiness" are one and the same, for as the eye is formed, so it sees. For the Navaho the eye inwardly open to inner form is able "to see holiness" precisely because it can "see according to holiness."

As a result of the movement we have described as a return to origin, the patient or initiate and the medicine man become identical with the heroes of the creationtime, with Holy Man and the Holy People, who represent the essential form of the durative origin as it ever incarnates itself in our changing world. And before we leave the Navaho, we must mention another tale of the ever reincarnate source of form and creation that harks back to and preserves an ancient shamanic symbolism. This is the story of Holy Man and the Buffalo People. Sandner encapsulates the tale as follows. He informs us that "Holy Man went on one more adventure, this time to the Buffalo People":

Holy Man saw a group of these animals [buffalo] and followed them a long way, until they revealed themselves to him as Buffalo People. They taught him their prayers and paintings so they might be included in the ceremony. They also gave him two of their women for his wives. Holy Man had intercourse with the buffalo women, and because this broke ceremonial restrictions he became ill, but the Buffalo were able to heal him with their magic herbs.

The buffalo women were wives of the great Buffalo-Who-Never-Dies, who was on his way to avenge the indignity. That night was very long; when Holy Man called for the dawn, it came in a red glare instead of the usual white light, indicating the greatest danger. Buffalo-Who-Never-Dies saw Holy Man and made a mighty charge, but Holy Man with his two wives escaped to one of the sacred mountains and waited there. Each time he charged, Buffalo-Who-Never-Dies was able to demolish part of the mountain, but Holy Man was always able to move to another part; as he did so, he shot a powerful arrow into Buffalo. On the fourth charge the arrows took effect and Buffalo-Who-Never-Dies rolled over and died. Since he embodied the life of all the Buffalo People, they all died with him except the two wives of Holy Man. With their encouragement, Holy Man set about restoring the great Buffalo to life. He pulled out the arrows with prayers and rituals. This took much effort, but finally Buffalo-Who-Never-Dies began to move. When he was completely restored, he recognized Holy Man's superior power and relinquished all claim to his wives. Holy Man stayed with the Buffalo People for some time, learning more of their lore. Then, with all that he had learned, he made his way back to those who were waiting for him at Whirling Mountain.[157]

This sacred act of restoration is often the subject of sand paintings in the form of a mandala, and thus the restoration is understood as a "restoration according to the ideal," a return to the generative source that the mandala represents. We see behind this drama of Holy Man and the Buffalo the ancient symbolism of sacrifice, return to the source, and eternal regeneration performed by the shaman. The episode of learning from the therianthropic Buffalo People, particularly the arts of healing, is typically shamanic.

Buffalo-Who-Never-Dies is, of course, the master animal spirit of the buffalo, and it is traditional that the shaman visits the realm of such master spirits to gain power. Some traditions represent this sojourn as involving sexual relations with the animal forms or taking them in marriage. The mortal confrontation between Holy Man and the buffalo repeats the shaman's sacrifice of the individuated form of the sacred animal, which returns, together with the entranced shaman, to the source to be regenerated by their eternal forms—the essential "inner form" of man, Holy Man, and the essential "inner form" of the buffalo, his master spirit, or Buffalo-Who-Never-Dies. This is yet another expression of the eternal dance at the heart of the creation, where enduring form ever incarnates itself in the world of time and change and where time and change, mythically transformed, are subsumed in the world of eternal form. And this process of transformation again occurs at, and symbolizes, the central axis uniting the realm of the Sun with its eternal forms and the world of Changing Woman. This is the very path of ascent traced by the inward journey of the twins through the sacred cave hole of the Spider Woman that, in the same manner as we have seen in each of the shamanic traditions discussed in this chapter, "unites the cosmos with itself" and shows the two realms, in essence, to be one.

Symbols are, as Jung said, "bridges thrown into the unknown," but they are produced in secret complicity with the unknown, and like the Apache spiderweb bridge, lead those who can follow their often thin and fragile thread to the Otherworld. We remember that in the face of the perils of the journey the twins "trusted their feather," their shared essence with the Source. "We will know where we are going when we get there," they said with an intuitive awareness of the inner purposiveness guiding their journey. They are, as an inspired Zarathustra recognized himself to be, "riding on many a symbol toward many a truth," for the symbolic structure of the journey is the universal way in which the plenitude that invests our mind and the cosmos leads us, through an innate and universal symbolic capacity, back to itself. Even today the Navaho produce small mandalas known as God's eyes. As the German mystical theologian Meister Eckhart understood, "The eye with which I see God is the eye with which God sees me," that is, the strong eye and mythic symbols are experienced as reflexive expressions of the Source that both effect and reflect the transformation of consciousness through which its form and power become open to human experience.

It is because the axis marks this universal way uniting the two worlds that it lies at the cosmic center, the center of formal power. And it is for the same reason that the feathered wand, which symbolizes it, can open a way into the mythic realm, back to the creationtime source, and be a sure guide through the perils along the way. As an expression of the Source, this path itself has a profundity, permanence, and universality comparable only to Nature herself, as we have witnessed in this chapter. We have seen in far-flung shamanic traditions distant in time and place, whether in initiation rites, dreams, shamanic lore, rock painting, or monumental sculpture, mankind riding on precisely the same symbols to precisely the same truths or, we might say, experiences. In the process, the initiatory cave hole everywhere opens into luminosity. It connects back to the Source and becomes itself the origin of illumination and power, of psychic and physical regeneration and inner orderedness, and of mythic form and beauty, beauty that is a reflex of the "Beauty supreme" that informs it.

In the shamanic traditions we have studied, the cave journey reveals the source of illumination and gives rise to symbols of ascent. The serpent that grows feathers and ascends to the celestial realm, the bird-topped World Tree, the feathered pole or axis, or an equivalent symbol (mountain, astral cord, and so forth) becomes manifest within the cave. These symbols are archaic but still powerful. We see them enduring today in the winged pole, the caduceus, up which two entwined serpents ascend. This was originally the staff of the psychopomp Hermes. Today it still signifies regenerative power and health in our modern medical traditions as well as the illumination or gnosis that is at the heart of the Hermetic traditions, the same dual significance we find associated with the component symbols in shamanism.

In this light we may remember that it is a pair of coupling intertwined serpents that greet the shaman at the entry to the Australian luminous cave and herald the illumination and regeneration it represents, as discussed earlier in this chapter. And lest any doubt the long-lasting power of these symbols, we close this chapter by noting that when the old Navaho shaman, Jeff King, was asked from where he received the images represented in the sand paintings that accompany the stages of the twins' heroic journey, he replied that they were, in fact, painted upon the walls of an ancient cave in the area. "He said he had visited the cave in his boyhood," Joseph Campbell tells us, "and could visit it again when he wished to refresh his memory of the painting." Campbell speculates as to whether it was an actual cave or "is to be allegorically understood as the cavern of the soul." In any case the shaman could recognize it because outside this luminous cave of shamanic enlightenment was "a stone carving of two snakes intertwined."[158]

Chapter 5

THE DOOR TO THE HEAVENS

Strive to bring back the god in yourselves to the
Divine in the universe.

Plotinus

We have followed the inward journey of the shaman and the transformation of consciousness it evokes into the inner grottoes of the
luminous cave as the portal to the durative, transpersonal reality
experienced by the shaman. We have seen the elements of this
visionary reality in strikingly similar structural and functional forms
in a variety of cultures scattered around nearly the entire globe
and often widely separated in distance and time. Before returning
to reexamine the caves of the Upper Paleolithic, I would like to
call attention to one more shamanic tradition, which survives
among the Tukano Indians of South America. Tukano shamanism
is an interesting example of an enduring shamanism that maintains a startling continuity with the images and stories we have
studied and manifests a nucleus of symbols that seems to point
right back to the cave walls at Les Trois Frères and Lascaux. And
though it is strongly influenced by the inflections of local culture,
it provides a living proof of that common formative force that, as
Joseph Campbell has told us, is "spontaneously working, like a
magnetic field, to precipitate and organize the ethnic structures
from behind, or within" into forms we can now recognize as universal. Moreover, because Tukano mythology carefully places all

of these symbols within the context of the cosmic creative process, as expressed in and through the shaman, it is clear that for the Tukano this formal archetypal force is the formative force of the cosmos itself.

The Tukano Indians inhabit the Territory of Vaupés in Colombia, South America. This area lies in the northwest Amazon region of Colombia and has long been characterized by its inaccessibility. Riverine travel, for centuries the only viable means of transportation, was hazardous at best, owing to large waterfalls and dangerous rapids. The jungle is lush, dense, and difficult to penetrate. For this reason, the Tukano have lived in an insulating isolation that has helped preserve their culture and their shamanism. The Tukano and, more particularly, a phratry of the tribe, the Desana, were the subject of fieldwork by Gerardo Reichel-Dolmatoff. Reichel-Dolmatoff developed a close rapport and sympathy with the natives and personally participated in some of their ceremonies. Shamanism, he notes, is a well-developed phenomenon among the Indians of the Vaupés. The shaman, or payé, as he is commonly called, is an important specialist who establishes contact with the supernatural powers for the benefit of society.[1] As we have seen in other contexts, there are certain qualities that mark a person as a potential payé. He must possess an innate ability to master the tribe's traditional lore, as well as "a deep interest in myth and tribal tradition, a good memory for reciting long sequences of names and events, a good singing voice, and the capacity for enduring hours of incantations during sleepless nights preceded by fasting and sexual abstinence." But most important, he tells us, "a payé's soul should 'illuminate,'"[2] a prerequisite precisely akin to that called for in other shamanic cultures and particularly reminiscent of the Aboriginal Australian shamanic novices we discussed earlier.

This luminescence of the spirit is integral to Tukano myth, for here, as elsewhere, the shaman is a conduit of formal power. "This supernatural luminescence of the payé is said to manifest itself when he speaks or sings, or when he explains his or others' hallucinatory experiences. . . . This powerful emanation is thought to be directly derived from the sun, and to have a marked seminal character. The sun's fertilizing energy is transmitted to the payé in the sense that he himself becomes a carrier of a force that contains procreative and fortifying components."[3] The sun, for the Tukano, is the pre-eminent creative force and the mythological creator of mankind. Like Campbell's magnetic force working from behind to give transpersonal shape and meaning to local experience, this creative force vests the shaman with an uncanny ability to interpret the myths and visionary experiences of his people. And among the Tukano it is precisely this luminescence that enables the payé to have insight into and interpret mythological passages as well as the dreams or other portents experienced by his tribesmen. "The payé's interpretations thus 'shed light' upon these matters, in the strict sense of the expression."[4]

To perform his office properly, the payé must obtain certain instruments of his practice, which are believed to come from a realm parallel to and more potent than our phenomenal world. The "essence" of these instruments preexists in the celestial sphere, and it is from that sphere that the shaman receives their essential and sometimes even material form. During his narcotic trance these power objects are said to "fall out of the sky" and appear before the apprentice. The now familiar quartz crystals, a special hoe, his snuffing apparatus of bird bone, his feather crowns, and the seed rattles that he ties to his legs when dancing are among these celestially sanctioned accoutrements of the shaman's vocation.[5] But most essential is the shaman's staff or scepter, for it becomes in every sense the center of the Tukano world.

This scepter is both the vehicle and symbol of trance ascent. One end forms a rattle, the rhythmic application of which assists in inducing ecstasy. It is mythically associated with hallucinogenic substances that further impel the trance ascent. Moreover, in a series of interwoven symbols it becomes the image of the axis mundi at the cosmic "center" from which the shaman's trance ascent begins and by virtue of which he ascends to the source and origin of creation. It is topped with the feathers of the hummingbird or oropendola bird. In this mythology, the scepter is associated with this bird. This is not just any bird, however, but the bird form of the Cosmic Creator, for in his creative exploits the Sun himself adopted the shape of the oropendola bird. And the feathered Tukano shaman in trance will assimilate the spiritual condition of the Sun as the supreme source of power.

Thus, the bird-topped staff can be associated with the bird-topped tree or feathered pole archetype that we have so often found marks the axis mundi at the center of the world, suggesting the penetration of human consciousness into the transpersonal realm and symbolically connecting the different levels of the shaman's universe. We may note that this axis also partakes of a sexual generative symbolism. This is clear from a number of contexts, but most patently from the Tukano creation myth. In this myth the Sun originally had to search for the proper place to create mankind. As he proceeded up a particular river, he used a ceremonial staff with which he probed the river bottom for a place where the staff would stand vertically. "The solar deity," Reichel-Dolmatoff tells us, "is a fertilizing male principle, phallic in nature." This phallic baton, "symbolized by the Sun's rays and the shaman's ceremonial staff, at a certain moment in time placed itself vertically upon a fixed topographic point at the equator. . . . From this phallic staff (the Sun's ray) drops of semen fell to earth and became man."[6]

This event is associated by the Tukano with certain sacred areas, the rocks of Ipanore and the Rock of Nyí, both of which lie almost exactly on the equatorial line. At certain times on the equator the sun's rays fall vertically upon the earth, that is, symbolically the phallic staff is positioned upright. In so placing his staff, "the Sun Father was 'measuring the center of the day'" Reichel-Dolmatoff informs us.[7] These sacred areas represent the central point where the Sun fertilized the earth, for at noon on the day of the vernal equinox the upright faces of certain rocks in the area cast no shadows and thus mark the place of primordial creation.[8]

At the Rock of Nyí, ancient petroglyphs memorialize this seminal event. One is particularly revealing. It depicts the erect staff in the form of an anthropomorphized winged phallus (Figure 30). The structure is characterized by a quaternity symmetrically surrounding a central axis and seems to grow from a central point. The central point in Tukano mythology is the point of cosmic origin penetrated by the Sun's staff, as is clear to us from the myth. In a larger context, bird, staff, erect phallus, center of the world, point of creation, axis mundi, and zone of verticality all coalesce in this depiction, which stands at the central point of creation, marking this as a sacred revelation of cosmogonic power.

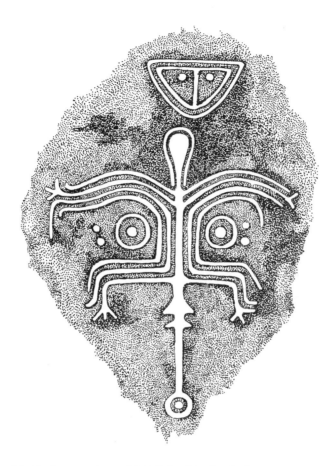

FIGURE 30. *Rock engraving at Nyí, Colombia, South America.*

For the Tukano the concept of finding the "center" plays an important role in myth and ritual. The center is associated with a female principle and also with the now familiar concept of the axis mundi as a connecting link between the earth and other cosmic levels that may lie above or below it. The center marks the spot where an object can be placed, for example, a staff, a house beam, a tree, a vine serving as a ladder, which serves as axis mundi and thus becomes a means of both communication and, at the same time, of fertilization or creation.[9] We remember that this has been a familiar attribute of the cosmic axis in the shamanic traditions we have examined; it is simultaneously the vehicle of ascent and communication with the Otherworld and the conduit through which the plenitude of the cosmos flows into creation. Thus, the Tukano shaman's staff, as representative of the central axis, also becomes both the emblem and vehicle of ascent to the realm of essence and of the source of the power that the shaman carries into this world.

When the Sun created mankind, he reasoned that man needed a means of communication with the source of his creation. It was for this reason that the Sun Father searched for *yajé*, a hallucinogen utilized to induce the shaman's trance. "In all cases, it seems, yajé is thought to provide a means of being transported to another dimension of consciousness, which, in the daily life of the individual or of the group, acquires great importance," Reichel-Dolmatoff tells us.[10] The same symbolism extends to the other major trance-inducing agent of the Tukano, *vihó*, a narcotic snuff prepared from *virola* sap. In some nearby cultures this snuff is carried in the scepter of the shaman. The Tukano carry this narcotic powder in a tube designated as the "penis of the sun."[11] As we know, the solar phallus is symbolized by the shaman's staff and the axis mundi of the creation. The distribution of the snuff takes place at the center, in mimesis of the sun's establishing the central axis of creation.

It is from the axis-center that the shaman begins his trance journey under the auspices of *Vihó-mahsë*, the master of snuff, who leads his ascent to the Milky Way. Here "the horizon opens like a door," and the payé is led to his ultimate destination, *Vaí-mahsë*, master of game animals, who is also regarded as a payé,[12] and lives in a celestial "hill-house" the description of which is markedly similar to other images with which we are familiar. It is a cosmic reservoir of life. A hill inhabited by Vaí-mahsë is imagined as having four doors located at the cardinal points. In his trance, the payé arrives at the hill and approaches the northern entrance, where he knocks three times with his baton. The house is filled with innumerable animals "crouching as if asleep . . . jaguars and snakes are lying on the floor, and brightly colored birds sit on the rafters." The shaman asks for food, and the master of game animals gives his assent. "The payé fills two large baskets with certain species of game animals and carries them to the door. There the animals awaken as if from a stupor and scurry away into the forest, always in pairs, a male and a female."[13] Here again we have an image of the cosmic source of life with its eternal animal forms, and the image bears a clear resemblance to !Kung, Siberian, Australian, and Navaho images of what Eliade calls the cosmic fount. And when we learn that in trance the shaman perceives not only the Master of Animals but also "the gigantic prototypes of the game animals," we cannot help but remember the animal essences inhabiting the walls of the Paleolithic caves visited by ancient entranced shamans in millennia past.

The narcotic role of yajé is hallowed by its own mythic foundations, and the hallucinogen is cast in the role of the primordial divine child and victim whose sacrifice creates the trance condition. Behind this belief lies the related conception that the sacrifice is also, in fact, the individuated or profane consciousness of the entranced person. This becomes clear from the larger mythological context. The myth tells us that "in the beginning of time . . . there appeared the Yajé Woman." Yajé Woman was mystically impregnated through the eye by the Sun Father "in the house of waters." Initially she confronted the first men of creation, and "when the men saw the woman with her child they became benumbed and bewildered. It was as if they were drowning as they watched the woman and her child." The Yajé Woman then asks, "Who is the father of this child?"[14] Surprisingly all aggressively assert their paternity. Arguing over who should possess the child, they tear it to pieces. Several important ideas are capsulized in this incident. The first element is the tearing apart of the divine child, the yajé. Sacrifice and transformation of consciousness are symbolically associated. We remember that after creating man, the Sun Father established yajé as a means of communion between creator and creation. Yajé is, of course, the narcotic that precipitates trance communication. Several associations are implicit in this mythic event: the loss of self, a return to primordiality as the source of authenticity, and the same return as a source of fecundity and illumination associated with the Sun Father's original act of creation through the womb of being, the "manifestation house." The myth also recalls several others where a trance-inducing agent or intoxicant is depicted as the sacrifice. We recall the Soma of the Soma sacrifice in India and the Deer-Peyote sacrifice of the Huichol. We might also think of the myth of Dionysus, himself a god of intoxication and ecstasy, who is torn to pieces by the Titans in Greek mythology.

The comparison with Dionysus serves as a catalyst for the remaining observations concerning the myth. Keeping in mind that it is also the individuated consciousness that is sacrificed under the effect of the narcotic, we might remember Nietzsche's description of this Dionysian experience in *The Birth of Tragedy*. Quoting Schopenhauer, he describes the individuated, or Apollonian, consciousness as being like a man sitting "in a little row boat" amid a raging sea that constantly threatens this "frail craft" with annihilation. Dionysian rapture, "whose closest analogy is furnished by physical intoxication," shatters the frail craft of individuated consciousness. "The mystical jubilation of Dionysus," he tells us, ". . . breaks the spell of individuation and opens a path to the maternal womb of being." Dionysus produces in the human being a state of consciousness that, "though the way passes through annihilation and negation . . . he is made to feel that the very womb of things speaks audibly to him." The analogy is fruitful because Nietzsche's description of the initially threatening aspect of the sacrifice of individuated consciousness and the resultant sense of exultation and of a person being united with "the maternal womb of being" very well captures the archetypal experience implicit in the myth of the tearing apart of the yajé divine child.

We remember that as the Yajé Woman approached the first men in "the house of waters" with her newly revealed son they were benumbed and bewildered. "It was as if they were drowning," we are specifically informed by the myth. Reichel-Dolmatoff points out that when Yajé Woman "drowns" the men the text actually reads *"gahpí noméri miria-vaya"*—"yajé images she drowned them with." The original experience contains the threat of "losing oneself."[15] The "frail craft" of individual consciousness is overwhelmed in the drowning welter of hallucinatory yajé images. The myth, however, has a complex symbolism that, like the trance experience itself, "opens the path to the maternal womb of being." The transition is effected by two sets of symbolic associations.

In the first association, "drowning," as used in this context, is also associated with coitus and has a sexual aspect. "According to my Indian informants, the term alludes to procreation or coitus, an act which the Tukano often compare to a state of drowning, drunkenness or hallucination," Reichel-Dolmatoff explains. "During the sexual act a man 'drowns' or 'sees visions.'"[16] In fact, hallucinatory trance is itself assimilated with the sexual act. The trance experience, one educated informant told Reichel-Dolmatoff, is a form of "spiritual coitus." How can we understand such a statement as it applies to our yajé myth?

The answer lies "in the beginning," that is, the beginning of the myth, which is the beginning or origin of creation and constitutes the very reality to which yajé was mythically appointed to open the human consciousness. For in this second symbolic association the womb is "the maternal womb of being." In this instance we may take our initial guidance from Carl Kerényi, who, in *Essays on a Science of Mythology*, examines the meaning of beginnings or origins in myth and particularly in the myth of the divine child. Such myths provide "a giving of grounds," that is, of ontological grounds.[17] "Primordiality is the same thing for him [the teller of myth] as authenticity."[18] "This return to the origins and to primordiality is a basic feature of every mythology."[19] The events described in myth form the ground, or foundation, of the world, because everything rests on them. They are the first principles "to which everything individual and particular goes back and out of which it is made, while they remain ageless, inexhaustible, invincible in timeless primordiality—in a past that proves imperishable because of its eternally repeated rebirths."[20]

The answer, indeed, lies "in the beginning," in the maternal womb of being. We remember the yajé myth tells us that "in the beginning of time" there appeared the Yajé Woman. Reichel-Dolmatoff informs us that this phrase, "in the beginning of time," or *neo gorare*, carries a complex set of meanings and connotations. "The root *go* expresses a uterine concept, the idea of origin and birth; *goró* is vagina, *gobé* is a cavity or hole, and *gorá* expresses the idea of a vital force emerging from somewhere. *Gorosiri* means 'place of origin.'" More important, he further notes that *gorare* means "true, authentic, legitimate, pure," and the related term *gorata* means "truly, in reality." "The initial expression *neo gorare*—in the beginning of time—contains therefore the idea of truthfulness, of the true and legitimate origins," he concludes.[21] In this context primordiality is equivalent to authenticity; it is the true, the real, and the source of reality. It is also the locus of vital force and impetus to all creation. It is not surprising that this symbolism plays an essential role in the Tukano creation myth, for in the beginning, when Sun Father created mankind by means of his scepter, the myth employs similar ideas.

On the petroglyph depicted earlier (see Figure 30), above the winged phallic staff is a triangular object the Tukano identify as a vagina. When Sun Father's scepter penetrates the earth, it enters the cosmic womb. Reichel-Dolmatoff tells us that "Tukano ideas connected with the generative powers of this cosmic womb are highly involved."

> The key word around which these ideas revolve is *taër ro* / "that which is constant, that which is a beginning." According to our Desana informants, the related verb *tariri* / "to happen," "to come to pass," and, in a wider sense, "to manifest itself," is connected with this concept. The womb . . . is designated as *taëró-víi* / "manifestation-house," in the sense of its being a place wherein the supernatural essence manifested itself in a visible, human form.[22]

Here, in this intrauterine world penetrated by the Sun Father's phallic scepter, the world of essence enters manifestation, the potential becomes actual, "that which is constant" becomes that which happens, that which will "come to pass." In a manner akin to the large number of myths described by Eliade in *The Two and the One*, the combined masculine and feminine symbolisms imply primordial totality, absolute reality, and illumination on the one hand and on the other an "immersion in the limitless ocean of power that existed before the Creation of the World and rendered the creation possible."[23] Yajé as the divine child, the representative of primordiality, is the symbol of and vehicle to this reality, for in trance the shaman penetrates the maternal womb of essence and the primordial power that informs it.

Generative symbols and symbols of the uterine world where essence becomes manifest pervade Tukano thought. In fact, the native term for payé, *ye'e* (Desana) or *yaí* (Tukano), is derived from the verb *yéeri*, meaning "to cohabit." As Reichel-Dolmatoff points out,

> The phallic attributes of the payé's office are obvious. In the first place, *Vaí-mahsë's* houses in the hills or under the water are, in all

essence, uterine deposits, an idea well recognized by the Indians, and the payé's penetration into these womblike abodes carries the connotation of a fertilizing act. Occasionally a payé might even cohabit with the female game animals that inhabit a hill and are "like people." *Vaí-mahsë* and *Vihó-mahsë* will sometimes celebrate a *dabucurí*, wherein the animals dance and sing in human shape, drink yajé, and behave in every respect like human beings. Quite often a payé, in his trance, will participate in these feasts, to which a great fertilizing power is attributed. . . .

In the second place, the payé's stick rattle is a phallic rod from which, according to the Creation Myth, the Sun Father's sperm dropped down to earth. The cylinder of whitish quartzite the payé wears suspended from his neck is called the "sun's penis" (D: *abé yeeru*).[24]

We now understand why the shaman's initial penetration of the uterine world of the Master of Animals is with his phallic baton, as we described earlier. It is a reentry into the world of primordial totality and creative plenitude such as was symbolized in the myth of creation, a return to origins with all that this implies. And the yajé trance, as the vehicle to this reality, shares a similar symbolism. Yajé is prepared in a pot, and the preparation together with the vessel itself recapitulate familiar images.

The yajé pot (*gahpí soró*) should be made by an old woman who smooths and polishes the inner and outer surfaces with a hard, smooth yellow stone. The Tukano view this stone as "a phallus which shapes" the vessel, which in turn is considered to be a uterine receptacle. As a matter of fact, the yajé pot represents the uterus, the maternal womb, and hence is a cosmic model of transformation and gestation. On the cylindrical base there is sometimes painted a vagina and clitoris, symbolizing the "door."[25]

This is a familiar symbol to the Tukano, which Reichel-Dolmatoff describes as a U-shaped element said to represent a "door," or "entrance," to the uterus, and, in a wider sense, to "the heavens." "It symbolizes the break from one cosmic level and the transportation to another dimension of perception."[26]

The shaman enters this door when he imbibes the trance-inducing yajé. Symbolically the shaman first enters this uterine world and then ascends to "the heavens." This entry into the womb describes the same path we have encountered in so many forms of shamanism. The shaman enters a cave, hole, or the womb as an image of "inwardness," for it is in the inner world of trance that he encounters the power that informs the creation. The first spatial metaphor is inward, into the cosmic womb of creation. Yet the heavens touch us from within, and just as the cave becomes luminous and the portal to the Otherworld, so does the symbolic womb. Yajé is mythically associated with light (the myth tells "the child had the form of light, it was human but it was light, it was yajé"), and the early stages of taking yajé are characterized by a state of "undefined luminosity."[27] Reichel-Dolmatoff informs us, "To describe the onset of the hallucinatory trance with the words 'The horizon opens like a door' is fairly common. The expression tries to convey the idea of a sudden luminous phenomenon which lights up a previous state of darkness."[28] In the luminosity of hallucination and illumination the door of the heavens opens to the eternal source of creation itself, and the participant is projected into the mythical era signified by the phrase "in the beginning of time."

Reichel-Dolmatoff himself took this inward and upward journey, personally participating in a Tukano yajé ceremony. The results are interesting. He first notes that songs and dances, different musical instruments, red torch lights, and ritualized conversation and repetitions all provide a certain frame of mind for the procedure. Preliminary to this, if the yajé is being taken by a novitiate payé, he will have undergone exhaustive dietary restrictions, endured a lack of sleep, and suffered the toxic and disorienting effects of prior drug experiences. But this state of extreme physical and psychological stress is said to be a necessary prerequisite and constitutes the true test of the payé's calling, according to the Tukano.

Reichel-Dolmatoff, from his own experience and from his research among natives well familiar with the yajé trance, notes that the first significant stage of the experience is fairly uniform and relates back to the myth of the Yajé Woman. We remember that the loss of individuation mythically attributed to the introduction of yajé was described as "*gapí noméri miria-vaya,* yajé images she drowned them with." Reichel-Dolmatoff tells us that *noméri* in this context signifies "to paint with red dots," and the initial stage of the yajé experience is specifically characterized by seeing such "red dots" and very simple abstract designs. Reichel-Dolmatoff, citing the regularity of the recurrence of these images, identified them as phosphenes. Phosphenes are momentary perceptions of dots, specks, and starlike or irregular patterns that appear in our visual field in darkness or in half-light and are thought to be caused by neurochemical impulses that pass through the eye, the cortex, or the subcortex of the human brain. They are subjective images resulting from a self-illuminating power of the visual sense owing nothing to any external source of light, and they are potentially common to all men. The production of phosphenes can be induced by various means, including trance, exposure to prolonged darkness, or by hallucinogenic drugs, as has been proved in laboratory experiments. Reichel-Dolmatoff was able to relate the regularity of these shapes that he found among the Tukano to laboratory experiments with phosphenes conducted by Max Knoll and to correlate these forms with those that Knoll found in the laboratory to be typical forms of spontaneously produced phosphenes.

A few observations warrant our attention here. First is the spontaneous production of these simple designs when the eye is deprived of light. As products of the "self-illumination" of the visual sense independent of an external light source they are fitting heralds of the illumination that characterizes the shaman's inward journey. Also of note is the prevalence of dancing red dots. And, finally, the Tukano uniformly recognized in these phosphenes specific "male" or "female" shapes. In fact, the pairs male and female and the cultural principles they imply dominate and provide the emphasis to the entire hallucinatory imagery.[29]

Moreover, the Tukano use the designs and patterns described by these phosphenes as an art form, as decorative elements that adorn various objects they produce. Among the most typical of these configurations, the rhomboid, or diamond shape, is interpreted as the female organ (Figure 31A). The addition of a dot in the center expresses the concept of fertilization (Figure 31B). And, in combination with other diamondlike designs, lineage and relationship between various exogamic groups are implied (Figure 31C). An oval-shaped design containing circles or semicircles represents the fertilized uterus (Figure 31D). Concentric rectangles, generally elongated in shape (Figure 31E), are said to be female or uterine elements. Rows of dots or small circles are thought to represent drops of semen, and by implication they indicate descent and life itself and are regarded as being a male shape (Figure 31F). The male organ is indicated by a triangle accompanied on each side by a vertical line that ends in an outward-turning volute or spiral (Figure 31G). Two more configurations are noteworthy because they relate in an important way to the mythology that provides the context for the trance experience. One is the U-shaped design that we saw at the top of the petroglyph in Figure 30, which is also placed on the base of the yajé pot. As described previously, it represents a door, an entrance to the uterus and, in a wider sense, to the heavens. As noted, it symbolizes the break from our cosmic level and the transportation to another dimension of perception (Figure 31H). And, finally, there is a pattern of small dots, said to represent the Milky Way: an image of trance experience (Figure 31I).[30]

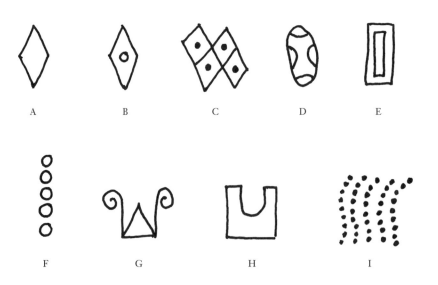

A   B   C   D   E

F   G   H   I

FIGURE 31. *Tukano phosphene motifs.*

The second stage of the yajé trance experience begins when the red dots and elementary patterns of the phosphenes begin to dissipate. At this stage larger forms suggestive of animals, people, or unknown creatures begin to crystallize.[31] Those who know how to interpret these iconic visions see in them various mythological elements. When the visions are discussed, the payé helps the participants understand their import and mythic significance, thus imprinting a certain cultural predisposition for the interpretation of future visions. As Reichel-Dolmatoff points out, the vision is the product, at least in part, of the projection of cultural contents on the hallucinatory subject matter. When we examine the vision, however, we can see that there is a deeper transpersonal factor at work, for the ultimate vision shares a certain universality with the traditions we have been examining. Behind the cultural inflections we see Campbell's magnet at work, drawing the individual elements into conformity with the archetypal template of the human mind.

The second stage of the yajé experience was generally interpreted as a return to the maternal womb. First the individual enters the vessel's vagina as a phallus. But this entry is also a transformation of consciousness and a regenerative return to the source of cosmic creative power, for within the womb he assumes an embryonic state that eventually leads to his rebirth.[32] "Once inside the receptacle he becomes one with the mythic world of Creation."[33] For the individual this is experienced as a rebirth from his own primal creative source. As it is for the Australian dreamtime heroes, "born from their own eternity," the act of entering the cosmic womb, the eternal creationtime source, is equivalent to "becoming his own progenitor, [he] is reborn."[34]

The symbolism retains its generative and uterine components, but the components are projected onto a cosmic level. This is consistent with the cosmogonic symbolism we examined earlier. As portrayed in the petroglyphs at Nyí and described in the local lore, it is within the womb, the point where essence becomes manifest, that the winged staff as axis mundi is to be found. For this is also the phallus of the Sun, which penetrates the womb of being, the manifestation house, and is symbolic of the point of creation and of communication with the source. As Reichel-Dolmatoff tells us, this is "a visit to the place of Creation, the *fons et origo* of everything that exists, and the viewer thus becomes an eyewitness and a participant in the Creation story and the moral concepts it contains."[35]

Here the entranced Tukano Indian perceives the creation of the cultural paradigms that inform his life, the ancestors, "the origin of the ornaments used in dances, the feather crowns, necklaces, armlets, and musical instruments." He witnesses the division into phratries and the origins of the laws of exogamy. But, most important, he sees the cosmic fount itself, the continuing source of creation as a reality accessible in trance:

> The Milky Way appears and the distant fertilizing reflection of the Sun. The first woman surges forth from the waters of the river, and the first pair of ancestors is formed. The supernatural Master of the Animals of the jungle and waters is perceived, as are the gigantic prototypes of the game animals, the origins of plants—indeed, the origins of life itself.[36]

What we would regard as history becomes more akin to ontology. The source and its paradigms as archetypes accessible to the human mind are ever present and informing realities. The participant is witness, in Kerényi's terms, to those first principles "to which everything individual and particular goes back and out of which it is made, while they remain ageless, inexhaustible, invincible in timeless primordiality—in a past that proves imperishable because of its eternally repeated rebirths." Yajé, associated with the shaman's baton and the Sun Father's phallic stick as axis mundi, is the vehicle by which the payé ascends to the source and in turn communicates its reality to the tribe. And over the whole presides Eros, a mighty demon, in his cosmogonic form as Eros Protogonos.

> For the Indian the hallucinatory experience is essentially a sexual one. To make it sublime, to pass from the erotic, the sensual, to a mystical union with the mythic era, the intra-uterine state, is the ultimate goal, attained by a mere handful but coveted by all.

And we find the most nearly perfect expression of this objective in the words of the missionary-educated Indian quoted earlier. "To take yajé is a spiritual coitus; it is the spiritual communion which the priests speak of."[37]

Chapter 6

A RETURN TO THE LUMINOUS CAVE OF THE UPPER PALEOLITHIC

> *We shall not cease from exploration*
> *And the end of all our exploring*
> *Will be to arrive where we started*
> *And know the place for the first time.*
>
> T. S. Eliot

Our review of the Tukano and their shamanism has brought us into our own times, and armed with an understanding of the shamanic techniques and symbols we have gleaned from our overall study we can now turn back in time to approach an understanding of the role played by the initiatory cave in the Upper Paleolithic. We can now see that Eliade was correct in his assessment that the experience upon which shamanism is based is coeval with and coexistent with the human condition, for the structure of consciousness reflected on these cave walls beginning more than three hundred centuries ago is strikingly parallel to that which we have been able to discern in diverse shamanic traditions distant in time and location. We can see in these caves a well-orchestrated attempt to utilize them to effect a transformation of consciousness leading from the world of peripheral effects to that part of the human mind that experiences itself as continuous with the form-generating power and plenitude of the creation. This process follows a typical initiatory pattern: crisis; the death of the profane man; a return to the creative source, both of the mind and the cosmos; and a rebirth with enhanced power from this source. And it leads us along this path of transformation by employing the methods traditionally used by shamanic cultures throughout history, that is, ecstatic and traditional training techniques relying on psychophysiological methods of mind alteration and the symbols and beliefs of traditional lore to awaken the mind to its depths and achieve, in Eliade's terms, "deeply meaningful states of altered consciousness." In so doing the cave journey traces the stages of a transformation of consciousness written indelibly in the human mind that have survived into this present century and by virtue of which the Paleolithic temple caves themselves became luminous and portals to the Otherworld, the enduring creationtime reality that supports human experience. This is because the cave journey itself is a product of the durative realm to which it points the way, for like other shamanic initiatory structures it is a device for inducing transformation, but at the same time it reflects the spontaneously engendered autoinitiatory patterns of the human mind seeking its own deep roots. In either case, it bodies forth the mystical itinerary of the shaman's journey.

We have noted that some commentators view these caves as possible places of initiation. We have seen ceremonial objects, such as horse- or bird-headed batons, phallic rods, and pendants, that are strongly suggestive of shamanism. We have also witnessed depictions of masked, horned, dancing therianthropic figures that very much resemble the shaman as he has survived into historical times. Our full conviction that the shaman was indeed present in the Upper Paleolithic period, however, depends on our understanding the shamanic structure of consciousness outlined in the caves themselves.

ECSTATIC TRAINING: PSYCHOPHYSIOLOGICAL METHODS OF MIND ALTERATION

Throughout our study of shamanism we have found that the various societies used as an aspect of ecstatic training various psychophysiological techniques to foster an altered state of consciousness in the postulant. In the Upper Paleolithic we can detect a similar pattern. Of course, there may have existed forms of ecstatic training accompanying the cave journey of which history has left no trace. Enough remains, however, to enable us to discern the manner in which the caves were intended to evoke the familiar stages of a transformation of consciousness conducive to illumination and how they lent themselves to this experience. The inceptional phases of initiation, we have noted, are often marked by the postulant's exposure to liminal structures of reality meant to dissolve the mind's normal orientation to the real. This phase is meant traditionally to loosen our attachment to the world as we normally experience it and to break down the categories of consciousness that habitually lead to its creation and acceptance. It is meant to refocus the locus of reality inward and to reveal an aspect of the real that is indeed a form of the mind's self-revelation.

The dark, labyrinthine, and disconcerting nature of the cave journey naturally helps effect the disorientation evoked in the liminal phase of shamanic initiation and has the same structural and functional values as does this inceptional phase in shamanic initiations elsewhere. As we have discussed, the cave itself is the perfect natural analogue to the journey inward. Its entry is, indeed, "a break with the universe of daily life," the light world of the "outward Creation," and the human being's obsessive involvement with the world of everyday values and pressing needs. Being swallowed into the earth both reflects and effects the ego death of shamanic initiation and simultaneously suggests the larger process of a return to the womb of rebirth. This experience, which has the greater resonance of suggesting that the shaman is being engorged by forces associated with the preconscious, is one we have witnessed repeatedly in conjunction with the cave of initiation.

In addition, as we have noted, several authors point out that many shamanisms typically employ such techniques as prolonged exposure to darkness, sensory deprivation, and restricted mobility to help effect a transformation of consciousness. These are often complemented by methods promoting physical exhaustion and various ordeals meant to lower the threshold of consciousness and create a condition of anxious anticipation and susceptibility. Each of these transformative processes is naturally inherent in the journey through these caves. Many of the caves chosen for embellishment were only to be initially entered by passing through a long, low, and extremely constricting passageway, immediately exposing the entrant to darkness, sensory deprivation, and restricted mobility, often for prolonged periods of time. Likewise, as the accounts of the cave journeys of André Leroi-Gourhan at Etcheberriko-Karbia Cave and of Herbert Kühn at Les Trois Frères revealed, the caves' epiphanies were often only to be reached after the most laborious, exhausting, and sometimes terrifying ordeals—purposefully employing harrowing and arduous physical effort in a thoroughly effective manner. Moreover, the initiatory paths along which they led the novice were clearly intended to maximize these effects.

In addition, other psychophysiological techniques that we have encountered in our study may be implicit in these Paleolithic initiations. We remember the sweat lodge of the Winnebago Indians associated with the bear as spirit guide and the initiatory swallowing represented by the bearskin hut containing the sweat bath. The sweat bath among certain Indian tribes was a common preliminary to the vision quest, itself often accompanied by many of the very techniques of ordeal, deprivation, and exhaustion clearly present in the cave journey. In this context we recall that Leroi-Gourhan found what he regarded as evidence of a primitive sweat bath at Pincevent dating back to the Upper Paleolithic. While we have no certain knowledge, the sweat bath may well have been employed to help foster a condition with a distinct tendency to open the mind to visionary experience, just as it has been employed by many shamanic cultures over the centuries. In this way, it would complement, as it has traditionally, other techniques leading to the inner revelation that the caves were intended to evoke.

We have noted that prolonged periods of hypermotility, such as dance, and of auditory driving, such as drumming and chanting, have been recognized to yield similar transformative results. We have evidence of footprints that may indicate such initiatory dances, for example, those before the coupling bison deities within the cavern at Le Tuc d'Audoubert. More to the point, the shamanic figures depicted, especially those within the caves, are repeatedly portrayed as dancers—and not just dancers but dancers who seem to be approaching a state of ecstasy. We have evidence of instruments of percussion from the period. Horst Kirchner sees certain of the batons as drumsticks,[1] and primitive flutes from hollowed bird bone exist from the period. The buffalo-shaman at Les Trois Frères himself dances with what appears to be a bow or stringed instrument in his mouth. It is likely that dance, drum, flute, chant, and perhaps rattle played their traditional roles in lowering the threshold of the conscious mind and opening it to its preconscious source as an integral part of the ceremonies within the caves' inner grottoes.

The Paleolithic cave is thus a well-devised tool of transformation employing darkness, sensory deprivation, restricted mobility, physical ordeal and exhaustion, and perhaps hypermotility, auditory driving, and other preliminary techniques as well, in much the same way as historical forms of shamanism have done, and to the same apparent end. Employing a spatial metaphor, we described these techniques as fostering a process in which the attention feels as if drawn backward into the brain. Interestingly, this description found an echo in Michael Winkelman's determination that the various techniques used in shamanic practice trigger activities that rely on the hippocampal-septal region of the mind, "part of the phylogenetically older part of the brain," which "includes terminal projections from the somatic and autonomic nervous systems." He also noted that these activities tend to evoke patterns of response that can lead to "erasure of previously conditioned responses, changes of beliefs, loss of memory and increased suggestibility." This, of course, promotes the ego death associated with this phase of initiation and fosters the process of inward relocation of what is perceived as real.

If we adopt Jung's psychological model, we can envision this as a penetration of the rhizome level of consciousness, its deep and abiding archetypal patterns with their roots in nature. And as we discussed in chapter 3, the world's shamanisms utilize the rhythm and patterned movement of dance in much the same way. They are employed to awaken an identity with the rhythm and patterned movement of the creation itself and to articulate a connection between the two. Each of these factors functions simultaneously to foster an identity between the individual's consciousness and the greater force of which he experiences himself to be an expression. We have seen these psychophysiological transformative techniques employed by cultures around the globe, and in chapters 4 and 5 we found them specifically employed as an adjunct to the symbol of the cave initiation. They are all inherent in the Upper Paleolithic cave journey and play the same structural and functional roles in relationship to the cave initiation and awakening the shaman's mind to the plenitude that supports it. In awakening the experience of the immense creative plenum, they everywhere complement the autosymbolism at the heart of the cave journey as opening the portal to the Otherworld and foster the ultimate awareness that we are participants in the creationtime or in the reality of the paradigmatic Otherworld—that we are, in fact, sons of the Sun and share his power and luminescence.

In Tukano mythology, we recall that at the time of "the beginning" the Sun, as Creator, endowed humans with a special vehicle to enable them to partake of his luminescence and to return to the source of creation. This was, of course, the hallucinogen yajé, which helped foster the shaman's trance experience; the use of such psychoactive substances to awaken a sense of identity between man and the creative ground is common in many shamanic traditions. Some commentators have seen evidence of trance experience, perhaps drug aided, in the swirling welter of overlaid and chaotic images sometimes found within the Paleolithic caves. The palimpsest-like effect of multiple outlines, the existence of composite or hybrid animal forms, and the sense of form emerging from and evaporating back into the cave walls may be evidence of a sort of trance or drug-induced dreamscape. Interestingly, facets of the painting of the animals may have been done by a sort of oral spraying—blowing pigments dissolved in saliva onto the cave walls. The manganese oxide base of some of the black pigments used in the painting is known to be toxic and to act on the central nervous system. Michel Lorblanchet, director of France's National Center of Scientific Research, provocatively suggests that "spitting is a way of projecting yourself onto the wall, becoming one with the horse you are painting. Thus the action melds with the myth. Perhaps the shamans did this as a way of passing into the world beyond."[2] The creative act and contact with the creative ground become simultaneous and coalesce. This "passing into the world beyond" is intimately related to the creative act itself, for in creating these animal forms the shaman and his initiates "merge," in Nietzsche's terms, "with the primal architect of the cosmos" and in this way affirm the common source shared by both cosmic and human creation.

We further noted the possible presence in the Paleolithic caves of what might be considered entoptic phenomena, of which we have seen examples in the phosphenes of the Tukano that accompany the initial stages of altered consciousness. As we recall, phosphenes are subjective images, independent of an external light source, that are the result of the self-illumination of the visual sense. They originate within the eye and brain, and are common across cultures. As we noted earlier, the Tukano regard these forms as significant and, reducing them to the most common types, to typical representative forms, use them as symbols of trance experience for artistic decoration of their dwellings and artifacts. Reichel-Dolmatoff compared these typical forms with laboratory-induced phosphenic forms and found a significant correlation. When I first saw this correlation, I immediately juxtaposed its results with the signs that so interested Leroi-Gourhan from the Paleolithic caves. Again the results were striking. Later I found that others had made the same correlation. We would not expect this correlation to be exact because these are only momentary, fleeting phenomena in the first place. And in each system they have undergone further development and stylization as they came to assume significance within their particular culture, for in the Paleolithic period these forms are to be found not only within the caves but also inscribed on material instruments, tools, and mobiliary art.

Not only is there a striking coincidence in the use of these simplified abstract designs in similar contexts, but in many cases the actual patterns are very close. As discussed previously, the diamond shape with a dot in the middle (Figure 32A) is a key sign for the Tukano, the diamond representing the female and the point indicating penetration and fertility. If we examine the Paleolithic engraved reindeer antler, as shown in Figures 8B and C in chapter 2, we note a very similar sign (Figure 32B), which T. G. E. Powell suggests is also a fertility symbol.[3] Another female sign among the Tukano is shown in Figure 32C, a striking analogue of which is present in the Upper Paleolithic (Figure 32D), also recognized to be a female sign. The rectangle within a rectangle as a female sign among the Tukano (Figure 32E) finds numerous analogues from the Upper Paleolithic that Leroi-Gourhan recognizes to be female signs (Figure 32F). The U and V shapes, familiar Tukano female signs (Figure 32G) are recurrently found in the Paleolithic and are regarded as female figures, as noted in Figure 32H. Figure 32I is a familiar stylized male sign among the Tukano and Figure 32J, which indicates a design composed of two male signs, may be a related Paleolithic form, as may be the design we see inverted in Figure 20 just above the horse's head (Figure 32K) or the similar design preceding the "Falling Cow" in Figure 21. And most predominant in each culture are groups of dots, both in single rows and in clusters, thought to be male signs in each tradition: Tukano (Figures 32L and 32M), and Paleolithic (Figures 32N and 32O).[4]

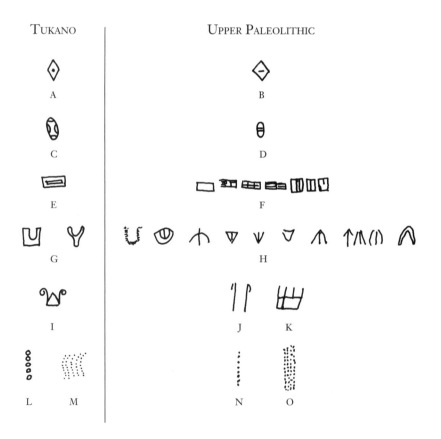

FIGURE 32. *Tukano phosphene motifs and Upper Paleolithic signs.*

Thus in each society we have 1) simple abstract designs; 2) stylized; 3) vested with a significance that makes them worthy of inscription or painting on important cultural objects; 4) found in contexts that suggest altered states of consciousness and shamanism; and 5) sharing a marked similarity of form, though separated in some instances by thirty thousand years, with 6) the same forms in each society being given a masculine or feminine identification, and 7) this identification being largely consistent in each society with the analogous configuration of the form of the other culture.

Since Reichel-Dolmatoff's work, similar phosphenic signs have been found in certain other societies that also shared a shamanic rock art. J. D. Lewis-Williams and T. A. Dowson find them present in San rock art in southern Africa and among the Shoshonean Coso of the western Great Basin in North America. Others have found them in other American Indian tribes with a shamanic heritage. Lewis-Williams and Dowson recognize their general correspondence with the laboratory work of Max Knoll and others and see a correspondence with Upper Paleolithic art, indicating that "there is thus a strong suggestion that at least a significant component of Upper Paleolithic art also derives from altered states of consciousness and that many of the signs depict entoptic phenomena in the various transformations we have described."[5] They note that these forms can be generated by psychoactive drugs or other means, such as fatigue, sensory deprivation, intense concentration, auditory driving (for example, drumming), hyperventilation, rhythmic movement, and flickering light. These are elements often associated with shamanism, and certain of them are naturally inherent in the cave journey, making it "possible that the painted caves of Western Europe provided circumstances especially conducive to the generation of entoptic phenomena and hallucinations."[6]

Viewing the signs in the caves as being related to phosphenes provides another explanatory key to the visionary experience of the caves. In altered states of consciousness that produce phosphenes or entoptic phenomena, such products generally constitute only a preliminary first stage in the experience and give way to iconic forms of vision. Lewis-Williams and Dowson observe, "In Upper Paleolithic Western Europe, southern Africa, the Great Basin, and elsewhere, entoptic phenomena were intentionally associated with iconic images simply because that is the way the human visual system works; the association is intrinsic to altered states of consciousness."[7] This is precisely what Reichel-Dolmatoff found among the Tukano and in his own yajé experience. The simple floating designs gave way to visionary hallucinatory images that, for the Tukano, were filled with significant mythological forms, such as the Master of Animals and the animal prototypes. Typically, the phosphenes precede the iconic forms, though "iconic imagery is 'often projected against a background of geometric forms.'"[8] Indeed, for Lewis-Williams and Dowson, the abstract shapes often seem to generate the more complex iconic figures from their own rudimentary forms in a manner that recalls the panels of outlines discussed in chapter 2 and their rudimentary representations of the basic forms, which gave rise to the great animal murals in the Paleolithic caves.

In addition, in the experimental work of some scholars, both with regard to trance induction and the use of hallucinogens, this stage of altered consciousness also tends to promote the production of tunnel-like images, sometimes with a bright light at the end or center.[9] This finding, of course, is interesting in relation to the spontaneous production of the luminous cave image especially in conjunction with phosphenes and more complex iconic imagery. And all of these observations bring us very close to what we find depicted in these caves, for the signs tended to precede the iconic depictions, though they sometimes accompany them or follow them. They roughly either herald these forms or are a background against which they lie. At the very least, they seem to be intentionally associated with the iconic forms and with the cave image itself because each—phosphene, cave image, and iconic form—is a natural stage of a transformation of consciousness and the phosphenic figures are experienced as harbingers of a process that opens the mind to its own inner depths and the autogenous images that arise from the dreamtime substratum.

As we remember from the inward journey of the Tukano, however, this process is also experienced as a return to origin and to the creationtime, for the entranced shaman feels himself projected into the very place of creation, the *fons et origo* of everything that exists, as previously related by Reichel-Dolmatoff:

The Milky Way appears and the distant fertilizing reflection of the Sun. The first woman surges forth from the waters of the river, and the first pair of ancestors is formed. The supernatural Master of Animals of the jungle and waters is perceived, as are the gigantic prototypes of the game animals, the origins of plants—indeed, the origins of life itself.

This same experience of return to the origin and source of creation was also typical of the other cave journeys we have examined. We see a continuum—whether induced by trance experience or hallucinogens or both—from simple, abstract phosphenic forms to iconic forms associated with a luminous tunnel or cave image, leading to the experience of the creationtime. This is a pattern of experience that thoroughly complements those we have previously examined in this section, which, through the vehicle of the various psychophysiological techniques we have discussed, likewise evoke the experience of an identity between the postulant and the greater force of which he now experiences himself to be the expression.

The pattern of experience effected by these techniques of transformation accords very well with the other evidences within the cave indicating that it is a return to the source of essence and power, just as were the cave journeys and equivalent symbols that we have studied. In Australia the cave opens to the creationtime, and the animal figures of their art were the prototypes of all living creatures, like "father" to "brothers," both their generative source and essential form. Just as the hole from which the shaman receives the spirit of his voice leads Sereptie to the cosmic fount of "the master spirits of all the running and flying birds and game" or Spider Woman's cavern opens to the cosmic source of plenitude with its animal forms in the Navaho visionary world or as the Apache shaman penetrated the holy cave of animal essences to Medicine's home and the source of power, so is this cave journey a return to the creationtime generative source, the very creative ground that the psychophysiological techniques we have examined allow the postulant to penetrate in altered states of consciousness. We shall see this spelled out in image and symbol in the remainder of this chapter.

But what is here important is that it is the penetration of this durative formal source in the world's shamanic cultures that fosters

208 THE STRONG EYE OF SHAMANISM

the emergence of archetypal and universal patterns in the mind, patterns with their own purposiveness that, as products of the source of power, lead back to the source of power. Such practices lead the postulant backward into the brain to that place in the mind where flux resolves itself into pattern and pattern becomes translucent to its creative, enduring source.

We remember that among the Tukano this sense of participation in the formal source was referred to as the shaman's luminescence. It was a product of the creative force of the cosmic creator, and it allowed the shaman to understand the inner significance of myth and vision and the manner in which they can be understood to lead to revelation. For the Navaho the repetition of the genesis of cosmic form and order in their creation myth was the necessary prelude to the recitation of the story of the twin heroes, which was the further expression of the world-creative source. Among the Australians myth and ritual were the direct products of the creationtime. In fact, in the nation's Aboriginal languages the terms for myth and creationtime are one and the same, for to experience the myths is to enter the creationtime.

Earlier, Eliade observed that the shaman is able to "interiorize" myth, to transform that which for others is merely traditional belief "into a concrete mystical experience." So interiorized, the lore becomes the actual vehicle by which the inner cosmos becomes a mode of direct communication with the informing source. As its lineaments crystallize, it carries the shaman to his destiny. It is here that the forms of the mind's own self-revelation grow into the organs of the spirit, the strong eye of the shaman. The shaman touches the universal source in his initiation and ecstatic experiences, and the universal forms he brings back derive from his experience in this realm. The power he receives, which he experiences as an expression of cosmos, works—like Campbell's magnetic field—from behind, marshaling individual and local experience into an archetypal visionary cosmos with its own form and direction. It is because the shaman becomes the expression of this creationtime formal force that the forms of his initiation share similar structural and functional features around the globe and over vast periods of time, as we have seen in this study. It is for this reason that we can expect to find a similar structural and functional pattern written in the Upper Paleolithic caves thousands and thousands of years ago.

THE SYMBOL AS A TOOL OF THE GODS

Mircea Eliade informs us that "the essential function of the symbol is precisely in disclosing the structures of the real inaccessible to empirical experience."[10] In the Upper Paleolithic caves we find these "structures of the real" articulated into a universe with its own form and significance, a realm that is autosymbolic, purposive, and reflexive. It represents humanity's first extensive surviving Hermetic use of myth and symbol to awaken or effect an anamnesis of the profoundest depths of the soul from which these salutary symbols emerge and to which they in turn appeal. And it is a universe the structural and functional features of which are now familiar.

In previous chapters we have examined examples of the cave of initiation, sometimes used ritually and sometimes produced in spontaneous autoinitiatory visions, which becomes luminous and a portal to the Otherworld marked by symbols of ascent paradoxically encountered within the cave depths. We noted a striking consistency of form over time and the ages associated with this symbolism for the inward journey to the durative realm: the cave itself, initiatory death or ordeals, the penetration of the unconditioned realm through the Symplegades or some variation of the *coincidentia oppositorum*, the mediating role of the spirit guide, a descent that becomes an ascent marked by avian transformation or symbols of ascent within the cave, the cave's symbolic luminosity, and the journey as a penetration of the creative source and a return to origin, an origin most often characterized as a realm of animal essences, the form-generating nucleus of creation where "that which is constant" becomes that which will "come to pass." All of these stages of the journey are expressed in a fairly constant structural and functional grammar of symbols. In the process the cave becomes the portal to the Otherworld and simultaneously the source of the generation and regeneration of this world. It articulates the relationship between the world of inner or essential form and the world of creation, natural and human, including artistic and mythic forms of creation. In penetrating the source of power, the shaman becomes a conduit of power. Throughout our study we have noted that certain of these features are inherent in the structures and symbols to be found within the Paleolithic cave, but now we can perceive them as an integrated whole and, supplying additional key elements, discern the features of an enduring and meaningful visionary world.

The harrowing early stages of penetrating the cave become the equivalent to the symbolism of the perilous journey, which we have seen related to the inceptional phases of the shaman's visionary quest in many societies. The cave journey also quite naturally appropriates to itself associations suggesting a reversal of the birthing process, a return to the womb and ultimately rebirth. In many instances of initiation this stage was accompanied by images of the postulant being engorged or swallowed by a figure representing the anterior forces of the preconscious mind, which often later became his own spirit guide, frequently in close association with the symbolism of entering the cave. After such engorging he emerges empowered as a shaman. The Paleolithic cave and the internal forces that it reveals also symbolically duplicate this process and through the mediation of the spirit guide transform the novice into a man of power.

We have frequently witnessed symbols of death, dismemberment, or piercing associated with the cave initiation. These reinforced the break with the everyday world and the correlative dissolution of the "old self" implemented by the techniques conducive to altering the initiate's state of consciousness. In the Upper Paleolithic we have seen the symbolism of dismemberment suggested in the mutilated hands outlined on the cave walls. We have seen a similar symbolism in other shamanic societies in which dismemberment symbolism plays a prominent role. Given the role played by dismemberment symbolism in the shaman's initiation elsewhere and the full structural and functional schema of symbols we detect in the cave, it seems evident that these mutilated hands are, in fact, images of initiatory dismemberment.

It may be, however, that there is more direct and more convincing evidence for the symbolism of initiatory death in the Paleolithic caves. As we shall discuss later, one of the most frequently depicted scenes in the Paleolithic involving humans or humanoid creatures portrays what Leroi-Gourhan called the "wounded man" motif. Interest in this enigmatic theme was recently rekindled by the discovery at Cosquer Cave, "the cave beneath the sea," of the depiction of a wounded or killed man or what can be viewed as a composite human and animal form. Jean Clottes and Jean Courtin inform us that it is an individual depicted as lying on his back with arm and leg extended upward. The figure is pierced once through the chest by a lightly engraved straight line and then more noticeably by "a long projectile weapon—arrow, spear, or harpoon. . . . The weapon hits the figure in the back, passes through the body, cuts off the front of the head, and extends considerably beyond it." In fact, "the nose can just be made out beyond the enormous spearhead" that penetrates from the back into what would be the neck and mouth cavity.[11] The figure is located in the eastern part of the cave which is clustered with handprints, many themselves of the "mutilated" variety suggestive of initiatory death.[12]

While there are certainly tenable interpretations of this mysterious figure other than that which would see it as an image of initiatory death or piercing within the Paleolithic cave, this creature does seem to be reminiscent of images with which we are familiar. For instance, we might remember the Tungus shaman's Siberian ordeal, when he tells us the deceased ancestors "stood me up like a block of wood and shot at me with their bows until I lost consciousness," which led to his further initiation. Or we might recall the similarly described ceremonies among the Amerindians, originally derived from their shamans, wherein the neophyte began his initiation by being shot by the ancestors with a sacred shell or arrow until unconscious.

We have seen from various parts of the world similar examples of such piercing associated with the shaman's initiation—Figure 33 depicts an interesting Inuit example. And, of course, there is the Mayan ahau pierced through the tongue in his vision quest. Most intriguing is the description of the piercing of the Australian shaman recorded by Baldwin Spencer and F. J. Gillen. The potential shaman leaves his camp and goes to sleep outside a cave. Here he is shot with a lance by a spirit being. The lance "pierces his neck from behind, passes through his tongue and emerges from his

FIGURE 33. *Inuit carving of pierced shaman, by Charlie Ugyuk.*

mouth," very much like our "killed" man at the cave of Cosquer:

> The tongue remains throughout life perforated in the center with
> a hole large enough to admit the little finger; and, when all is over,
> this hole is the only visible and outward sign remaining of the

treatment. A second lance then thrown by the spirit pierces his head from ear to ear, and the victim, falling dead, is immediately carried into the depths of the cave, within which the spirits live in perpetual sunshine, among streams of running water.

It is here, in the luminous cave, that the shaman's initiation by the spirits takes place as it may have at Cosquer.

In some Australian traditions the initiating spirits, the Wondjina, who are frequently inscribed on cave walls along with the essential animal forms that generated and still regenerate the living animal species in Aboriginal lore, bear a curious resemblance to those strange figures referred to as "ghosts" (see Figure 14) that we noted briefly in chapter 2. Their images are also recurrently found on the walls of the Paleolithic caves. Each type is frequently depicted in an anthropomorphic form with eyes and nose but no mouth. While the name ghosts is somewhat arbitrary, their oddly spectral form suggests that they are, in fact, initiating ancestral spirits within the cave, as the term "ghosts" seems to imply. Certainly, initiating ancestral forms have been associated again and again with the cave journeys we have examined. And images of initiatory death within the cave may give credence to this observation.

Now we may be able to understand some of the other enigmatic and crudely drawn anthropomorphic forms depicted within the caves. Clottes and Courtin note that the figure of the "Killed Man" at Cosquer calls to mind the "wounded man" theme discussed by Leroi-Gourhan and finds its closest analogues in the "bird men" of Pech-Merle and Cougnac and a related scene depicted at Sous-Grand-Lac Cave in Dordogne (see Figures 10–13), which we briefly discussed in chapter 2.[13] In looking at these creatures we must not forget that for reasons we do not understand, human and humanoid figures were conventionally depicted by apparently crude artistic techniques as opposed to the exquisitely portrayed life of the animal world. The depictions seem to be more nearly ideograms than attempts at realistic portrayal. However, crudeness of portrayal and pictographic significance are not necessarily mutually exclusive in the Paleolithic artistic idiom and, as Leroi-Gourhan recognizes, the wounded man theme was of apparent significance.

Several commentators familiar with this idiom, including Clottes and Courtin, have seen in Figures 10 and 12, from Pech-Merle and Cougnac, respectively, men with beaked faces riddled by spears or similar projectiles. Although it is headless, the other figure from Cougnac is also regarded as illustrative of such piercing, as is the ithyphallic figure from the cave at Sous-Grand-Lac. In fact, other cave figures, often less distinct, seem to point to a similar piercing or killing.[14] Interpretations of the meaning underlying such depictions vary from the attempted portrayal of scenes of destructive magic to the representation of specific mythic or legendary events now lost to time. Clottes and Courtin, noting that the figures "were intentionally drawn in an obviously crude way," provocatively suggest that "perhaps they represented extraordinary beings, shamans or spirits in human form who could be depicted only in a somewhat indirect way."[15] Other authors recognize "bird-men," akin to those portrayed here, illustrated in other examples of Paleolithic art in the apparent role of the shaman. Shamans, we know, are frequently associated with animal and particularly avian transformations as well as with "composite" animals seen in vision and trance. Given all these factors and the well-articulated initiatory structure of the caves, it seems convincing that these pierced figures at Pech-Merle, Cougnac, Sous-Grand-Lac, and Cosquer portray shamanic initiation and the initiatory death or piercing that is found in so many shamanisms. So envisioned, this symbolism becomes continuous with and complements the symbols and techniques discussed in the section of this chapter on ecstatic training, implying the death of the old self and evoking a transformation of consciousness. We shall return to this idea later in this chapter with further observations and examples to support this approach.

Another provocative interpretation of these figures penetrated by lines, or at least those at Pech-Merle and Cougnac, is that the lines represent what are commonly referred to as "power lines," often wavy projections emanating from a figure that traditionally allow us to identify the possessor as a shaman. Such representations have a widespread distribution and occur in a number of diverse shamanic societies. Perhaps the case for this interpretation is bolstered by the fact that in some rock art portrayals, these projections accompany a sort of penumbra around the head of the figure such as can also be seen in Figures 10 and 12. These lines appear to represent the empowerment of the shaman and are sometimes associated with his transformation and the spirit guide that helps impel his empowerment. As representing the empowerment and transformation at the heart of shamanic initiation, the idea that these depictions carry, at least in part, this sense of meaning within the context of the cave initiation would be consistent with and may complement the motif of initiatory death that is clearly preliminary to transformation and empowerment. Rock art in shamanic societies is often abstract and ideographic, and several significances can inhere or be conflated in a single representation, which will be readily recognized by the initiated viewer. These figures may represent a complex of ideas: initiation; piercing, dismemberment, or initiatory death; transformation; empowerment. These are, of course, stages on the shaman's path, and we shall see how they converge as we proceed. However, history may have left a clue as to the manner in which these motifs coincided in a shamanic context. We remember that among the Sioux the shaman's death was symbolized by his being shot or pierced until unconscious, after which he was initiated. In rock art depictions of the Dakota Sioux, the shaman's ability to shoot objects into a person is denoted by a wavy line, which also indicates "spirit" or "wakan," power associated with that investing the cosmos, that is, shamanic power. The Dakota symbols for medicine men also include wavy lines.[16] Here piercing, initiation, and empowerment converge around the symbol of the wavy line, suggesting a symbolic correlation between initiatory death and the shaman's ultimate power.

And now we might discern a similar complex of ideas surrounding the hand images in the caves, both mutilated and intact. We have suggested that the mutilated prints imply dismemberment within a context meant to elicit the experience of liminality and the death of the profane structures of consciousness. But what about the hand image itself, mutilated or whole? Why was it projected upon the wall? We have indicated that it implied a sense of presence and enduring participation in the cave ritual. Eliade, however, has informed us that in Australia touching the images of the rock paintings is a participation in the power and plenitude of the dreamtime source. And Lewis-Williams and Dowson make a very similar observation with regard to rock art among the southern

San Bushmen. "The supernatural potency that San shamans activate to enter trance is named after powerful animals and things,
supreme among which is the eland," an animal frequently depicted
in their rock art. Part of the function of these depictions was explained by an old woman, "probably the last survivor of the southern San." "She demonstrated how dancers seeking power turned to
face the paintings on the wall of the rock-shelter and how some
people placed their hands on the paintings of the eland to gain
power. The paintings, she said, had been put there by shamans and
contained power."[17] Because these caves are receptacles of power
and regeneration, touching the cave wall, I believe, played a similar
role in the Paleolithic times, a touching memorialized in the hand
image. It would seem that we again have a similar complex of ideas—
initiation, dismemberment, transformation, and ultimately empowerment—implicit in the imprint of these hands upon the cave walls.

That symbols of initiatory death with prefigurations of transformation and empowerment should appear in these caves is consistent with the overall pattern we have discerned in the cave initiation
in other cultures. It also complements the psychophysiologically
induced experience of the dissolution of the profane structures of
consciousness that the cave evokes at this point in the inward journey. And it also may reflect another symbolic aspect that we have
seen marking the inner purposiveness experienced at the heart of
initiatory structures. We recall that in many instances images of
death, dismemberment, or piercing had autosymbolically appropriated an element that augured a more distant goal. Bone revealed in
dismemberment became a symbol of indestructible essence in Siberia, a role played by quartz in Australia and blood in the Mayan
world. In the Upper Paleolithic, these symbols of death and dismemberment likewise seem to incorporate an aspect that looks forward to transformation and empowerment, a presentiment of the
teleological directedness of the initiation process symbolically
glimpsed and bodied forth in these archaic images. We shall add to
these observations and indicate how these prefigurations are developed as we proceed, but first we must leave the profane self behind
and attempt to understand the entry into the zone of shamanic empowerment presented in the Paleolithic cave.

The cave journey everywhere has been a return to the source, to the nucleus of generative and regenerative power that sustains our temporal and spatial world but lies beyond it and is itself unconditioned, atemporal, and outside the ordinary laws of dimensionality. Breaking through the plane to this realm of power is symbolized by the passage through the narrow aperture or the clashing gates, which the profane mind conditioned according to ordinary worldly experience and dimensionality cannot penetrate. This symbolism is necessarily related to the process of the dissolution of the profane self, with its traditional methods of organizing and being bound within the "outward Creation" of our temporal and spatial world of linear causation. In breaking the plane, linear paradigms of causation are transcended, and creation is understood to be an immanent or "vertical" process opening to an ever present source.

We have seen repeated instances of various forms of this symbolism in relationship to the cave initiation. Generally known as the Symplegades motif, it took the form of passing in the timeless and dimensionless interval between clashing rocks, reeds, or knives, through the closing cloud gates, past the borderline that lies between two daybreaks, or between the rivers of life and death. For the Wiradjuri Australian shaman it is "the place where doctors go through," which keeps "opening and shutting very quickly" and prevents those unworthy of initiation from entry. In other spontaneous incarnations it is "the hole-too-small-to-enter," which turns out to be the entryway to initiation and the return to the source for Sereptie and for the Navaho twins. It is here that the !Kung Bushman, Old K"xau, tells us, "When you go there, friend, you make yourself small like this. Friend, when you go there, you do not go standing up straight. You make yourself small so that you are a mamba [a snake]." We remember that K"xau has entered a hole in the ground and must pass beneath a very low metal barrier that "grabs" him if he even slightly lifts his head as he proceeds on his journey to the source of creation. At times, as with the Apache cave journey, as a transcendence of the laws of dimensionality this symbolism takes the form of an entry where there was apparently no aperture at all, into the blank face of a rock wall, which somehow opens the inner world to the initiate.

We have worked under the premise that these caves were selected and their embellishments organized in the manner in which they were to effect and reflect the transformation of consciousness that lies at the heart of the shaman's initiation. They became the objective correlative of the same structure of consciousness, often spontaneously produced, which we have seen so often. The cave features were most carefully chosen and adroitly employed to reproduce the shamanic initiatory schema, including that of the Symplegades, particularly in its variation as "the hole-too-small" or the narrow aperture, as a representation of entering a realm without dimension.

This symbolism is inherent in the cave journey as penetrating a dark, dimensionless "realm beyond," a world within. But it is particularly apparent in the repeated choice and employment of caves with long, narrow, confining entrances through which the initiate had to squeeze his groping and uncertain way, "made small" by the narrow confines to which he had committed himself. Entering there you do not go standing up straight, but slither through like Old K"xau's mamba. And both André Leroi-Gourhan and Joseph Campbell note that the entrance to the great sanctuaries was usually through a particularly narrow part of the cave.[18] Similar effect was achieved by placing the most important cave epiphanies in locations only visible after the initiate had inched his way through extended confining tunnels such as those found at Lascaux, Les Combarelles, and Les Trois Frères.

However, these narrow apertures of the Paleolithic caves are preliminary to the inner chambers of illumination, and with further initiation and emergent insight the narrow aperture will expand and the hole that is too small will lead to revelation, as it did for Sereptie and the twin heroes. This follows a traditional pattern —as Ananda Coomaraswamy points out, the apparent obstacle becomes the "Gateway of Truth" through the realized experience that it is the "narrow gate" between the conditioned and unconditioned worlds, the point in the mind where the polarities of the conditioned world coalesce in unity. In this symbolism the narrow way, the dimensionless point that the mind somehow fathoms, having left its "old self" behind, is, as Coomaraswamy further informs us, the cardinal "point" that has no fixed position, since the distinction of the correlated members of any pair of contrary qualities (e.g., long and short) is only to be found where we actually make it; and without extent, seeing that it is one and the same "limit" that simultaneously unites and divides the contraries of which it is no part—"strait is the gate, and narrow is the way, which leadeth unto life, and few there be that find it."

This narrow way leads "from the world of time (i.e. past and future) to an eternal Now,"[19] to the world of inner or essential form characterizing the ever present origin from which the shaman receives his illumination and power.

It is thus appropriate that in the cave journeys that we have studied we find this symbolism within a larger context suggesting the mythological expression of the *coincidentia oppositorum*. We have seen this coincidence of opposites articulated in too many ways to rehearse here, but we may recall a few examples that will be pertinent to this discussion: the spirit guide with chthonic characteristics who becomes a unifying symbol with "celestial" attributes, the dark cave that becomes luminous and a portal to the Otherworld, the paired animal opposites that the Apache shaman must encounter in the cave journey to enlightenment, and, perhaps most salient to our purpose, the symbolism of male and female polarity that has played a part in most mythologies we have looked at but most prominently in that of the Huichol and the Tukano.

In the Huichol and Tukano incarnations of this archetypal structure, we can discern several stages that bind together our journey so far in this chapter and point us forward. The Huichol shaman undergoes a perilous journey and an initiatory death of the profane self aided by peyote. He uses his feathered scepter, the prayer arrow, as a phallic symbol to unite male and female opposites and suggest not merely coitus but also plenitude and unity on a cosmic level. This is done in close identity with his spirit guide as he traverses the Symplegades—the clashing cloud gates—to reach the creative source itself, the realm of animal essences characterized by the perpetually incarnated Master of the Deer Species. The Tukano shaman, called the payé, or "cohabitor," to emphasize his sexually uniting character, follows a similar path with his phallic baton. This is a path that has many sexual resonances, the most important of which lead him through the opposites to the "intrauterine" realm of animal essences that he enters with his phallic scepter, or, in a related ceremony, into the vagina of the yajé bowl, the womb through which the door of the heavens opens to the generative and regenerative nucleus of original creation penetrated in ecstasy and characterized by gigantic animal prototypes.

Now let us continue our examination of the Upper Paleolithic symbolism. We have seen cave features and images that reproduce the experience of initiatory death and the perilous journey and that recurrent variant of the Symplegades symbolism represented by the "hole-too-small" as the entry into the unconditioned realm of unity. We have previously indicated how these are reinforced by psychophysiological experiences that complement them and how they parallel other versions of the shamanic cave journey. If our approach is correct, we might expect the Upper Paleolithic cave journey to express what Eliade described as the mythological representation of the *coincidentia oppositorum*, which we have seen in so many other expressions of the shamanic structure of consciousness.

We can, in fact, see this coincidence expressed on several levels, including the uniting of the sexual opposites. First of all, penetration of the cave itself has an obvious intrauterine significance. This is reinforced by images of vulvas on many of the cave walls, including recently discovered examples at Chauvet, and such sexual images as Herbert Kühn found surrounding the coupling bison at Le Tuc d'Audoubert. We recall that Leroi-Gourhan found this significance implicit in the cave and the specific manner in which it was embellished:

> The cave as a whole does seem to have had a female symbolic character, which would explain the care with which narrow passages, oval-shaped areas, clefts, and the smaller cavities are marked in red, even sometimes painted entirely in red. This would also explain why these particular topographic features are marked with signs from the male set, which thereby become complementary. A few dots in the last small chamber of an immense cave then take

on the same significance as the more complex groupings on the big panels, and this would account for the care with which, almost invariably, Paleolithic men placed some mark on the cave's innermost recess.

We also remember that the shamanlike figures within the cave are markedly phallic or ithyphallic. And we noted in chapter 2 that a comparatively large number of batons surviving from the period are most graphically and unambiguously phallic (Figures 2A, 2B and 3). The feminine characteristics of the cave suggest a penetration by the costumed shaman, whose ithyphallic character may have been represented by carrying these ceremonial phallic batons. This relationship would supplement the symbolism of sexual complementarity noted by Leroi-Gourhan and be consistent with initiation imagery throughout the world, particularly the phallic batons of the Huichol and Tukano shamans.

These observations are reinforced by the fact that much of what had traditionally been described as early Upper Paleolithic art in fact did consist of unambiguously female and male symbols, which seem to be basic to their symbolism. And we remember that Leroi-Gourhan found two other pervasive examples of what he regarded as systems of balanced sexual complementarity in the caves—the "signs" and the animal art itself. According to him, the two major systems of representation within the caves were characterized by a carefully devised schema of balanced sexual polarities. That the signs, which some regard as examples of phosphenes, should be regarded as having a sexual significance is interesting because the Tukano representations of phosphenes are also clearly vested with sexual attributes.

We noted in chapter 2 that such a system of balanced sexual complementarity within the context of the cave had cosmogonic implications suggestive of the many age-old myths in which male and female cosmic principles create a cosmos and original unity becomes divided into and generates a world of individuated form, thus making the caves conduits of generative power. And, conversely, for the initiate penetrating the cave, the sundered opposites become united in illumination to suggest the unitive reality that underlies them. We concluded our discussion of the sexual complementarity by noting that Eliade's work has repeatedly shown that the shaman's journey is itself a return to the cosmogonic source and that in doing so he unites and transcends the duality symbolized by the sexual opposites. "For the shaman," Eliade tells us, "unites in himself the two contrary principles [male and female], and since his own person constitutes a holy marriage, he symbolically restores the unity of Sky and Earth [the world's parents, the cosmic generative source] and consequently assures communication between Gods and men." As we noted earlier, the combined male and female principles imply primordial totality, absolute reality, and illumination and also an "immersion into the limitless ocean of power that existed before the Creation of the World and rendered creation possible."

This immersion lies at the heart of the cave journey as a return to origin, for as Eliade has elsewhere reminded us, "for archaic societies life cannot be *repaired*, it can only be *re-created* by a return to sources. And the 'source of sources' is the prodigious outpouring of energy, life and fecundity that occurred at the Creation of the World." In penetrating the maternal cave with its eloquent forms that everywhere testify to their source, the ithyphallic shaman and his initiates are symbolically returning to the miracle and mystery of the generative source of all form. He becomes the conduit of that regenerative plenitude and power with which he is united and taps the common formative force that animates both the cosmos and the human mind, especially in its artistic and mythic products represented so well by the majestic creations within the cave. As in the other shamanic cave initiations we have studied, here also the experience of initiatory death, penetrating the Symplegades, and uniting the opposites will lead the shaman across the cosmic threshold to the generative and regenerative source characterized by supernatural animal essences, thus following a pattern of experience that has persisted for millennia.

As part of the perilous cave journey productive of a transformation of consciousness, the Paleolithic initiate was made to crawl through long, dark, and narrow passageways often immediately preliminary to some parietal epiphany. We also remember that stages of the cave journey were often marked by cryptic signs that were frequently in the form of red or black dots. A particularly good example is the entry into the Sanctuary at Les Trois Frères described earlier:

> The ground is damp and slimy, we have to be very careful not to slip off the rocky way. It goes up and down, then comes a very narrow passage about ten yards long through which you have to creep on all fours. And then again there come great halls and more narrow passages. In one large gallery are a lot of red and black dots, just those dots.

Passing this gallery the visitant is forced to traverse a long, extremely low tunnel, approximately forty yards long and, in places, barely a foot high. "We placed our lamp on the ground and pushed it into the hole," and, "With our arms pressed close to our sides, we wriggle forward on our stomachs, like snakes," its explorers explain in a manner reminiscent of old K"xau's description of crawling like a snake through the visionary Symplegades. Then, suddenly and miraculously ("It is like a redemption," they tell us) the narrow passage opens to reveal the Sanctuary with its panoply of animal forms presided over by the numinous form of the therianthropic Sorcerer of Les Trois Frères (see Figure 22).

We can now understand the well-orchestrated and sophisticated manner in which the cave features and symbols are employed. We have discussed various psychophysiological techniques as being conducive to a transformation of consciousness, the initial stages of which are characterized by disorientation and the loss of ego consciousness preliminary to the penetration of the psychoid realm symbolized by the therianthropic form of the spirit guide. Here we can discern the role played by physical exhaustion, isolation, and sensory deprivation in inducing these effects in this portion of the cave journey and particularly in the final forty-yard-long slither through this version of the narrow aperture, this extremely constricted cave passage. In a real sense, this journey reverses the birthing process, taking us back through the contraction of the birth canal to the uterine world of the inner cave. We can also understand the role played by the burgeoning animal forms within the sanctuary and the half-human, half-animal Sorcerer in symbolizing the human experience of an entry into the deep level of the mind, where it seems to touch the form-producing principles of its psychophysical organic substratum, the womb or matrix of life itself. But why, we might still ask, is the experience heralded by the gallery filled with dots, "a lot of red and black dots, just those dots"?

In Tukano shamanism the same loss of self is induced by taking yajé. It is likewise associated with the symbolism of a return to the womb and the therianthropic realm with its mixed human and animal forms. But more to the immediate point we remember the myth of Yajé Woman and the description of her primal encounter with mankind. The men feel as if they are "drowning," which Reichel-Dolmatoff associates with a "loss of self." More specifically, the myth tells us, "yajé images she drowned them with" (*gaphí noméri miria vaya*). In this context *noméri* signifies "to paint with red dots." This signification is telling, for the initial stage of the altered consciousness produced by yajé, and often by trance experience in general, is characterized by seeing dots, particularly red dots, along with other simple abstract designs. We also recall that among the Tukano these dots were a paramount male symbol.

If something similar is depicted upon the Paleolithic cave walls, we can now see a complex symbolism inherent in the gallery full of red and black dots that was encountered before entry of the tunnel and Sanctuary at Les Trois Frères. On the one hand, as phosphenes that mark the loss of individuated consciousness and accompany the first stage of visionary experience, these signs properly mark the antechamber to the visionary iconic forms of the Sanctuary and to that point where the cave becomes luminous and a portal to the Otherworld. They are here, as elsewhere, the heralds of vision. On the other hand, remembering that these dots are also, according to Leroi-Gourhan, male signs, we can discern that they augur the transformation of consciousness symbolized in penetrating the tunnel to the uterine world of self-generating form represented by the Sanctuary proper. Male and female cosmic principles combine to suggest the "original oneness" of the Dionysian world portrayed on the walls of the Sanctuary that the shaman penetrates inwardly.

Now we can envision the ithyphallic Paleolithic shaman, such as we have seen depicted on the cave walls, passing with his phallic baton from the initial chamber of red and black dots that presage his transformation of consciousness, back through the narrow aperture of the cave tunnel into the womb where the animals of eternity miraculously appear in the Sanctuary, the uterine world where essence becomes manifest. Here are the Sorcerer and the animal throngs he commands. But the similarity of this visionary experience with others we have examined is much more striking still. For also depicted on the ancient Sanctuary walls is another creature resembling a shaman in animal costume who marks the penetration of the threshold to the world of generative form and essence (see Figure 15). We can now view this figure in a larger context (Figure 34). Within the womb of the Sanctuary, dancing and playing music, is a curious bacchanalian celebrant. As Mario Ruspoli describes the scene:

> The Trois Frères sanctuary also contains another figure of a shaman, disguised and masked as a bison and holding a curious instrument shaped like a bow which seems to be coming out of his mouth, possibly representing the emission of a sound. He advances as a suitor, displaying his intentions to a female reindeer, but, as if jokingly, the head she turns toward him is that of a bison.[20]

Leroi-Gourhan also notes that the figure is "following a strange creature with the body of a reindeer, very visibly provided with an anus and a prominent vulva. What we see at the level of the rump might be a very indistinct female silhouette, but this symbolism is not even needed to illustrate the proximity of two composite figures of the opposite sex."[21] In other words, it looks as if this shamanlike figure who advances like a suitor, penis erect, is about to have sexual intercourse with the female animal essence depicted. This, of course, is a fitting complement to the initiate's penetration into the womblike abode of the Sanctuary and to the symbolism of male and female complimentarity.

Given the full context surrounding this figure, we can discern even more—this is the very nucleus of generation and regeneration, the creationtime source itself. This is a world burgeoning and

FIGURE 34. *Bison shaman at Les Trois Frères with supernatural mate and surrounding animal forms, with inset, above, isolating bison shaman and mate.*

composite forms like those associated with shamanism elsewhere. And it is a scene overtly suggestive of the fertilizing act on a cosmic plane. Moreover, as Alexander Marshack notes, it contains images that imply that it is the regenerative source itself. Prominently displayed nearby is a bison that appears to have been "killed" by numerous spears or darts but also is symbolically "renewed" by the later addition of a second tail and by the indication of molting on its sides, suggestive of seasonal renewal.[22] In this larger context the bison-shaman very well captures the full significance and function implicit in Eliade's observation with regard to the shaman's projection of himself into the mythic animal spirit guide, who becomes "the center at once of the existence and renewal of the universe" and "showed the shaman his power and brought him into communion with cosmic life."

And here we might recall other renditions of this recurrent experience of penetrating the generative source, which help us identify its archetypal significance. We remember that among the Huichol, after the shaman, carrying his ceremonial bow, has marked the mandala pattern at "the cosmic threshold" with his phallic feathered scepter, he makes the dangerous passage through the clashing cloud gates to the land called Vagina and finally into the realm of the Master Deer. Let us repeat the precise images with which Peter Furst relates the scene:

> Ramón stepped forward, lifted the bow, and, placing one end against his mouth while rhythmically beating the string with an arrow, walked straight ahead, stopped once more, gestured (to *Káuyumarie*, we were told later, to thank him for holding back the cloud doors with his horns, at the place called "Where the Clouds Open"), and set out again at a more rapid pace, all the while beating his bow. The others followed close behind in their customary single file.

It is Ramón, bow lifted with one end held in his mouth and beating a rhythm with an arrow, and the antlered Káuyumarie who penetrate the cosmic threshold. We remember that Káuyumarie is Ramón's spirit helper, a reality speaking through and identifiable with the shaman. As we have learned, as the shaman completes his journey, he approximates an identity with or, in Eliade's terms, "projects himself into" his spirit guide. Furst tells us that Káuyumarie "is conceived both in deer form and as a person wearing antlers," a well-documented costume of the shaman throughout the ages. Understanding this underlying identity between shaman and spirit guide, with a shiver of uncanny realization that collapses millennia we recognize this antlered composite figure penetrating the cosmic threshold to the uterine realm of the animal essences, one end of the bow in his hand and the other held in his mouth, beating time with a ceremonial arrow. It is precisely similar to the horned, half-human and half-animal celebrant at Les Trois Frères, who also stands bow lifted with one end in his mouth, beating time with his forelimb, or perhaps with a stick or arrow. He has crossed the cosmic threshold to the uterine realm of animal essences and leads the antlered throng of the animals of eternity on the ancient cave walls from the Upper Paleolithic era.

This dancing ithyphallic creature cohabiting with the part-bison figure in this world of teeming animal essences is otherwise familiar also. We might, of course, think of Holy Man from the Navaho universe and his sojourn and sexual relations with the wives of the Master Buffalo, from whom he learned their wisdom. A more striking analogy, however, lies closer to hand. Let us return to the phrase "yajé images she drowned them with" and examine its other component, the Tukano understanding of drowning. As we know, drowning connotes loss of self and also coitus or cohabitation, hallucinatory trance, and a return to the womb. An important variation in this symbolism is found when the shaman, taking yajé, enters in hallucinatory trance with his phallic baton the uterine hill house of *Vaí-mahsë*, the Master of Animals. Let us repeat what was previously said in this respect:

> The phallic attributes of the payé's office are obvious. In the first place, *Vaí-mahsë*'s houses in the hills or under the waters are, in all essence, uterine deposits, an idea well recognized by the Indians, and the payé's penetration into these womblike abodes carries the connotation of a fertilizing act. Occasionally a payé might even

cohabit with the female game animals that inhabit a hill and are "like people." *Vaí-mahsë* and *Vihó-mahsë* will sometimes celebrate a *dabucurí*, wherein the animals dance and sing in human shape, drink yajé, and behave in every respect like human beings. Quite often a payé, in his trance, will participate in these feasts, to which a great fertilizing power is attributed.

After the initial phase of altered consciousness, where the shaman's vision is characterized by "red dots," he enters the realm of animal essences, the realm of *Vaí-mahsë*, the Master of Game Animals. The entry is through the vehicle of his phallic baton and is characterized as a cohabitation, a joining into a bacchanalian celebration and union with the dancing and singing supernatural animal forms—with some of whom he may literally have coitus. The entry into these womblike abodes carries the connotation of a fertilizing act and is a source of power.

This is very much what we see at Les Trois Frères. Here the ecstatic shamanic celebrant in animal guise likewise dances and plays music accompanied by these teeming animal forms and, advancing as a suitor toward a female game animal who inhabits this world, is about to perform a similar fertilizing act. From the red dots to the pervasive sexual complementarity, from the ecstatic celebration of dancing half-human, half-animal forms to the cohabitation with animal essences, this vision portrayed at Les Trois Frères marks the same experience of crossing the cosmic threshold in precisely the same images as those employed more than one hundred and fifty centuries later by the Tukano. It is almost as if the human mind at its deep levels, the levels galvanized by initiation, does in fact contain "the whole spiritual heritage of mankind's evolution born anew in the brain structure of each individual," as Jung observed. Like the other shamans taking the inward journey, in approaching the Sanctuary the Paleolithic initiate has experienced initiatory death—the loss of individuated consciousness indicated by the myriad red dots—passed through the narrow aperture, united the male and female opposites, and penetrated the barrier to the realm of essence, the fateful cosmic threshold that only the shaman is able to perceive.

Throughout the process of transformation of consciousness involved in penetrating the cosmic threshold to the world of essential form, the symbol of the therianthropic shamanic spirit guide serves as the great mediating force, just as it does in the form of the Sorcerer at Les Trois Frères. These revelations (see Figures 15–17 and 22), found primarily in the deepest parts of the caves, manifest themselves to the postulant only after the ardors of the perilous journey and its attendant psychological stimuli have worked their effect on the mind, lowering the threshold of consciousness and opening the way for the revelations of the preconscious in the manner we examined in detail in chapter 3. It is under their auspices, or under the guidance of the reality they represent, that the initiate enters the cave a novice and leaves a man of power, for they are the keepers of the symbols of the journey that act as tools of the gods, unlocking the symbolic capacities of the mind and becoming emissaries of an emergent inner orderedness that the shaman begins to serve in the process of attaining an altered form of consciousness.

As such, these creatures of the depths continue to articulate the elements of the symbolism of the coincidence of opposites evoked by the experience of penetrating the cave and become, as mediators, the great uniting symbols of the cave journey. They unite the person of the costumed shaman with the reality represented by the guide, for as the journey progresses the figures become one. As ithyphallic cave dwellers, these creatures join masculine and feminine principles and suggest the very process of cave penetration that is simultaneously an initiation and a fertilizing act with cosmic resonances of a return to origin. Ecstatic, they bring individuated consciousness together with the transpersonal ground that creates and sustains it. Dancing, they suggest the point in the mind where movement becomes pattern and repeated pattern suggests eternal form. And as half-human and half-animal, they unite us with the psychoid realm that opens into the world of instinct, nature, and cosmos. In a very real sense they are, in Nietzsche's terms, "prophets of wisdom born from nature's womb." Like the archetype itself, as products of the psychoid realm, they "represent the uniquely human means whereby instinctual, biological energy is transformed into the meaningful symbolic life of the human psyche." As such they escort us to the durative and paradigmatic realm of myth and archetype and to the reality that myth and archetype reveal, a reality that everywhere leads back to and becomes translucent to its informing source. It is this very translucence to the source that makes the cave luminous.

We have spoken of the cave as representing the journey from the light world of our everyday reality into the darkness of the depths, but a darkness that also opens to a greater illumination. This is certainly a symbolic aspect of the Upper Paleolithic cave journey that initiates the mind to a reality made luminous by being open to its source. And this sense of luminosity may very well have been reinforced in a literal sense in several ways in these ancient caves; they are by their nature not only caves of darkness but also caves with a potential for the most resplendent illumination. We have discussed the fact that many of the caves in the area are lined with a white calcite. The sudden illumination of these dark grottoes by torch or firelight playing against the luminous walls would create a shock of sudden revelation reaching deep into the mind, an effect well-known to the world's rituals and mysteries.

First, imagining ourselves subject to prolonged darkness and sensory deprivation, we can perhaps catch a glimpse of the power potential in such a revelation from the impressions of the discoverers of Chauvet as they, lantern in hand, first explored this magnificent cave. The cave "is decorated with magnificent crystallizations and concretions," they relate in awe, "white in the first chambers, then astonishingly and brilliantly coloured beyond."[23] They tell us in detail of their exploration of one gallery:

> It was decorated with white, yellow and orange concretions, in often intense shades. We took the time to play our lights over this extravagant decor. Bear bones were strewn over the orange floor. Hearths made of big pieces of charcoal, thousands of years old, looked as if they had been extinguished the day before . . . the astonishing flows of red calcite, a waterfall of terraced hollows filled with clear water, eccentric and fistulous stalactites as pure as crystal, a stalagmite in the shape of a white candle (with a triangular

cross-section—a rarity for the experienced caver). We revelled in this magnificent spectacle.[24]

The trip further reveals "pillars of orange calcite . . . decorated with red dots" and a floor "made up of millions of sharp calcite crystals."[25] "We were dazzled," they tell us, "by a myriad crystals, white 'cacti' had grown on the floor and colonnades formed a barrier of very pure concretions."[26]

Ample evidence of torches and fires has been found in the caves. "If there were fires," Jean Clottes tells us, "they were for lighting purposes, like those known elsewhere, for example in Cosquer Cave, and not hearths for cooking food."[27] In fact, at Cosquer the presence of charcoal or charred traces on top of broken stalagmitic pillars has suggested to some fixed sources of light and even an organized lighting system. And we recall the evidence of charcoal on the pedestal holding the bear skull at Chauvet. It is likely these Paleolithic caves became luminous during ritual, perhaps suddenly, after long periods of utter darkness and sensory deprivation, to imprint on a mind already conditioned for revelation the epiphanies within a cave framed in gleaming calcite, a most eloquent and awe-striking correlative of the shaman's inner illumination and perhaps the most ancient example of the archetype of the luminous cave.

We have traced the journey of initiation of the Upper Paleolithic novitiate through the various stages that have marked the cave journey elsewhere: the entry into the cave, the perilous journey, and the symbols of initiatory death that harbor prefigurations of the overall structure of transformation and empowerment. We have made the entry through the narrow aperture into the zone of power, the unconditioned realm of the creationtime source with its corresponding symbols of the *coincidentia oppositorum* leading to the generative cosmogonic source. We have witnessed the fertilizing act implicit in the crossing of the cosmic threshold to the realm of inner or essential form symbolized in the ever reincarnate animal essences, a realm everywhere mediated by the symbolic aspects of the spirit guide. And all these stages of the inward journey are expressed in images that are remarkably familiar to us and that have endured into our present day. Each element marks a stage in an archetypal process portrayed in symbols that are autosymbolic of the phases through which the mind is led back to its own fructifying inner depths. The symbols have their own inner purposiveness; they are indeed "tools of the gods."

Jung once stated, "The decisive question for man is: Is he related to something infinite or not?" The archetypal symbols of these ancient sacred caves work in conjunction with the psychophysiological techniques we have described to act as psychopomps, articulating this relationship with something infinite. Products of the source, they lead the initiated mind back to the source. Ultimately, the cave journey unites the three realms—the daylight world of our ordinary reality, the inner depths of the initiatory cave and the human mind, and the realm of the principle of permanence beyond the world of time and change. It is thus that the cave becomes luminous and a portal to the Otherworld. We shall see this expressed at the famous cave of Lascaux by symbols of ascent within the cave depths. Before we proceed, however, let us examine one more important aspect of the cave's luminescence that marks it as the portal to the Otherworld.

The Paleolithic caves are a testament to luminosity in another important sense, a sense that closely parallels the other forms of shamanism we have examined as a participation in the formal creative power of the cosmos. We have previously called attention to the manner in which the cave journey functions to awaken the mind to its deep levels, to that point where the energies of *bios* and cosmos rise to meaningful symbolic form in myth, dream, and vision and unite the human being with the transpersonal realm of essential form and meaning. It is at the conclusion of the journey inward that—for the awakened mind—myth, symbol, and visionary experience open the portal to the Otherworld and reveal themselves as the shaman experiences them to be, that is, as the expression and guarantee of the durative realm.

But perhaps this sense of luminescence is best captured by what we remember these caves for most, their magnificent art. The caves seem to capture the eternal paradox of all great art, which somehow must travel to an inward source to find the true perfection of the forms it has encountered in the external world. While art may gather its raw material from the world of the senses, the "truth" it expresses is that of the inward eye. "The 'truth' of traditional art," Coomaraswamy states, "is a formal truth"; it is "not a truth that can be tested by comparing the work of art with a natural object."[28] Or as Blake more poetically announced, "He who does not imagine in stronger and better lineaments . . . than his perishing and mortal eye can see, does not imagine at all."[29]

Plotinus very well captured the essence of the artistic function of the strong eye in works of art:

> We must recognize that they [works of art] give no bare reproduction of the thing seen but go back to the Reason-Principles from which Nature itself derives, and, furthermore, that much of their work is all their own; they are holders of beauty and add where nature is lacking. Thus Pheidias wrought the Zeus upon no model among things of sense but by apprehending what form Zeus must take if he chose to become manifest to sight.[30]

The eye of the artist is somehow able to intuit and to instantiate the essential forms "underlying the technic of nature," as Kant recognized. Great art does not portray the single individual but captures the essential form "to which no separate individual, but only the race as a whole, is adequate." As such, the image presented in such art can best be described as "a floating image for the whole genus."[31]

We have noted repeatedly in various forms of shamanism that the cave becomes the source of the generation and regeneration of this world. It articulates the relationship between the world of inner or essential form and the world of creation, both natural and human. In chapter 2, we observed that the Paleolithic cave journey was a return to the source of that common formative force investing both cosmos and mind, inwardly experienced in the capacity shared by man and nature to create forms of beauty. We noted that the hand images on the walls, the manner in which the animal forms seemed to emerge mysteriously from the cave walls, and the panels of outlines, which in their concise reproduction of the formal essentials of the great panels seemed to pay tribute to and participate in the same power that produced the magnificent forms on the cave walls, all seemed to testify to this creative power. Here humans first experienced themselves as cocreators with the Divine. This was expressed most of all in the animal art of the great panels. For, as we have noted, these are not the animals of time but the forms of eternity. They precisely capture that artistic sense of ideal form that seems to intuit the underlying formal principles or technic of nature's creations. They are not portrayals of individual animal forms but, indeed, somehow take the form of "a floating image for the whole genus." Thus, Erich Neumann has told us, "each of these painted animals is a numinosum; it is the embodiment and essence of the animal species. The individual bison, for example, is a spiritual-psychic symbol; he is in a sense the 'father of bison,' the idea of the bison, the 'bison as such.'" And Joseph Campbell repeatedly points out that these paintings are "the prototypes, Platonic Ideas, or master forms of those temporal herds of the earth."[32] Like the inner forms of the Navaho or the essential forms of the Australians, which are "like father and brothers," they are the ideal source of the species they represent. They are not bison, deer, or bears, but Bison, Deer, and Bear, familiar creatures in our study of shamanism. The cave of the Upper Paleolithic again brings us to the realm of the "master spirits of all the running and flying birds and game," to "the cosmic fount itself."

Just as in the other shamanisms we have explored, the return to origin that is represented by the cave is simultaneously a return to essential or inner form. Here we may recall the Navaho phrase translated as "according-to-the-ideal may-restoration-be-achieved" and all that it implies. In a very real sense, art joins hands with ecstatic training and the symbolic aspects of the cave as a psychopomp opening the cave portal at that very place where essence becomes manifest in an art that is experienced as the expression of the primal architect of the cosmos. And we might speculate that the initiate not only "sees holiness" but, having awakened the strong eye to that intuitive sense of inner form from which all great art derives, he is able to "see according to holiness," that is, to experience a creation restored according to the ideal and to leave his initiation with something of the same impression as his Navaho counterpart thousands of years later:

The World before me is restored in beauty,
The World behind me is restored in beauty,
The World below me is restored in beauty,
The World above me is restored in beauty,
All things around me are restored in beauty,
My voice is restored in beauty,
It is restored in beauty,
It is restored in beauty,
It is restored in beauty,
It is restored in beauty.

SYMBOLS OF ASCENT WITHIN THE CAVE OF INITIATION

"To the center of the world you have taken me and showed me the goodness and the beauty and the strangeness of the greening earth, the only mother—and there the spirit shapes of things, as they should be, you have shown to me and I have seen. At the center of this sacred hoop you have said that I should make the tree to bloom."[33] Thus did the Oglala Sioux holy man Black Elk sum up the triumphant vision he had before falling under the forces of a worldview grown inimical to such visionary powers. During his youth, hard upon severe psychological and existential crises, Black Elk was blessed by the spirits with an extraordinary visionary experience of great beauty and symbolically significant of the unity of the creation. In the vision he sees "in a sacred manner the shapes of things in the spirit, and the shapes of all shapes as they must live together like one being. And I saw," he tells us, "that the sacred hoop of my people was one of many hoops that made one circle, wide as daylight and as starlight, and in the center grew one mighty flowering tree to shelter all the children of one mother and one father. And I saw that it was holy."[34]

At the heart of the sacred experience, he encounters a council of the ancestors or "grandfathers," the interior visionary forces we have seen as typically leading the shaman's ecstatic initiation. They are not old men, however, but "the Powers of the World." The "fourth Grandfather" addresses Black Elk:

"Younger brother," he said, "with the powers of the four quarters you shall walk, a relative. Behold, the living center of a nation I shall give you, and with it many you shall save." And I saw that he was holding in his hand a bright red stick that was alive, and as I looked it sprouted at the top and sent forth branches, and on the branches many leaves came out and murmured and in the leaves the birds began to sing. And then for just a little while I thought I saw beneath it in the shade the circled villages of people and every living thing with roots or legs or wings, and all were happy. "It shall stand in the center of the nation's circle," said the Grandfather, "a cane to walk with and a people's heart; and by your powers you shall make it blossom."[35]

This is a hierophany of the creative plenitude that fires the cosmos. The Powers of the World are fourfold and describe a mandala around the sacred center. Invested with their visionary power, Black Elk is able to see "in a sacred manner the shapes of things in the spirit" and their underlying totality, "the shape of all shapes as they must live together like one being." And at the center of it all is the great flowering tree, the tree blooming at the "center of the world."

This tree at the center of the world is the emblem of the gift of shamanic vision and the rejuvenative power it represents. It is given to Black Elk by the fourth Grandfather in the form of a red stick, or staff, with the power to grow, and has birds perched in its growing branches. This recalls a familiar pattern, the gift of the shaman's feathered scepter that is the emblem of his successful quest and resultant power among the Apache and Navaho. The sacred pole of the Oglala Sioux medicine dance is also in the form of a tree and is painted red on its four sides with a symbolic bird's nest at the top.[36] It, too, marks the center of the world and the axis of the Sioux initiate's symbolic ascent. In fact, the feather-topped cane, bird-headed scepter, or bird perched on top of a pole or tree are familiar symbols in the world of American Indian shamans and shamans worldwide.

Eliade notes that the shaman's tree, a tree regarded as being at the world's center, is traditionally the main vehicle of vision in numerous shamanic cultures, and, coupled with ornithological imagery, represents the central ascent of the soul to its source. "For it will be remembered," he tells us, "in the mythologies of Central Asia, Siberia, and Indonesia the birds perched on the branches of the World Tree represent men's souls. Because shamans can change themselves into 'birds,' that is, because they enjoy the 'spirit' condition, they are able to fly to the World Tree to bring back 'soul-birds.'"[37] In some forms of shamanism the shaman's soul is prenatally nurtured in the World Tree. Repeatedly we have seen the role played by the central bird-topped tree, pole, or its symbolic equivalent as the unitive revelation in which the inward journey culminates. We recall the feathered ceremonial pole in Australia, the bird-topped central tree among the Olmec and the Maya, the World Tree with the shaman's bird at its top in the visionary universe of the Siberian shaman, the symbolically feather-topped axis of ascent unifying the Navaho cosmos, and the feathered staff used by the Sun Father as axis mundi and the central point of creation in the Tukano world.

And just as the bird-topped stick or staff given to Black Elk is meant to blossom into the central World Tree of the visionary universe in our Sioux example, so is the shaman's bird-topped or feathered scepter also traditionally symbolic of the World Tree or axis mundi. We can detect the equation between the World Tree or axis mundi and the shaman's scepter or baton in the shamanic cultures we have explored. It is epitomized in the Tukano visionary cosmos in which the central axis of creation, the Sun Father's staff topped by the Creator in the form of the oropendola bird, is emblematically reproduced in the shaman's feathered baton. As we saw, the baton specifically represents the central point of world creation and the path of the shaman's trance ascent. We found the same to be true of the feathered prayer stick given to the twins by Talking God as the emblem of their successful quest up the central feathered axis to the source of power. The scepter of the Olmec shaman, apparently depicted as feathered like the World Tree, is thought to have been ceremonially raised by the shaman from a horizontal position to a vertical axis as a repetition of the world creative act of the primal ancestor, who raised the World Tree at the sacred center to create a cosmos. Such a tree with the celestial bird at its top, of course, marks the path of the Olmec and Mayan shamans' visionary flights. The Huichol shaman uses his feathered scepter, as the center of a mandala configuration, to effect his magical flight through the clashing cloud gates. And, finally, the feather-topped *tjurunga* plays a similar role in Australia in relationship to the central axis represented by the Numbakulla pole connecting man with the eternal world. As is apparent from their similarity of symbolic function and form, World Tree, bird-topped pole, and feathered or bird-topped scepter or baton make up a continuum of equivalent symbols worldwide. And this recognition leads us back to the Upper Paleolithic and helps us understand the central mystery revealed in the cave journey at Lascaux, the elements of which we discussed at the conclusion of chapter 2 (see Figure 23).

We remember that next to the recumbent figure in the famous Shaft at Lascaux lies what appears to be the representation of a stick with a bird perched on its top. Commentators have differed as to the significance of this object and the scene of which it forms a part. It is clear, however, that such an object, functioning as a baton or scepter, is a traditional instrument of the shamanic vocation in a number of widespread cultures. Very similar batons still survive from the Upper Paleolithic period (see Figures 4 and 5). Understanding its relationship to the World Tree symbolism, we can see that it precisely complements the symbolism inhering in the structure of the cave as the portal to the Otherworld, expressed by the revelation of symbols of ascent paradoxically present in the cave depths. We can now perceive that all the symbols in the Shaft at Lascaux converge upon the bird-topped scepter, understood as the symbolic equivalent of the World Tree; it is another incarnation of the archetypal revelation of symbols of trance ascent within the cave of initiation. The Shaft itself, the bird, soul flight or trance, the bird costume of the entranced shaman, his erect penis, the slain bison, and the "animals of eternity" englobing the whole scene form a coherent grammar of universal symbols with which we are now familiar. Properly understood, they harmonize with and unify a larger context of Upper Paleolithic symbolism. We can see them as the essential forms of the individual soul's expression of the cosmic source, encountered through its archetypal forms within the human mind. In this symbolism the heavens touch us from within, just as they have touched and awakened human beings since they first cast the forms of epiphany upon the blank walls of the Paleolithic caves.

Eliade tells us that the shaman's trance and ecstatic flight take place from what is symbolically imaged as the center of the world.[38] The visionary Shaft at Lascaux with its entranced shaman represents just such a center. The centrality of the location is not geographic but is determined by its role in the sacred cosmos as a place of epiphany. As Eliade has extensively shown, in the visionary geography of the archaic mind, "Every microcosm, every inhabited region, has what may be called a 'Center'; that is a place that is sacred above all."[39] "The idea of a 'Center' followed from the experience of a sacred space, impregnated by a transhuman presence: at this particular point something from above (or from below) has manifested itself. Later it was supposed that the manifestation of the sacred in itself implied a break-through in plane."[40] "In cultures that have the conception of three cosmic regions . . . the 'center' constitutes the point of intersection of those regions. It is here that the break-through onto another plane is possible and, at the same time, communication between the three regions."[41] These archaic societies recognized an unlimited number of "centers." Moreover, each of these centers is considered and even literally called the "Center of the World."[42] In the world's shamanic traditions this center often takes the form of a hole penetrated by an axis of ascent, hence the archetypal propriety of symbols of ascent within the cave and also within the Shaft, which itself naturally implies a breakthrough to another plane. It is clearly trance experience that effects this breakthrough.

Consistent with the symbolism of the Symplegades and the union of sexual opposites, it is at the center, where all opposition unites, that the shaman transcends the conditioned universe. And it is at this very point in the mystical itinerary of the shaman that we have frequently found a principal symbol of ascent, or the breeching of the ontological plane, that is, the bird-topped tree, as represented at Lascaux by the shaman's bird-topped scepter. Like the cave journey itself, this symbol typically unites the three realms and establishes "the principle of verticality." In this way it marks this point as the interface between this world and the next, the central axis that opens the portal of the shaman's ascent.

At the same time, the World Tree is the sacred center of creation through which flows the plenitude of an origin of creation experienced as still accessible and effective and an all-sustaining source of revelation. Eliade tells us that it represents the cosmos in a perpetual process of regeneration; it is the "inexhaustible spring of cosmic life, the paramount reservoir of the sacred."[43] In the mythic universe it is at the World Tree that the order of creation unfolds and the seeds of time germinate in real events. Thus, according to him, the Cosmic Tree always embodies the very reservoir of life and is the master of destinies.[44] It is the source of prophecy, vatic inspiration, and human creativity. This symbol within the Shaft appropriately marks the cave journey as a passage to the Otherworld and simultaneously as an access to cosmic power and plenitude, to generative and regenerative force, the two traditional aspects of the shaman's journey everywhere and particularly of the cave journeys we have explored.

Traditionally, all the symbols in the Shaft at Lascaux are complementary, which helps support our view and furthers our understanding of the revelation within the cave. In the world's shamanic traditions, trance, the shaman's scepter, and the World Tree are symbolically interrelated on a number of levels other than those that we just discussed. As the focal point of the vision within the cave, they harbor traditional associations that for the initiated bring together both the mythic-symbolic facets of the process of transformation of consciousness implicit in the cave journey and its ecstatic aspects.

At the beginning of this chapter, we noted that psychoactive drugs may have aided the transformation of consciousness effected by the cave journey. In many shamanic cultures, the scepter-tree is symbolically associated with just such a transformation of consciousness. We noted that among the tribes neighboring the Tukano, it was the shaman's scepter that actually held the trance-inducing narcotic that impelled the shaman's ecstatic flight, making it both the symbol and the vehicle of the shaman's ecstasy. Among the Warao shamans of Venezuela, the *manaca* palm is the shaman's central tree of ascent, and it is from the epidermis of its leaf stalk that the Warao shamans make the *wina*, or tube, for their cigars. These are no ordinary cigars—they are between fifty to seventy-five centimeters long and are highly toxic. After smoking this prodigious cigar, the candidate falls into a deep trance sleep. The entranced shaman "travels in the smoke of his cigar to the zenith,"[45] meaning that he symbolically ascends the shaman's tree by virtue of smoking the tobacco enfolded in its leaves.

R. Gordon Wasson notes that in Siberia "the birch is preeminently the tree of the shaman," and he asks why:

> For me the answer is clear. The birch is revered wherever it grows in Siberia because it is the preferred host to the fly agaric [*Amanita muscaria*—a type of hallucinogenic mushroom]. This mushroom grows in mycorrhizal relationship with certain trees, and the tree that it prefers is the birch. It also grows at the foot of conifers, and I hold it to be no accident that the pine tree occupies a place second only to the birch as a cult focus for the forest tribesmen of Siberia.[46]

For Wasson and others the hallucinogenic role of the mushroom in its association with the World Tree symbolism may be ancient. "Its role in human culture may go back far, to the time when our ancestors first lived with the birch and fly agaric, back perhaps through the Mesolithic and into the Paleolithic. We have here a web of interrelated beliefs that give us a unified field in a major area of primitive Eurasian religion."[47] Thus the scepter-World Tree may symbolically be associated not only with the shaman's trance journey as an ascent but also with the psychoactive techniques that induce his ecstasy and become the vehicle of his ascent.

And this same larger pattern may extend to another set of associations. Horst Kirchner has argued that the batons of the Upper Paleolithic, of which the shaman's scepter at Lascaux is a type, were in fact used as drumsticks. The scepter becomes not only a symbol of ascent, but its very instrument; it supplies the auditory driving that helps implement the transformation of consciousness essential to the shaman's experience. In this function it is traditionally brought into association with the World Tree, for the drum that it beats is frequently said to be made from the World Tree. This drum depicts the "mystical itinerary" of the shaman's journey on its sides and frequently the Cosmic Tree itself as axis mundi. As Eliade notes, the shaman, through his drumming, is transported to the vicinity of the Tree; to the "Center of the World," where he can ascend to the sky.[48]

The scepter also sometimes doubles as a rattle in many societies. The rattle, whose rhythm helps induce the shaman's ecstasy, is also a symbol and a vehicle of ecstasy and this role is sometimes made explicit. Let us take the single and beautiful example of the Tlingit Raven rattle, which is another variant of the bird-topped scepter (Figure 35). This particular rattle is an example of a general type that employs the same basic mythic motifs. Here the bird-topped scepter motif is dominated by the shape of the raven that carries on its back a shaman. The shaman is accompanied by the kingfisher, his spirit guide, who provides him sustenance—power—on the ecstatic flight. Raven in Tlingit mythology is said to have founded shamanism. Here he is the instrument of the soul's flight to its inner source, the breaking of the plane to the Otherworld. As such the body of the Raven rattle, like the World Tree, incorporates the symbolism of uniting the three realms, for the kingfisher dives beneath the surface of the sea, lives on the land, and soars above it.

FIGURE 35. *Raven rattle with traditional motifs of a shaman carried in ecstatic flight on the back of a raven while receiving power from a kingfisher, Sitka, southeast Alaska.*

Scepter, trance, and World Tree everywhere reinforce one another and reveal themselves to be familiar complementary forms— precisely what we should expect to find at this central point of hierophany at Lascaux. They bring together both the ecstatic and mythic aspects typical of the shaman's journey everywhere and potentially opened a whole universe of associations for the initiates who viewed them. As representations of trance ascent within the cave, they mark it as the portal to the Otherworld in precisely the same manner as they do in the other shamanic traditions we have examined. Here we would again expect to find another widespread symbol for breaking the ontological plane, the shaman's avian transformation, an image that is, of course, implicit in both the Raven rattle and the bird-topped scepter.

"The natural property of a wing is to raise that which is heavy and carry it aloft to the region where the gods dwell," Plato tells us, and this is precisely what the shaman experiences. The result of his transformation of consciousness induced by the cave journey is a state of spiritual exaltation, a transcendence of the profane condition, most often symbolized by the creature at the top of the axis of transcendence, the celestial bird. It has often been noted that the recumbent figure in the Shaft at Lascaux has the face or wears the mask of a bird. We have noted the many humanoid creatures with birdlike features in roles implying those of the shaman to be found in Upper Paleolithic art. The figure here also has hands that resemble the feet of a bird. Annette Laming-Emperaire points out that the bird mask, or transformed face of the man, resembles that of the bird on the scepter.[49] This similarity underlines the theme of magical flight at the central axis of creation. Of course, it recalls the same flight at the world center and its associations with avian transformation that we found among the Aborigines, the Olmec and Maya, the Navaho, the southern San, and in Siberia.

We might specifically recall the Siberian shaman's magical flight, a flight that is indicated on shamans' costumes in Siberia by symbols of avian transformation and in recognition of which, Andreas Lommel tells us, Siberian shamans still wear bird costumes. When this costume is employed, "the appropriate head ornament is a bird's head, while the shoes are made to look like bird's claws."[50] This is precisely what we see depicted at Lascaux fifteen millennia earlier.

In each of the shamanisms we have examined, we have seen avian transformation or equivalent symbols of magical flight marking the inward penetration of the cave journey in a symbolism most eloquently expressed over the entrance to the Olmec cave at Oxtotitlan (see Figure 28). Here the shaman with bird mask and bird costume, representing—according to Kent Reilly, "a specific moment in a shamanic flight or cosmic travel ceremony" or, more exactly, "the precise moment before he will lift off and fly through the thin membrane of the cosmic portal into another reality"[51]—is graphically depicted with the cave journey itself as the symbolic vehicle for his magical flight to ecstasy.

"Strive to bring back the god in yourselves to the Divine in the universe," Plotinus entreated an increasingly profane world. As the result of the cave initiation, the human soul and the formal essence of the universe are experienced as being kindred in essence. The shaman's transformation, his hard-won ability to soar upon the previously latent "wings of the soul," symbolizes the innate identity of the human soul with the essential form unfolding in the universe, as represented by the World Tree as the birthplace and true home of the soul. This experience expressed in symbols of avian transformation lies at the heart of the transformation of consciousness that characterizes the shamanic quest and nearly everywhere marks its successful conclusion.

We thus recognize in the Shaft at Lascaux a coherent grammar of symbols consistent with the initiatory structure of the cave journey itself and with the archetypal structure of the same journey in shamanic traditions from diverse ages and places. Yet, as we noted earlier, there is still a real division of opinion as to what this scene signifies, and much of it centers upon the presence of the wounded or eviscerated bison depicted on the mural. Unwilling to view it in a shamanic context, some of the most eminent authorities on cave art have seen the recumbent figure as having been wounded by the bison, which he has perhaps attempted to kill. The explanation gains strength from the fact that it appears to be in agreement with what has been referred to as the "wounded or endangered man" theme found in a number of instances where human or humanoid figures have been depicted. Leroi-Gourhan saw this theme expressed in three related groups of images: humanlike creatures pierced by lines probably representing spears or similar missiles; humanoids apparently knocked down or threatened by a bison, of which the Lascaux scene is an example; and similar creatures confronting a bear. Seeing the mural as expressive of this general theme has given rise to diverse theories: for instance, that it represents a hunting accident, a situation not without its own drama in a hunting culture, or some mythical event in the history of the ancestors of the group. The question is important not only with regard to Lascaux but also for our understanding of the Upper Paleolithic period in general, because, while many disagree as to what its significance was, almost all agree that the wounded man motif was significant. It was, according to Leroi-Gourhan, "probably the most pictographic theme in Paleolithic art."[52] "By this he meant," Clottes and Courtin elaborate, "that it is the theme that comes closest to telling a story."[53] Moreover, they stress that the frequency of its portrayal argues for its significance:

> André Leroi-Gourhan often stressed the recurrence of the theme of the Wounded Man and therefore its importance in the Paleolithic iconography. In 1962, Annette Laming-Emperaire called attention to what she termed "bird-men" because of the curious shape of their heads and their short, winglike arms. They were, she said, always in a difficult situation, wounded or struck dead, and must represent a mythical or legendary Paleolithic character. Even if only those of Cougnac and Pech-Merle are unquestionable, the fact that the same theme was repeated and has come down to us in several caves, to which the Cosquer cave has just been added, suggests that it must have been depicted a considerable number of times.[54]

What then was the meaning for the Upper Paleolithic peoples of these three groups of depictions recognized as constituting the wounded man theme? I believe these three groups are, in fact, symbolically related, are of paramount significance, and can be consistently and coherently explained in relation to the initiatory cave journey, its attendant symbols, and related ideas from other shamanic traditions. Furthermore, the same approach will serve to harmonize the conflicting elements surrounding the "killed man" at Cosquer and the other depictions that we discussed as examples of initiatory death at the beginning of this chapter. And, finally, it will likewise serve to clarify the vision in the Shaft at Lascaux and prove that it is, indeed, an entranced shaman who lies in the mysterious Shaft deep within that famous cave. If these varied elements can be harmonized within the framework of the Paleolithic cave journey and the larger context of shamanism, we shall have unified an important aspect of Upper Paleolithic symbolism and given it sense and significant meaning.

Let us return to the controversy surrounding the wounded bison at Lascaux. This animal has at times been seen as sacrificial, and we may recall that the concept of sacrifice was associated with many of the shamanic traditions we have traced. Moreover, symbols of sacrifice are recurrently present in association with the tree or bird-topped pole as an axis mundi symbolism. For instance, before the Buryat shaman's ascent of the central birch tree, a goat is sacrificed, the Tungus shaman places a pelt of the sacrificed animal on the shamanic tree, and among the Dolgan a bird-topped tree marks the road to the sky for the shaman and the soul of the sacrificed animal.[55] During shamanic ceremonies the Koryak of Siberia sacrifice reindeer to Big Raven, who among their people replaces the eagle as the principal shamanic figure. Among the Maya and Olmec, apparently, human sacrifice was made at the sacred center associated with the shaman's trance, and the sacrificial victim among the Olmec was clad as the divinity to whom the sacrifice was made—god sacrificed to god. Among the Mapuche of Chile, before the shaman ascends the seven levels of their shaman's tree, a ritual pole called the *rewe*, "lambs are sacrificed and the heart of one of the sacrificed beasts is hung from a branch of a brush enclosure." In trance the blindfolded shaman uses a white quartz knife to draw blood from herself and the candidate for initiation, which is mixed together. "Then the troop of shamans make their ascent up the *rewe* accompanied by continuous chanting and drumming."[56] Similar sacrificial effigies are hung on the central feathered pole of the Sioux and, accompanied by drum and dance, young Sioux, on the instruction of their shamans, "sacrifice themselves" in the torturous ritual known as the Sioux sun dance.[57]

In the sacrifice, the sacrificial soul returns to its source, and the shaman's own ascent is magically aided in the process. Eliade points out that "the ascension to heaven is one of the specific characteristics of Siberian and central Asian shamanism. At the occasion of the horse sacrifice, the Altaic shaman ascends to heaven in ecstasy in order to offer to the celestial god the soul of the sacrificed horse. He realizes this ascension by climbing the birch trunk, which has nine notches, each symbolizing a specific heaven."[58] The birch, of course, incarnates the central World Tree in Siberia. The sacrificial animal is an incarnation of the mythical animal ancestor, which, according to Eliade, is conceived as the inexhaustible matrix of the life of the species.[59] The sacrifice's death is a return to this source of fecundity, which is also the source of the shaman's power. So viewed, we can recognize in the Shaft at Lascaux the archetypal sacrifice at the center, which not only aids the shaman's trance flight but also articulates the relationship between the world of individuated form in which the animal is incarnated and the world of essential, or inner, form that the return to center traditionally symbolized. And now we can see this scene as having a larger resonance complementary to the transformation of consciousness that the cave journey effects, which will help unify the various exemplars of the wounded man theme within the context of shamanism.

In the symbolism of shamanic sacrifice, as in Vedic sacrifice, in an important sense "the initiate is the oblation." The shaman himself, or his everyday individuated or profane consciousness, is sacrificed to experience the "higher" state of consciousness symbolized by the ecstasy of trance ascent and the state of unity it apprehends. Sacrifice and sacrificer are purposely conflated on a symbolic level. Thus, in numerous traditions we have explored, the shaman himself symbolically dies or is dismembered before his ascent. Blood is drawn from the Mayan and Mapuche shaman, and the Sioux initiate is himself "sacrificed" under the shaman's auspices on the central tree. We may recall the shamanic antecedents of the Norse god Odin, who sacrifices himself to himself, god to god, on the central tree in order to gain the wisdom of the runes. Huichol Indian shamanism is another excellent example. The shamanic sacrifice is symbolically the deer, but the deer is also specifically identified with the shaman himself and with peyote, which becomes the vehicle of the shaman's own trance, his sacrificing his individuated structures of consciousness in ascending to the source of power. Finally, however, the deer is *Wawatsári*, "master of the deer species," who incarnates himself as a deer. Lifting the veil of individuated form, which is simply a reflex of the source of power, we now recognize that the sacrifice, the sacrificer (or his individuated consciousness), and the deity to which the sacrifice is made are one, and we celebrate the mythical eternal circular sacrifice of god to god at the world's center.

Given that in the state of ecstasy the initiate is in some sense the oblation, that is, that there is a deliberate identification of the shaman and the sacrifice, can we see the different exemplars of the Wounded Man theme so central to Paleolithic symbolism in a context that makes them complementary to one another and fit into the overall schema of shamanism and the cave journey as a transformation of consciousness? Let us begin with the most common examples, the men or birdlike humanoids pierced with arrows or spears and the birdlike men involved in some sort of "confrontation" with the buffalo. We initially dealt with the first theme in the second section of this chapter, indicating that it pointed in the direction of initiatory killing or piercing with implications of transformation and empowerment in a shamanic context, which would be consistent with cave initiation. We further noted, along with Clottes and Courtin, that one of the features attending most of these representations is that the pierced figure is a composite being, partly human and partly animal or bird. These authors illustrate further examples of the theme, one being the bisonlike shamanic figure from Gabillou Cave discussed earlier (see Figure 16). Leroi-Gourhan also placed this figure in his group of wounded men, presumably based on the projectile-like lines that appear to pierce its body and what may be blood coming from its mouth.[60]

We noted in chapter 3 that the cave journey was meant to effect a rapprochement with that level of consciousness that we termed the psychoid realm, where the human mind experiences its deep inward connection with the creative matrix of nature and even the cosmos itself. We further noted that the therianthropic form, human and animal combined, symbolically articulates the elements of this transformation of consciousness, and we called attention to such hybrid creatures as the Sorcerer of Les Trois Frères and the dancing shamanic figure at Gabillou Cave as examples. The transformation of consciousness leading to the therianthropic form is the correlative of the cave journey itself. As we have seen, as the shaman more closely approaches the altered state of consciousness that is his goal, he approximates an identity with or transforms into the half-animal spirit guide.

At the same time, the trance experience is itself equated with death. We saw this specifically set forth among the !Kung and Tukano and symbolically expressed in other types of shamanism in rites of initiatory death. The animal sacrifice that accompanies the trance ascent is also a death. But as we noted earlier, the two are often symbolically conflated. Thus the !Kung shaman gains the power for his trance from a slain eland. While superficially we have sacrificer and sacrifice, in visionary experience the two are identical, and, as the rock painting of the related San Bushmen makes clear by a series of graphic transitions, in their trance ascent the shaman and the eland combine in ecstasy into a hybrid winged creature known as an *ales*. Sacrificer and sacrifice, shaman and spirit guide, become one in sacrificial death, for to enter a trance is also symbolically to die among the !Kung. Death, trance, spirit guide transformation, and sacrifice are interwoven as symbols of the shaman's transformation of conscious and ecstatic experience. Again "the initiate is the oblation," or the two are symbolically one in their therianthropic composite forms. And what we find in the Upper Paleolithic in these pierced birdlike or otherwise composite forms is a similar conflation of the shaman's initiatory death, transformation, trance, and sacrifice expressed in the transformation into the therianthropic animal spirit whose "death," or piercing, symbolizes the trance state. Whereas at Lascaux we have distinct forms of the sacrificer and sacrifice, buffalo and shaman, leading to trance ascent, in these representations the shaman's trance, shamanic transformation, and sacrifice combine into a single symbol much as they do among the Bushmen, the Huichol, and others to indicate access to the transcendent condition experienced in ecstasy.

If these are indeed symbols of the shaman's transformation of consciousness and ecstatic trance ascent, we ought to be able to

FIGURE 36. *Engraved bone fragment depicting humanlike creatures confronting an oversized bison, Les Eyzies.*

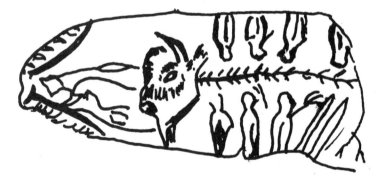

FIGURE 37. *Engraved bone fragment depicting humanlike figures and head of a bison with skeletal spinal column and detached front legs, Raymonden.*

discern a similar dialectic between the shaman and the bison, the figures represented at Lascaux, in the art of the period. This will in turn shed light on that aspect of the wounded man theme in which birdlike men recurrently have some relationship to a bison. Bird-like men have been recognized in certain contexts as suggesting shamans, an observation that receives support from the almost universal theme of avian transformation in the world's shamanic traditions. And there are also numerous depictions of buffalo pierced by lines, which some have thought to be arrows or spears that may suggest animal sacrifice. They may also portray other forms of killing, or the penetrating lines may symbolize something else entirely. However, Marshack notes several examples of animal art that seem to point to sacrifice and suggest a shamanic context. In one example of mobiliary art, crudely portrayed anthropomorphs approach a supernaturally large bison (Figure 36). The birdlike men may be "struck through by spears or darts," Marshack notes, reminding us of the bird-men of Pech-Merle and Cougnac. He concludes, "The image might be of the bison sacrificed or worshipped at the 'proper time.'"[61] He also draws our attention to a bone slate composition containing a bison and humanoid figures (Figure 37). The bison's head is intact and well portrayed, but its body is reduced to a skeletal spinal column, and its disarticulated front legs lie in front of it. Marshack notes that the "image need not represent a hunt for food but, as seems more likely, a myth and rite in which the bison, or bison parts, and the manlike figures are related. In such a storied ceremony, any 'killing' would be also storied and probably 'sacrificial.'" Particularly interesting here is the observation that these birdlike men are themselves pierced, "struck through," as Marshack asserts based upon microscopic analysis, by what may be "spears or darts."[62] Elsewhere we have suggested that this piercing is symbolic of an initiatory death, itself a form of sacrifice. In this light, both this depiction and the one we described earlier appear to assert symbolically an underlying identity between sacrificer and the sacrifice, the shaman and his bison spirit guide, which we have seen expressed elsewhere.

But the underlying identity in the state of ecstasy between the shaman and the buffalo, the initiate and the oblation, is more obvious and easier to find. We have encountered numerous depictions where in ecstasy the shaman and buffalo symbolically combine as one: the dancing buffalo shamans of Les Trois Frères (see Figures 15 and 17), the buffalo shaman of Gabillou Cave (see Figure 16), and the exquisitely portrayed buffalo shaman recently discovered at Chauvet. Each of these therianthropes, knees bent in a dancing position, is a creature of ecstasy and initiation into the realm of essence that the shaman penetrates in trance. That found at Chauvet is the mediator to the revelation of the panoply of essential forms on the magnificent lion panel, just as that at Les Trois Frères introduces us to the myriad animal forms with which the Sanctuary of that cave is adorned.

Some of these buffalo shaman figures seem to imply even more. The dancing buffalo shaman at Gabillou Cave, revealed to the initiate only when he has reached the deepest chambers of the cave, is himself thought to represent a figure pierced with projectiles and is included by Leroi-Gourhan as an example of the wounded man theme. If this is so, we can see that in this portrayal shaman and buffalo symbolically combine as the sacrifice in the ecstatic state. Here shaman and animal sacrifice together ascend in ecstasy to the inexhaustible matrix of life and the life of the animal species. This is, of course, a direction in which all the shamanic traditions we have studied point, the familiar realm of "the master spirits of all the running and flying birds and game," which the shaman penetrates in trance. And it is both telling and appropriate that it is also a buffalo shaman who penetrates the cosmic threshold to this matrix of creation at Les Trois Frères in a symbolism that we discussed earlier (see Figure 34).

Here in Dionysian ecstasy the ithyphallic buffalo shaman has coitus with (that is, unites and becomes one with) the master spirit of the animal species in the form of his supernatural part-buffalo partner. As we discussed, the surrounding symbolism suggests the eternal sacrifice and restoration of the bison form at the source of creation, where *sub specie aeternitatis* it becomes the eternal animal ancestor. Now we recognize the significance of the epiphany of the source deep within the cave at Le Tuc d'Audoubert, with its coupling bison pair, and why it provoked the ecstasy of dance that the ages have preserved in the footprints surrounding it. And the depths of the mind cast up the recollection of another avatar of this experience, another visitant to the essential forms of the Buffalo People, who himself had coitus with the buffalo wives and learned their wisdom, who also killed and then restored the Master Buffalo at the mandala-formed center of creation. For this is the eternal dialectic between Holy Man and Buffalo-Who-Never-Dies that we experienced among the Navaho, bearing the same features over millennia. And whether the Upper Paleolithic scenes involve sacrificer and sacrifice, shaman and bison, brought ritually together in trance-death, as at Lascaux and in the examples presented by Marshack, or whether they are found in composite forms as creatures united in the ecstatic state, the significance is the same. Each poetically expresses the eternal dance at the center of creation, where eternity becomes incarnate in the world of time and transient man ever attempts to rearticulate his relationship with the eternal through the central ecstatic experience in which the shaman's journey culminates.

It would seem then that Leroi-Gourhan was correct in recognizing the importance of the wounded man theme in the Upper Paleolithic period, but perhaps partly for the wrong reasons. It is now clear that this theme portrays the various forms of relationship between the shaman and the animal sacrifice and spirit guide. We can perceive that the birdlike men or composite figures wounded or pierced with spears or other projectiles are better understood within the context of shamanic initiation and the transformation of consciousness leading to ecstasy that this implies. And the birdlike men confronting a buffalo are indicative of the sacred relationship between shaman and buffalo, which we have shown at Lascaux and in the numerous roles of the buffalo shamans who also symbolize the shaman's transformation and empowerment. Seeing them in this way, they complement each other and fit within the larger context of the symbolism of the cave journey that we have attempted to elucidate. And, finally, they make it apparent that the scene in the Shaft at Lascaux is a representation of a shaman accompanied in trance-death and transformation by the sacred bison as sacrifice, the same animal with which he elsewhere becomes one in ecstasy and in his return to the source of life.

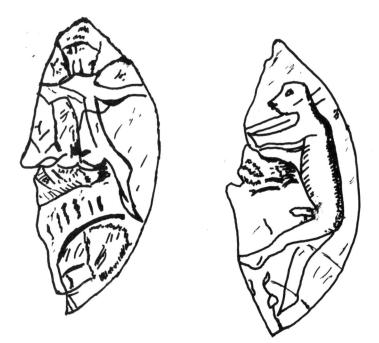

FIGURE 38. *Both faces of a broken engraved bone disk with humanoid figures and bear paws, Le Mas d'Azil.*

FIGURE 39. *Piece of engraved stone depicting a bear and two humanoid figures, Péchialet.*

Can we make similar sense of the remaining examples (Figures 38 and 39) of the so-called wounded man theme, men wounded or endangered by a bear? The figures on both sides of the fragment in Figure 38 are confronting a bear, although only the paw appears on the fragment; in Figure 39 the bear is fully represented. It is obvious that viewing these depictions as representative of scenes from the hunt in unsatisfying, for the men are either naked, ithyphallic, dancing, and perhaps pierced (Figure 38) or birdlike, dancing, and perhaps pierced (Figure 39). Marshack sees the ithyphallic character in Figure 38 as carrying a pole on his shoulder held in two outstretched arms. "The attitude of the man and the manner of carrying the pole in two hands indicates its use in dance ceremony or baiting," he notes.[63] Examining Figure 39 by microscope, he determined that it portrays "two dance-like human figures around a standing bear." One creature appears markedly birdlike. Marshack asks the obvious question, "Is this the image, then, of a ceremonial dance or of the ceremonial baiting of a bear? The presence of bear myths, ceremonies, and rites, almost always seasonal or periodic, from Scandinavia through Asia and into America in historic times, is enlightening."[64] We earlier noted, in relationship to the possible bear skull altars at Chauvet and Montespan, the existence of a circumpolar cult of bear ceremonialism stretching into the Americas and emphasizing bear sacrifice, often after a period of ritual and baiting, and the bear as master animal. These same areas tend to be marked by the presence of strong shamanic traditions.

There is evidence within the caves suggesting bear sacrifice. We remember the portrayal of a wounded bear just beneath the Sorcerer at Les Trois Frères, a position that Joseph Campbell says vests it with a special symbolic importance (Figure 40). Marshack draws our attention to further examples of bears shot with darts, displaying wound marks and what appears to be blood flowing from the nose and mouth (Figures 41 and 42). Noting that the bear, though perhaps eaten occasionally, was not a part of the usual diet of the times and that it was a difficult and dangerous prey as well, he concludes, "The intentional killing of any such animal must have been special; it required other techniques of hunting and a special allotment of time; it must have had some other intent and story

WOUNDED OR SACRIFICED BEARS

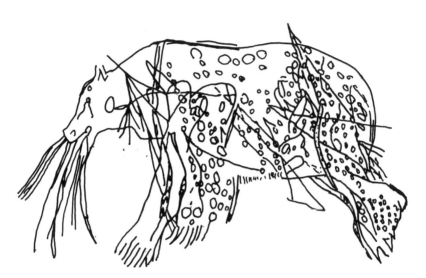

FIGURE 40. *Sanctuary of Les Trois Frères.*

FIGURE 41. *Les Trois Frères.*

FIGURE 42. *Le Portel.*

than was used for either the tundra or forest herbivore."[65] Viewing these representations together with the "bear altar" at Montespan, Marshack suggests that they are indeed images of ceremony and sacrifice. In support, he refers to the Abbé Breuil's famous description of the headless statue of a bear found in the cave at Montespan, upon which "a young Bear's head attached to the skin" was ritually placed and then "stabbed by more than 30 javelin thrusts of various size, entering very deeply," leaving their impression on the base of the "statue."[66] While some have disputed Breuil's account, its credibility received a recent boost from the discovery at Chauvet. Here, as we have noted, in the middle of one cave chamber on a block of stone that had fallen from the ceiling "the skull of a bear was placed as if on an altar," and all around it were more than thirty additional bear skulls.[67] The absence of other bones that would accompany a natural death implies that the skulls alone were intentionally placed for some unknown purpose. All of this seems to be evidence of bear ceremonialism and sacrifice and may point to a continuity with a circumpolar cult of bear sacrifice existing into historical times.

We may also recall that the bear as animal spirit guide has frequently figured in the shamanic traditions we have studied and played a distinctive role in the shaman's initiation. These shamanisms, it might be noted, often lie generally within the spread of the cult of bear ceremonialism discussed. We have described the symbolism in which the novitiate shaman is swallowed by the animal spirit guide. Among the Angmagsalik Eskimos of Greenland, Joan Halifax informs us, "all shamans are inevitably devoured by an *angakoq* bear. . . . At the end of the apprentice's probation, the *angakoq* bear makes a thorough meal of him, swallowing him whole and later regurgitating him bone by bone. The dismembered shaman is then reassembled and clothed with new flesh."[68] She also relates a similar vision from the accounts of Knud Rasmussen where the shaman is likewise devoured by a bear in the form of a helping spirit, who then regurgitates him. The shaman emerges with his powers increased. And in this example the process occurs within a cave.[69] We have seen the "swallowing" motif frequently connected with the cave and cave initiation. In a variation of this theme, we remember that the Winnebago initiate is swallowed by a bear in the form of the sweat lodge covered with bear skin. We might also recall the bear spirit guide who led the Apache shamanic initiate through the Symplegades and into the shaman's holy cave, a cave in which dwelled the sacred animal essences in paired forms and which became the portal to Medicine's home and to the source of power, the realm of the Master Bear and the power that made the initiate a bear-shaman.

We find the bear in various instances in the role of sacrifice or animal spirit guide associated with initiation, swallowing, and the cave symbolism. The two merge in the dancing grizzly bear spirit guides of the Winnebago Indians. In these immortals revealed in trance, who alternately pierce and heal each other according to their holy regenerative power, sacrifice, sacrificer, and source of power once more come together in a single image that suggests the eternal interchange between the world of individual form and the generative source, the *fons et origo* from which life and its regenerative power emerge ever anew.

We can thus see in these shamanic traditions the bear as sacrifice, as spirit guide, and as Master Animal marking the cosmic fount of creation. We have noted that the age and widespread distribution of these practices and symbols have suggested to some a possible continuity with the Upper Paleolithic caves. And we have seen from this era images of birdlike men, that is, shamans, apparently ritually baiting or piercing bears; portrayals of bear sacrifice upon the cave walls; and evidence of bear skulls placed upon altars in the inner grottoes of certain caves, suggestive of ritual worship or sacrifice in a symbolism that may have antecedents going back seventy-five thousand years.

The cave journey is, as we have labored to illustrate, a return to the origin, to the source of creation itself. And at Les Trois Frères it is precisely at the cosmic fount of animal forms, the Sanctuary, that the bear sacrifice is depicted. Our study has shown—and Eliade's work has proved in detail—that for archaic societies bone signifies a similar return to essence and to the cosmic fount of creation. And shamanic sacrifice also marks the eternal interchange between the incarnated animal and enduring source of the life of its species. The cave journey as a return to origin and the symbolisms of bone and of sacrifice all seem to converge in the bear skull altars within the caves, suggesting that point which, opening the portal to the

Otherworld, again articulates the relationship between the world of individuated form and the creative plenitude of the source. We have seen this point where essence becomes manifest and, conversely, where the manifest world returns to essence repeatedly in the shamanic cultures throughout the world, and it would appear that the ritual of bear baiting, the images of bear sacrifice, and the bear altars deep within the cave are yet another expression of the opening of the cave portal to the source of plenitude.

This interpretation receives confirmation from two important pieces of art from the period. The first is a half-rounded engraved rod made of bone from La Madeleine, perhaps originally a shaman's baton. The other is an engraved baton of deer antler found at the site of Massat a short distance from Les Trois Frères. If Leroi-Gourhan is correct, these are not simply random examples but, like the wounded man theme, present an idea prevalent enough at the time that it was tending toward "a symbolism that already comes close to the ideographic"—it was evolving toward an abstract expression of a common underlying idea.[70] If we examine the example from La Madeleine, we see the head of a bear (Figure 43A and B). However, like the sacrificial bison in Figure 37, its body is reduced to the upper portion of the skeletal spinal column, suggesting sacrifice, and perhaps a disarticulated head similar to those deposited on the altars at Montespan and Chauvet. We noted that bear sacrifice within the cave was a return to the source of creation. Previously we saw that the coincidence of sexual opposites similarly marked the cave journey as a return to the generative source represented by their union. And this is precisely what we find on this rod in conjunction with the head of the sacrificial bear. For here, as Leroi-Gourhan recognizes, a graphically depicted phallus joins with a distinct vulva to point toward the sacrificial bear.[71] We have described how the shaman, perhaps with a phallic baton of which this may be an example, penetrated the feminine cave, often itself marked with vulvas and other female signs, unifying the sexual opposites and returning to the generative source of creation. We have also seen a similar symbolism implying a return to the source in the bear sacrifice and in the symbolism of bone as a return to essence. In this phallic bone rod uniting the sexual opposites and depicting the sacrificial bear's head, all these themes converge to

FIGURE 43A. *Half-rounded bone rod depicting bear's head, skeletal spinal column, and sexual symbolism. St. Germain-en-Laye, Musée des Antiquities Nationales.* © *photo RMN—M. Beck-Coppola, photographer.*

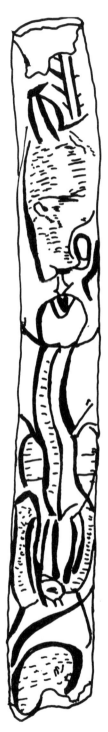

FIGURE 43B. *Drawing of above.*

suggest the very same symbolic pattern revealingly inscribed on the shaman's baton, which traditionally represents his continuing participation in the source of power to which these visionary symbols point.

And these themes are repeated on the baton from Massat, perhaps with an interesting additional twist (Figure 44A–D). Here we see once more the head of a bear. The marks around its mouth, resembling other images in which bears appear to be sacrificial, suggest, according to Marshack, "blood spouting from the mouth" and thus also imply sacrifice.[72] Marshack's microscope, in fact, reveals that the bear has a dart in its throat and is bleeding from its mouth and nose. According to Leroi-Gourhan, however, the design on the baton is an abbreviation of the very same symbolism found on the bone from La Madeleine (Figure 43B), abstractly suggesting with oval and barbed signs the same vulva and phallus configuration (Figure 44C).[73] Marshack questions whether such sexual symbolism is really implied by these engraved configurations and, looking at the other side of the baton as well, sees it as part of a pattern indicating the eyes and curved beak of a waterbird on both faces (Figure 44B and D).[74] Given symbolisms as complex as those we have already encountered in the Upper Paleolithic, however, and given the similarity to the rod from La Madeleine, there is no reason to believe that the symbols cannot overlap and that one must necessarily exclude the other. Their intentional combination would make sense in the context of familiar symbolisms. For now we can see the coalescence of animal sacrifice, the union of sexual opposites, and ornithological symbolism all relating to the baton. This ornithological symbolism is, of course, reminiscent of the bird-topped batons from Le Mas d'Azil and Les Trois Frères presented in chapter 2 (see Figures 4 and 5) and, more important, of that lying beside the bird-man shaman at Lascaux (see Figure 23), which all carry associations of the shaman's avian transformation and the magical flight of trance experience.

It seems clear that all the elements of the third category of the wounded man theme point to a shamanic context. Bear ceremonials performed by birdlike men, baiting, bear sacrifice, and the bear altars within the caves all fit into and reinforce a larger matrix of symbols, such as the prestige accorded to bone as a return to essence,

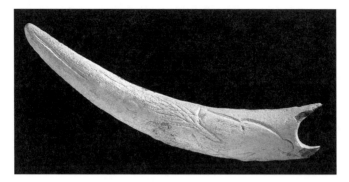

FIGURE 44A. *Broken engraved baton from Massat. St. Germain-en-Laye, Musée des Antiquities Nationales © photo RMN–Loic Hamon, photographer.*

FIGURE 44B. *Drawing of same.*

FIGURE 44C. *Drawing of same (after Leroi-Gourhan).*

FIGURE 44D. *Drawing of reverse side of same (after Marshack).*

the cave journey as a return to origin, and the function of sacrifice as a return to the generative source of the species. These features also fit within a larger context, perhaps reaching back seventy-five thousand years and surviving into historical times, in which the bear is sacrifice, spirit guide, and master animal often associated with the cave symbolism in the world of the shaman. In this context we can recognize in the pierced birdlike men in Leroi-Gourhan's schema as well as in the men confronting either a bison or a bear a common thread of significance that explains the continuing prestige accorded this theme in the Upper Paleolithic period.

From this vantage point we can perceive a unified system of visionary symbolism in the Upper Paleolithic and can recognize that it manifests a remarkable resemblance to the structural and functional stages inducing a transformation of consciousness in shamanic cultures worldwide and enduring into our own times. In the first section of this chapter we traced how the various psycho-physiological aspects of the cave journey served to erase existing patterns of thought and response and to awaken the mind to an experience of continuity with and empowerment by its deeper source, a source continuous with cosmic power and plenitude. In so doing it employed the same techniques to alter the state of human consciousness that we have traced across the globe and over the ages. In the next section we were able to discern a structure of visionary symbols that led the mind in the same direction, tracing with precision a pattern of shamanic "cave" initiation and the inward journey that we had seen repeatedly in various cultures. We can now perceive a striking cultural continuity pressing back to the very horizons of modern Homo sapiens in a system of practice and belief that the contemporary world is only beginning to understand but which has a meaning and experienced significance that offer a badly needed alternative to modern man's alienation from both his own preconscious resources and the infinite.

The entire direction of psychophysiological preparation, the symbol as psychopomp and tool of the gods, and the unified system of symbolism we have traced in this chapter realize a definitive expression and visionary culmination in the grammar of symbols expressed in the Shaft at Lascaux, to which we can now return with an understanding of the relationship between shaman and sacrifice embodied in the wounded man theme. It is evident that the bird-topped scepter, avian transformation, the entranced shaman and his animal sacrifice returning in ecstasy to the generative source all point in the direction to which all our shamanisms have led, the realm of "the master spirits of all the running and flying birds and game," the world of self-generating form represented by the animals of eternity that everywhere adorn the cave walls at Lascaux. Here life is indeed "born from its own eternity." Within the womb of the cave is the interface between eternity and time experienced in trance, the portal to the Otherworld as the source of generative and regenerative power. Here both scepter and cave unite the three realms as they have everywhere and establish the zone of verticality marking the origin as an effective and accessible source of the real. It is here that the axis of verticality penetrates the womb of creation and essence becomes manifest—"that which is constant" becomes that which "will come to pass," as the Tukano expressed this idea. We may note the almost startling similarity of this Paleolithic scene with the Tukano vision so many thousands of years later, where the cosmic scepter penetrates the womb of being, the "manifestation house," to mark the immense source of life and power that creates and sustains our manifest world. And thinking back to the Rock at Nyí (see Figure 30), we can recall the presence of the very same symbols as those found at Lascaux. There we noted that in a larger context, bird, staff, erect phallus, center of the world, point of creation, axis mundi, and zone of verticality all coalesce in this depiction that stands at the central point of creation marking this as a sacred revelation of cosmogonic power.

At Lascaux the entranced shaman also lies with penis erect at the axis of verticality within the womb of creation. Such symbolism complements the ithyphallic characteristics of the shamans we have seen elsewhere in these caves and the symbolism of the cave journey as uniting the opposites. In many of the cultures we have examined there has been an erotic aspect implicit in the shaman's ecstatic journey with his spirit guide. Lommel informs us of the shaman's magical flight in Australia. "These flight-dreams are of a special kind and distinctly sexual in character. During such a dream the shaman's power 'rises' in his body and causes his penis to become erect."[75] The shaman rides to the dreamtime upon the

Unggud snake in this condition. We recall the erect shaman with his spirit guide in the Olmec cave at Oxtotitlan (see Figure 26) and the bird-shaman from the African bush who is portrayed as ithyphallic in his ecstatic flight (see Figure 29). Penetrating the cosmic threshold in ecstasy, we have noted, is a fertilizing act of cosmogonic proportions. We have seen similar sexual imagery in a number of shamanic traditions: the payé and the female animal essences among the Tukano, Holy Man and the Buffalo Women among the Navaho, the entry into the land called Vagina among the Huichol, and the bison-shaman of Les Trois Frères with his supernatural bison mate in the Paleolithic. Ultimately, as Peter Furst informs us, it is not coitus but unity that lies at the heart of this symbolism and of the shaman's ecstatic experience. This is the mystical union of which the Tukano spoke as a sort of "spiritual coitus," the reunion of the soul with its sacred source. And it is precisely this same experience of the return of the soul to its source, the same communion with cosmic life made articulate in the very same symbols we have seen enduring over time and the ages, that is symbolized in the Shaft at Lascaux. And we can now recognize that here, deep within the cosmic womb of creation where the cave portal opens to the source of eternal form—human, natural, and cosmic—indeed lies an entranced shaman where he has lain for more than one hundred and fifty centuries rapt in ecstasy in spiritual coitus with the ever incarnated forms of Eternity.

NOTES

CHAPTER 1

1. C. Kerényi, as found in C. G. Jung and C. Kerényi, *Essays on a Science of Mythology*, trans. R. F. C. Hull (Princeton: Princeton University Press, 1969), p. 1.
2. Joseph Campbell, *Historical Atlas of World Mythology*, vol. 1: *The Way of the Animal Powers* (New York: Harper and Row, 1983), p. 8.
3. Mircea Eliade, *Shamanism: Archaic Techniques of Ecstasy*, trans. Willard R. Trask (Princeton: Princeton University Press, 1972), p. 4.
4. Ibid.
5. Ibid., p. 5.
6. Ibid., p. 8.
7. Ibid., p. 216.
8. Ibid., p. 8; Mircea Eliade, *Rites and Symbols of Initiation: The Mysteries of Birth and Rebirth*, trans. Willard R. Trask (New York: Harper Torchbooks, 1965), pp. 100, 101.
9. Joseph Campbell, *The Masks of God*, vol. 1: *Primitive Mythology* (New York: Viking Press, 1970), p. 350.
10. Ibid., p. 264.
11. Ibid., p. 263.
12. Eliade, *Shamanism*, p. 11.
13. Ibid., p. 504.
14. Mircea Eliade, "The Occult in the Modern World," in *Occultism, Witchcraft and Cultural Fashions* (Chicago: University of Chicago Press, 1976), p. 56.
15. Eliade, *Rites and Symbols of Initiation*, p. 96.
16. Johannes Wilbert, "Tobacco and Shamanic Ecstasy Among the Warao Indians of Venezuela," in *Flesh of the Gods: The Ritual Use of Hallucinogens*, ed. Peter T. Furst (Prospect Heights, Ill.: Waveland Press, 1990), pp. 81–82.

17. Eliade, *Shamanism*, p. 51.
18. Roger N. Walsh, *The Spirit of Shamanism* (Los Angeles: Jeremy P. Tarcher, 1990), p. 13.
19. Åke Hultkrantz, *The North American Orpheus Tradition: A Contribution to Comparative Religion* (Stockholm: The Ethnographic Museum of Sweden, 1957), Monograph series 2, p. 310 as found in Jay Miller, *Shamanic Odyssey: The Lushootseed Salish Journey to the Land of the Dead* (Menlo Park: Ballena Press, 1988), p. 104.
20. Campbell, *Primitive Mythology*, p. 251.
21. Eliade, *Shamanism*, pp. 510, 511.
22. A. C. Graham, *Disputers of the Tao: Philosophical Argument in Ancient China* (La Salle, Ill.: Open Court, 1989), p. 100.
23. Carl G. Jung, *Collected Works*, trans. R. F. C. Hull, vol. 13: *Alchemical Studies* (Princeton: Princeton University Press, 1983) para. 84.
24. Friedrich Schiller, *On the Aesthetic Education of Man*, trans. Reginald Snell (New York: Frederick Ungar, 1965), p. 40.
25. Arthur Schopenhauer, *The Fourfold Root of Sufficient Reason*, trans. E. F. J. Payne (La Salle, Ill.: Open Court, 1974), p. 76.
26. Bryan Magee, *The Philosophy of Schopenhauer* (Oxford: Oxford University Press, 1987), p. 101.
27. Schopenhauer, p. 114.
28. Karl Jaspers, *Kant*, taken from *The Great Philosophers*, vol. 1, trans. Ralph Manheim (San Diego: Harvest/HBJ, 1962), p. 51.
29. Ernst Cassirer, *Language and Myth*, trans. Susanne K. Langer (New York: Dover, 1953), p. 8.
30. Ibid., p. 99.
31. F. W. J. Schelling, *System of Transcendental Idealism*, trans. Albert Hofstadter, in *Philosophies of Art and Beauty: Selected Readings in Aesthetics from Plato to Heidegger;* eds. Albert Hofstadter and Richard Kuhns (Chicago: University of Chicago Press, 1976), p. 355.
32. Schelling, *The Philosophy of Art*, trans. Douglas W. Stott (Minneapolis: University of Minnesota, 1989), p. 45; Schelling, *Philosophie der Mythologie*, p. 136, as found in Jung and Kerényi, p. 1.
33. Schelling, *Sämmtliche Werke*, ed. K. F. A. Schelling, vols. 11 and 12: *Philosophie der Mythologie* (Stuttgart and Ausburg: J. G. Cotta'scher Verlag, 1856–1861), in Ernst Benz, "Theogony and the Transformation of Man in Friedrich Wilhelm Joseph Schelling," in *Man and Transformation: Papers from the Eranos Yearbooks*, vol. 5, ed. Joseph Campbell, trans. Ralph Manheim (Princeton: Princeton University Press, 1980), p. 217.
34. Ibid., p. 218
35. Schelling, *System of Transcendental Idealism*, p. 368.
36. Schelling, *The Philosophy of Art*, p. 4.
37. Schelling, *System of Transcendental Idealism*, pp. 367, 368; see also *The Philosophy of Art*, pp. 50–52.

38. Ibid., p. 368.
39. Schelling, *The Philosophy of Art*, p. 51.
40. Ibid., p. 52.
41. J. J. Clarke, *In Search of Jung* (London: Routledge, 1992), preface, p. xiv.
42. Jung, *Collected Works*, vol. 8, para. 423.
43. Ibid., vol. 11, para. 751.
44. Ibid., para 553.
45. Ibid., vol. 7, para. 292.
46. Ibid., vol. 8, para. 401.
47. Ibid., para. 435.
48. Ibid., vol. 14, para. 558.
49. Ibid., vol. 8, para. 436.
50. Jung, "Psychological Commentary on *The Tibetan Book of the Dead*," trans. R. F. C. Hull, in W. Y. Evens-Wentz, *The Tibetan Book of the Dead* (London: Oxford University Press, 1960), p. xliv.
51. Jung, *Collected Works*, vol. 7, para. 235.
52. Ibid., vol. 8, para. 230.
53. Ibid., vol. 8, para. 342.
54. Ibid., vol. 18, para. 280.
55. Jung, *Modern Man in Search of a Soul*, trans. W. S. Dell and Cary F. Baynes (San Diego: Harcourt Brace, 1933), p. 126.
56. *C. G. Jung Speaking: Interviews and Encounters*, eds. W. McGuire and R. F. C. Hull (London: Pan Books, 1980), p. 100, as found in Clarke, p. 104.
57. Jung, "Psychological Commentary on *The Tibetan Book of the Dead*," xlix.
58. Jung, *Collected Works*, vol. 9, para. 714.
59. Ibid., vol. 9, para. 717.
60. Ira Progoff, *Jung, Synchronicity, and Human Destiny: C. G. Jung's Theory of Meaningful Coincidence* (New York: Julian Press, 1987), p. 83.
61. Jung, *Collected Works*, vol. 11, para. 440.
62. Ibid., vol. 8, para. 923.
63. Plato, *The Republic*, 518 bcd, as found in G. M. A. Grube, *Plato's Thought* (Indianapolis: Hackett Publishing, 1980), p. 234.

CHAPTER 2

1. André Leroi-Gourhan, *Treasures of Prehistoric Art*, trans. Norbert Guterman (New York: Harry N. Abrams, 1967), p. 205; see also Paul Bahn, foreword to *The Dawn of Art: The Chauvet Cave*, Jean-Marie Chauvet, Eliette Brunel Deschamps, and Christian Hillaire, trans. Paul Bahn (New York: Harry N. Abrams, 1996), pp. 9–10, for more detailed explanation of Leroi-Gourhan's chronology.
2. Ibid.
3. Jean Clottes and Jean Courtin, *The Cave Beneath the Sea: Paleolithic Images at Cosquer*, trans. Marilyn Garner (New York: Harry N. Abrams, 1996), p. 7.

4. Michael D. Lemonick, "Stone-Age Bombshell," *Time* (June 19, 1995).

5. Jean Clottes, epilogue to *The Dawn of Art: The Chauvet Cave*, pp. 121–26.

6. Abbé Henri Breuil, *Four Hundred Centuries of Cave Art*, trans. Mary Boyle (Montignac, France: Centre d'Etudes et de Documentation Prehistoriques, 1952), p. 238; Leroi-Gourhan, pp. 181, 182; Johannes Maringer, *The Gods of Prehistoric Man* (London: Weidenfeld and Nicholson, 1960), p. 126; see also Campbell, *The Masks of God*, vol. 1: *Primitive Mythology*, pp. 345–47; Alexander Marshack, *The Roots of Civilization* (Mount Kisco, N.Y.: Moyer Bell, 1991), pp. 240–41.

7. See discussion in Campbell, *The Masks of God*, vol. 1: *Primitive Mythology*, pp. 339–47; *Historical Atlas of World Mythology*, vol. 1: *The Way of the Animal Powers*, pp. 54–56, 62–63; Maringer, p. 40 ff., pp. 100–113.

8. Emil Bächler, *Das Alpine Paläolithikum der Schweitz im Wildkirschli, Drachenloch und Wildenmannlisloch*, Schwizerische Gesellschaft für Urgeschichte, Monographien zur Ur- und Fruhgeschichte der Schweiz, vol. 2 (Basel, 1940), p. 260, as found in Campbell, *Historical Atlas of World Mythology*, vol 1: *The Way of the Animal Powers*, p. 55.

9. Leroi-Gourhan, p. 31.

10. Ibid., p. 32.

11. Ibid., p. 150.

12. Mario Ruspoli, *The Cave of Lascaux: The Final Photographs*, trans. Sebastian Wormwell (New York: Harry N. Abrams, 1987), p. 76.

13. Leroi-Gourhan, p. 31.

14. Ibid., pp. 64, 69.

15. Marshack, p. 89.

16. Ibid., p. 88, quoting Paolo Graziosi, *Palaeolithic Art* (New York: Faber and Faber, 1960), p. 40.

17. Ibid., p. 91.

18. Ibid., pp. 260–62.

19. Leroi-Gourhan, p. 69.

20. Alexander Marshack, "Images of the Ice Age," *Archeology*, vol. 48, no. 4, July/August 1995, p. 34.

21. See Leroi-Gourhan, p. 131; it should be noted, however, that he feels some of these characteristics may have been artistic conventions of the time.

22. Ruspoli, p. 88.

23. Anne Baring and Jules Cashford, *The Myth of the Goddess: Evolution of an Image* (New York: Arkana, 1993), p. 38.

24. Joan Vastokas, comment on J. D. Lewis-Williams and T. A. Dowson, "The Signs of All Times: Entoptic Phenomena in Upper Paleolithic Art," *Current Anthropology*, vol. 29, no. 2, April 1988, p. 230.

25. Friedrich Nietzsche, *The Birth of Tragedy*, trans. Francis Golffing (Garden City, N.Y.: Anchor Books, 1956), p. 126.

26. Leroi-Gourhan, p. 164.

27. John Halverson, "Art for Art's Sake in the Paleolithic," *Current Anthropology*, vol. 28, no. 1, 1987, p. 67.

28. Leroi-Gourhan, *The Art of Prehistoric Man in Western Europe* (London: Thames and Hudson, 1967), as found in Mary Settegast, *Plato Prehistorian: 10,000 to 5,000 B.C. Myth, Religion, Archaeology* (Hudson, N.Y.: Lindisfarne Press, 1990), p. 23.

29. Leroi-Gourhan, p. 208.

30. Erich Neumann, "Art and Time," in *Man and Time: Papers from the Eranos Yearbooks*, vol. 3, ed. Joseph Campbell, trans. Ralph Manheim (Princeton: Princeton University Press, 1983), p. 6.

31. Breuil, pp. 170, 171.

32. Leroi-Gourhan, *Treasures of Prehistoric Art*, p. 181.

33. Herbert Kühn, *On the Track of Prehistoric Man*, trans. Alan Brodrick (New York: Random House, 1955), pp. 96, 97.

34. Campbell, *Historical Atlas of World Mythology*, vol. 1: *The Way of the Animal Powers*, p. 78.

35. Clottes and Courtin, pp. 66, 69–70, 79.

36. Leroi-Gourhan, *Treasures of Prehistoric Art*, pp. 182–85.

37. Brigette Delluc and Gilles Delluc, comment on J. D. Lewis-Williams and T. A. Dowson, "The Signs of All Times: Entoptic Phenomena in Upper Paleolithic Art," *Current Anthropology*, vol. 29, no. 2, April 1988, p. 224.

38. Leroi-Gourhan, *Treasures of Prehistoric Art*, p. 136.

39. Ibid., pp. 164–71.

40. Ibid., p. 137.

41. Ibid., p. 174.

42. *The Principal Upaniṣads*, trans. S. Radhakrishnan, *Bṛhadāraṇyaka Upaniṣad*, I.4, 4–5 (Atlantic Heights, N.J.: Humanities Paperback Library, 1992), p. 165.

43. *Bṛhadāraṇyaka Upaniṣad*, I.4, 5, trans. Joseph Campbell, *Masks of God*, vol. 1: *Primitive Mythology*, p. 105.

44. Mircea Eliade, *The Two and the One*, trans. J. M. Cohen (New York: Harper Torchbooks, 1965), p. 116.

45. Herbert Kühn, *Auf den Spüren des Eiszeitmenschen* (Wiesbaden, Germany: F. A. Brockhaus, 1953), pp. 91–94, as found in Campbell, *Historical Atlas of World Mythology*, vol. 1: *The Way of the Animal Powers*, pp. 73–75.

46. Kühn, *On the Track of Prehistoric Man*, pp. 108–9.

47. Leroi-Gourhan, *Treasures of Prehistoric Art*, p. 367.

48. Campbell, *Historical Atlas of World Mythology*, vol. 1: *The Way of the Animal Powers*, p. 76.

49. C. G. Jung, *Collected Works*, vol. 5, para. 261–64.

50. Ibid., vol. 5, para. 503.

51. Lancelot Law Whyte, *The Unconscious Before Freud* (Garden City, N.Y.: Anchor Books, 1962), p. 63.

52. Progoff, pp. 111–12.

53. Ruspoli, pp. 149–50.
54. Ibid., p. 146.
55. Leroi-Gourhan, *Treasures of Prehistoric Art*, p. 185.
56. Ruspoli, p. 29.
57. Ibid., p. 28.
58. Leroi-Gourhan, *Treasures of Prehistoric Art*, pp. 175, 511.
59. Breuil, pp. 135–37.
60. Settegast, pp. 109–10.
61. Campbell, *The Masks of God*, vol. 1: *Primitive Mythology*, p. 301.
62. Marshack, *The Roots of Civilization*, p. 278.

CHAPTER 3

1. Mary Schmidt, "Crazy Wisdom: The Shaman as Mediator of Realities," quoting, in part, Douglas Sharon, *Wizard of the Four Winds* (New York: Theosophical Publishing House, 1978), p. 16, in *Shamanism*, comp. Shirley Nicholson, p. 63.
2. Eliade, *Shamanism*, p. 32.
3. Schmidt, p. 64.
4. Ernst Cassirer, *The Philosophy of Symbolic Forms*, vol. 2: *Mythical Thought*, trans. Ralph Manheim (New Haven: Yale University Press, 1955), p. 169.
5. Paul Friedländer, *Plato: An Introduction*, trans. Hans Meyerhoff (Princeton: Princeton University Press, 1973), pp. 38, 41.
6. G.V. Ksenofontov, *Legendy i rasskazy o shamanach u. yakutov, buryat i tungusov*. Izdanie vtoroe. S. predisloviem S. A. Topkareva (Moscow: Izdatel'stvo Besbozhnik, 1930), trans. (into German) by Adolph Friedrich and Georg Buddruss, *Schamanengeschichten aus Siberian* (Munich, 1955), pp. 211–12, as found in Joseph Campbell, *The Masks of God*, vol. 1: *Primitive Mythology*, p. 252.
7. Eliade, *Shamanism*, p. 109, quoting, in part, Willard Z. Park, *Shamanism in Western North America* (Evanston: Northwestern University Press, 1938), p. 26.
8. Ibid., p. 18.
9. Vilmos Diószegi, *Tracing Shamans in Siberia*, trans. A. R. Babo (Oosterhout, The Netherlands: Anthropological Publications, 1968), p. 143.
10. Eliade, *Rites and Symbols of Initiation*, p. 87.
11. Eliade, *Shamanism*, p. 19.
12. Natalie Curtis, *The Indians' Book* (New York: Dover Publications, 1968), p. 39.
13. Eliade, *Rites and Symbols of Initiation*, p. 101.
14. Ibid., p. 87.
15. Schmidt, p. 64.
16. Ibid., pp. 64–65.

17. Michael Harner, "The Ancient Wisdom in Shamanic Cultures," in *Shamanism*, comp. Nicholson, p. 4ff.
18. Åke Hultkrantz, "A Definition of Shamanism," *Temenos*, vol. 9, 1973, p. 31, as found in Richard Noll, "Mental Imagery Cultivation as a Cultural Phenomenon: The Role of Visions in Shamanism," *Current Anthropology*, vol. 26, no. 4, 1985, p. 446.
19. D. Handelman, "The Development of a Washo Shaman," *Ethnology*, vol. 6, 1967, p. 457, as found in Noll, p. 446.
20. Richard Noll, "The Presence of Spirits in Magic and Madness," in *Shamanism*, comp. Nicholson, p. 49.
21. Eliade, *Shamanism*, pp. 223, 401.
22. Weston La Barre, "Hallucinogens and the Shamanic Origins of Religion," in *Flesh of the Gods*, p. 272.
23. Noll, "Mental Imagery Cultivation as a Cultural Phenomenon," p. 445.
24. Michael Winkelman, "Trance States: A Theoretical Model and Cross-Cultural Analysis," *Ethos*, vol. 14, 1986, pp. 176–77.
25. Eliade, *Rites and Symbols of Initiation*, p. 87.
26. Ibid., p. 89.
27. Ksenofontov, pp. 211–12.
28. Diószegi, p. 62.
29. A. A. Popov, *Tavgytsy. Materialy po etnograpfii i vedeyevskikh tavgytsev* (Moscow and Leningrad: Akademia Nauk Soyaza Sovetskikh Sotzialisticheskikh and Trady Instituta Anthropologii i Etnografii I, 1936), p. 84ff, trans. and summarized by Mircea Eliade, *From Primitives to Zen* (New York: Harper and Row, 1977), pp. 436–37.
30. Knud Rasmussen, *Intellectual Culture of the Iglulik Eskimos*, trans. William Worster (Copenhagen: Glydendalske boghandel, 1930), p. 114, originally found in Eliade, *Shamanism*, p. 62.
31. Eliade, *Shamanism*, p. 63.
32. A. P. Elkin, *Aboriginal Men of High Degree: Initiation and Sorcery in the World's Oldest Tradition* (Rochester, Vt: Inner Traditions International, 1994), p. 21.
33. Baldwin Spencer and F. J. Gillen, *The Native Tribes of Central Australia* (London: Macmillan, 1899), pp. 523–25.
34. Knud Rasmussen, *Across Arctic America* (New York: G. P. Putnam's Sons, 1927), pp. 84–85, as found in Campbell, *The Masks of God*, vol. 1: *Primitive Mythology*, p. 244.
35. Paul Radin, *The Road of Life and Death: A Ritual Drama of the American Indians* (Princeton: Princeton University Press, 1991), pp. 75, 197, 339.
36. Ibid., p. 4.
37. Ibid., p. 341, ftnt. 11; see also p. 221.
38. Campbell, *The Masks of God*, vol. 1: *Primitive Mythology*, pp. 229–30.
39. Sally J. Cole, *Legacy on Stone: Rock Art of the Colorado Plateau and Four Corners Region* (Boulder: Johnson Books, 1990), p. 144.

40. Ibid., p. 153.
41. Eliade, *Rites and Symbols of Initiation*, p. 92.
42. Eliade, *Shamanism*, p. 63.
43. Eliade, *Rites and Symbols of Initiation*, p. 93.
44. Campbell, *The Masks of God*, vol. 1: *Primitive Mythology*, p. 255.
45. C. G. Jung, *Memories, Dreams, Reflections*, trans. Richard and Clara Winston (New York: Vintage, 1989), p. 4.
46. Walsh, p. 207.
47. Eliade, *Shamanism*, p. 265.
48. Campbell, *The Masks of God*, vol. 1: *Primitive Mythology*, p. 471.
49. Oliver La Farge, foreword to Gladys A. Reichard, *Navaho Religion: A Study of Symbolism* (Princeton: Princeton University Press, 1990), p. xv.
50. Jung, as found in Jung and Kerényi, *Essays on a Science of Mythology*, p. 79.
51. Ibid., p. 93.
52. Noll, "Mental Imagery Cultivation as a Cultural Phenomenon," p. 445.
53. Ibid., p. 449.
54. Ibid. p. 448.
55. Heinrich Zimmer, *Artistic Form and Yoga in the Sacred Images of India*, trans. G. Chapple and J. B. Lawson (Princeton: Princeton University Press, 1984), pp. 18–19.
56. Jay Miller, p. 173.
57. Larry G. Peters, "Trance, Initiation, and Psychotherapy in Tamang Shamanism," *American Ethnologist*, vol. 9, no. 1, 1982, p. 21.
58. Ibid., p. 22.
59. Ibid., p. 25.
60. Andrei A. Popov, "How Sereptie Djaruoskin of the Nganasans (Tavgi Samoyeds) Became a Shaman," in *Popular Beliefs and Folklore Tradition in Siberia*, ed. Vilmos Diószegi and trans. Stephen P. Dunn (Bloomington: University of Indiana Press, 1968), pp. 137–46.
61. S. M. Shirokogoroff, *Psychomental Complex of the Tungus* (London: Kegan, Paul, Trench, Truebner, 1935), p. 271.
62. Eliade, *Shamanism*, p. 27.
63. Ibid., p. 31.
64. Jung, *Collected Works*, vol. 8, para. 415.
65. Radin, pp. 339–40, ftnt. 21.
66. Eliade, *Shamanism*, p. 460.
67. The peyote hunt has been perceptively studied by, among others, Peter T. Furst, "To Find Our Life: Peyote Among the Huichol Indians of Mexico," in *Flesh of the Gods*, and Barbara G. Myerhoff in *The Peyote Hunt: The Sacred Journey of the Huichol Indians* (Ithaca: Cornell University Press, 1974).
68. Furst, p. 138.
69. Ibid., p. 141.
70. Ibid., p. 152.
71. Ibid., p. 149.

72. Myerhoff, p. 103.
73. Ibid., pp. 133, 240–53.
74. Furst, p. 160, ftnt.
75. Joan Halifax, *Shaman: The Wounded Healer* (London: Thames and Hudson, 1982), p. 37.
76. Furst, p. 165.
77. Myerhoff, p. 135.
78. Myerhoff, pp. 202–3.
79. Furst, p. 170.
80. Myerhoff, p. 253ff.
81. Furst, pp. 174–75.
82. Ibid., pp. 175–76.
83. Michael Harner, *The Way of the Shaman* (New York: Harper and Row, 1990), p. 58.
84. Campbell, *The Masks of God*, vol 1: *Primitive Mythology*, p. 292.
85. Ibid., p. 378.

CHAPTER 4

1. Erich Neumann, "Art and Time," p. 3.
2. Ernst Cassirer, *The Philosophy of the Enlightenment*, trans. Fritz C. A. Koell and James Pettegrove (Princeton: Princeton University Press, 1951), p. 326.
3. Campbell, *The Masks of God*, vol. 1: *Primitive Mythology*, p. 398.
4. E. Nandisvara Nayake Thero, "The Dreamtime, Mysticism and Liberation: Shamanism in Australia," in *Shamanism*, comp. Nicholson, p. 223.
5. Elkin, p. 18.
6. Jeremy Beckett, foreword to 1976 edition of Elkin, p. xvii.
7. Elkin, p. 86.
8. Ibid., p. 4.
9. E. Nandisvara Nayake Thero, p. 227.
10. Elkin, p. 152.
11. Ibid., p. 147.
12. Eliade, *Shamanism*, p. 51.
13. Elkin, p. 113.
14. Mircea Eliade, *Australian Religions* (Ithaca: Cornell University Press, 1973), p. 14.
15. Andreas Lommel, *Shamanism: The Beginnings of Art*, trans. Michael Bullock (New York: McGraw-Hill, 1967), pp. 50–51.
16. Ibid., p. 51.
17. Eliade, *Australian Religions*, p. 146.
18. Joan Halifax, *Shaman: The Wounded Healer*, p. 70; see also Joseph Campbell, *Historical Atlas of World Mythology*, vol 1: *The Way of the Animal Powers*, p. 137.

19. Elkin, p. 105.
20. Ibid., pp. 20–21.
21. Ibid., p. 106.
22. Ibid., p. 105.
23. Ibid., p. 128.
24. Eliade, *Australian Religions*, p. 79.
25. Eliade, "Shamanism and Cosmology," in *Shamanism*, comp. Nicholson, p. 17.
26. Elkin, p. 145.
27. Lommel, p. 146.
28. Andreas Lommel, *Die Unambal: Ein Stammin Nordwest-Australien* (Hamburg, Germany: Museum für Volkerkunde, 1952), pp. 10–12, following commentary in Eliade, *Australian Religions*, p. 68.
29. Ibid., as found in Campbell, *Historical Atlas of World Mythologies*, vol. 1: *The Way of the Animal Powers*, p. 141.
30. Eliade, *Australian Religions*, pp. 76–78.
31. Ibid., pp. 80–81.
32. Ibid., p. 84.
33. Ibid., pp. 51–52; see also Mircea Eliade, *The Quest: History and Meaning in Religion* (Chicago: University of Chicago Press, 1969), p. 83.
34. Campbell, *Historical Atlas of World Mythology*, vol. 1: *The Way of the Animal Powers*, pp. 144–45.
35. Eliade, *The Quest*, p. 84.
36. Elkin, p. 4.
37. Elkin, p. 33.
38. Eliade, *The Quest*, p. 86.
39. Elkin, p. 146.
40. Henri Bergson, *The Creative Mind: An Introduction to Metaphysics*, trans. Mabelle L. Andison (New York: Citadel, 1946), pp. 124–25.
41. Andreas Lommel and David Mowaljarlai, "Shamanism in Northwest Australia," *Oceania*, vol. 64, no. 4, June 1994, p. 283.
42. Ibid.
43. Ibid. p. 281.
44. Ibid., pp. 286–87.
45. Linda Schele and David Freidel, *A Forest of Kings: The Untold Story of the Ancient Maya* (New York: Quill, 1990), p. 17.
46. Shamanism has traditionally been found in "simpler" cultures, and its association with more complex civilizations, such as the Olmec and Maya, has caused some difficulty. As F. Kent Reilly III observes, "Shamanistic trance is rarely the basis for political authority in societies that are more complex than a tribe or, perhaps, a chiefdom. Recent hieroglyphic discoveries demonstrate conclusively, however, that Classic period Maya kings validated their right to royal power by publicly proclaiming their ability to perform the shamanic trance journey and transform into power animals. Linda Schele's

and David Freidel's iconographic and epigraphic discoveries successfully show how shamanism's ideology was the foundation of Classic period Maya political validation. Formative period Mesoamerica was not alone in validating political authority through shamanic authority. In the Old World, Shang Dynasty China (1766–1122 B.C., early Yamato period Japan (ca. A.D. 50–300), and Silla Dynasty Korea (A.D. 668–935) are prime examples of state-level political authority based on shamanism." ("Art, Ritual and Rulership in the Olmec World," in *The Olmec World, Ritual and Rulership*, ed. Michael Coe, Princeton: The Art Museum, Princeton University, in association with Harry N. Abrams, New York, 1996, p. 30.)

47. David Freidel, Linda Schele, and Joy Parker, *Maya Cosmos: Three Thousand Years on the Shaman's Path* (New York: William Morrow, 1993), p. 48.
48. Barbara Tedlock, *Time and the Highland Maya* (Albuquerque: University of New Mexico Press, 1992), p. 50.
49. Ibid., p. 49.
50. Ibid.
51. Ibid., p. 158.
52. Schele and Freidel, p. 66.
53. Michael Coe, *The Maya* (New York: Thames and Hudson, 1993), p. 181.
54. Ibid., p. 182.
55. Mary Miller and Karl Taube, *An Illustrated Dictionary of the Gods and Symbols of Ancient Mexico and the Maya* (New York: Thames and Hudson, 1993), p. 42.
56. Freidel, Schele, and Parker, pp. 202–7, 244; see also Linda Schele and Mary Ellen Miller, *The Blood of Kings: Dynasty and Ritual in Maya Art* (New York: George Braziller, 1986), p. 181.
57. Schele and Miller, p. 285.
58. Schele and Freidel, p. 89.
59. Miller and Taube, pp. 181–82.
60. J. Eric Thompson, "Ethnology of the Mayas of Southern and Central British Honduras," *Field Museum of Natural History*, pub. 274, Anthropological Series, vol. 17, no. 2 (chicago, 1930), pp. 68–69, as quoted in Freidel, Schele, and Parker, pp. 208–9.
61. Ibid., pp. 109–10, as quoted in Freidel, Schele, and Parker, p. 209; first bracket added by quoting authors.
62. Freidel, Schele, and Parker, p. 448.
63. Karen Bassie-Sweet, *At the Edge of the World: Caves and Late Classic Maya World View* (Norman, Okla: University of Oklahoma Press, 1996), p. 9.
64. Ibid., pp. 4, 41, 42, 111, 131.
65. Ibid., p. 81ff.
66. Freidel, Schele, and Parker, p. 151; see also Coe, p. 181.
67. Schele and Freidel, p. 427, ftnt. 16.
68. Ibid., p. 72.
69. Ibid., p. 417.

70. Miller and Taube, p. 181.
71. Coe, p. 175.
72. Schele and Freidel, p. 407; see also pp. 415–16.
73. Richard A. Diehl and Michael D. Coe, "Olmec Archaeology," in *The Olmec World: Ritual and Rulership*, p. 19.
74. Andrea Stone, *Images from the Underworld: Naj Tunich and the Tradition of Maya Cave Painting* (Austin: University of Texas Press, 1995), p. 20.
75. Ibid., p. 47.
76. Ibid.
77. Ibid.
78. Ibid., p. 49.
79. Ibid.
80. F. Kent Reilly III, "Art, Ritual and Rulership in the Olmec World," in *The Olmec World: Ritual and Rulership*, pp. 39–41.
81. Stone, p. 49.
82. Schele and Freidel, pp. 66–67.
83. Freidel, Schele, and Parker, p. 53.
84. Miller and Taube, p. 186.
85. Schele and Freidel, p. 418.
86. Ibid., p. 67.
87. Ibid., p. 427.
88. Ibid., p. 68.
89. Ibid., p. 72.
90. Peter Dunham, personal communication to David Freidel, as found in Freidel, Schele, and Parker, p. 425, ftnt. 60.
91. Freidel, Schele, and Parker, p. 427, ftnt. 9.
92. Ibid., 128.
93. Ibid., p. 191.
94. Ibid., p. 273.
95. Ibid., p. 265.
96. Ibid., pp. 190, 422, ftnt. 43.
97. Schele and Freidel, p. 90.
98. Freidel, Schele, and Parker, pp. 210–13.
99. Ibid., pp. 411–12, ftnt. 19.
100. Jung, *Collected Works*, vol. 9, para. 291.
101. Clarke, *In Search of Jung*, p. 129.
102. C. G. Jung, "Approaching the Unconscious," in *Man and His Symbols*, ed. C. G. Jung (New York: Dell, 1968), p. 53.
103. Halifax, *Shaman: The Wounded Healer*, p. 43.
104. Peter T. Furst, "Shamanism, Transformation, and Olmec Art," in *The Olmec World: Ritual and Rulership*, p. 72.
105. Elkin, p. 87.
106. Eliade, *Australian Religions*, pp. 51–52.
107. Mircea Eliade, "Sacred Architecture and Symbolism," trans. Diane

Apostolos-Cappadonna and Frederica Adelman in *Symbolism, the Sacred and the Arts*, ed. Diane Apostolos-Cappadonna (New York: Crossroad, 1988), pp. 118–19; see also Eliade, *Australian Religions*, pp. 50–53.

108. Freidel, Schele, and Parker, pp. 52, 202, 442, 443; Dennis Tedlock, *Popul Vub* (New York: Simon and Schuster, 1986), p. 337.

109. A. W. Howitt, *The Native Tribes of South-East Australia* (London: MacMillan, 1904), pp. 406–8.

110. Eliade, *Shamanism*, pp. 120, 121, 269ff.

111. Uno Holmberg, *Finno-Ugric, Siberian Mythology*, vol. 4 of *The Mythology of All Races* (Boston: Marshall Jones, 1927), p. 351; Eliade, *Shamanism*, p. 272.

112. Eliade, *Shamanism*, p. 117.

113. Ibid., pp. 68–71.

114. Andreas Lommel, *Shamanism: The Beginnings of Art*, p. 111.

115. Eliade, *Shamanism*, p. 156.

116. Marguerite Anne Biesele, "Folklore and Ritual of !Kung Hunter-Gatherers" (Ph.D. diss., Harvard University, 1975), part two, p. 154. Originally found in Halifax, *Shamanic Voices*, pp. 54–62.

117. Ibid., p. 155.

118. J. David Lewis-Williams, *Believing and Seeing: Symbolic Meaning in Southern San Rock Paintings* (London: Academic Press, 1981), pp. 34, 81.

119. Biesele, p. 158.

120. Lewis-Williams, p. 77.

121. Biesele, p. 168.

122. Ibid.

123. Ibid., p. 163.

124. Ibid., p. 162.

125. Ibid., p. 171.

126. Thomas A. Dowson, *Rock Engravings of Southern Africa* (Johannesburg: Witwatersrand, 1992), p. 74.

127. Morris Edward Opler, *Apache Odyssey: A Journey Between Two Worlds* (New York: Holt, Rhinehart and Winston, 1969), pp. 41–46.

128. Rainer Maria Rilke, *Sonnets to Orpheus*, trans. M. D. Herter Norton (New York: W. W. Norton, 1962), p. 89.

129. Donald Sandner, *Navaho Symbols of Healing: A Jungian Exploration of Ritual, Image, and Medicine* (Rochester, Vt: Healing Arts Press, 1991), p. 242.

130. Joseph Campbell, commentary to *Where the Two Came to Their Father: A Navajo War Ceremonial*, ed. Joseph Campbell and Maud Oakes (Princeton: Princeton University Press, 1991), p. 64.

131. Ibid.

132. "Hovamol," in *The Poetic Edda*, trans. H. A. Bellows (New York: American Scandinavian Foundaton, 1923), p. 60.

133. Campbell and Oakes, p. 40.

134. Ibid.

135. Ibid., p. 41.

136. Ibid.
137. Ibid., p. 44.
138. Campbell, in Campbell and Oakes, pp. 65–67; see also Reichard, *Navajo Religion: A Study of Symbolism*, p. 20.
139. Ananda Coomaraswamy, "Symplegades," in *Traditional Art and Symbolism*, ed. Roger Lipsey (Princeton: Princeton University Press, 1986), p. 530.
140. Ibid., p. 529.
141. Reichard, p. 15.
142. Sandner, p. 127, quoting in part Leland Wyman and Bernard Haile, *Blessingway* (Tucson: University of Arizona Press, 1970), p. 112.
143. Campbell, in Campbell and Oakes, p. 78.
144. Reichard, p. 301.
145. Washington Matthews, "The Mountain Chant: A Navaho Ceremony" in *Fifth Annual Report of the Bureau of American Ethnology to the Secretary of the Smithsonian Institution*, 1883–84 (Washington, D.C., 1887), p. 467, as found in Sandner, pp. 272, 273.
146. Sandner, p. 62.
147. Washington Matthews, "The Prayer of a Navaho Shaman," *American Anthropologist*, Old Series, vol. 1, 1888, pp. 152ff.
148. Reichard, p. 112.
149. Sandner, p. 42.
150. Ibid., p. 71.
151. Mircea Eliade, *Myth and Reality*, trans. Willard R. Trask (New York: Harper Torchbooks, 1968), p. 30.
152. Plotinus, *The Enneads*, trans. Stephen MacKenna (New York: Penguin, 1991), I, 6–7; p. 53.
153. Matthews, "The Prayer of a Navaho Shaman," p. 163.
154. Sandner, p. 225; Sandner notes this is an approximate rendering. His commentary is based upon Washington Matthews, "Navaho Legends," *Memoirs of the American Folklore Society*, vol. 5, 1897, p. 299.
155. Reichard, p. 47.
156. Sandner, p. 225.
157. Sander, pp. 220–21, based upon and summarizing Gladys A. Reichard, *Navaho Medicine Man* (New York: J. J. Augustin, 1939).
158. Campbell, in Campbell and Oakes, p. 14.

CHAPTER 5

1. Gerardo Reichel-Dolmatoff, *The Shaman and the Jaguar: A Study of Narcotic Drugs Among the Indians of Colombia* (Philadelphia: Temple University Press, 1975), p. 76.
2. Ibid., pp. 76–77.
3. Ibid., p. 77.
4. Ibid.

5. Ibid., p. 78.
6. Gerardo Reichel-Dolmatoff, "The Cultural Context of an Aboriginal Hallucinogen: *Banisteriopsis Caapi*," trans. Michael B. Sullivan, in *Flesh of the Gods*, ed. Peter T. Furst., p. 93.
7. Reichel-Dolmatoff, *The Shaman and the Jaguar*, p. 141.
8. Reichel-Dolmatoff, "The Cultural Context of an Aboriginal Hallucinogen," p. 93.
9. Reichel-Dolmatoff, *The Shaman and the Jaguar*, pp. 140-41.
10. Ibid., p. 35.
11. Ibid., p. 111.
12. Ibid., p. 83.
13. Ibid., p. 85.
14. Ibid., pp. 134–35; see also "The Cultural Context of an Aboriginal Hallucinogen," pp. 93–94.
15. Reichel-Dolmatoff, "The Cultural Context of an Aboriginal Hallucinogen," pp. 94–95.
16. Ibid., p. 94.
17. Carl Kerényi, in Jung and Kerényi, *Essays on a Science of Mythology*, p. 14.
18. Ibid., p. 8.
19. Ibid., p. 7.
20. Ibid.
21. Reichel-Dolmatoff, *The Shaman and the Jaguar*, pp. 137–38.
22. Ibid., p. 145.
23. Mircea Eliade, *The Two and the One*, p. 114.
24. Reichel-Dolmatoff, *The Shaman and the Jaguar*, p. 101.
25. Reichel-Dolmatoff, "The Cultural Context of an Aboriginal Hallucinogen," p. 99.
26. Ibid., p. 108.
27. Ibid., pp. 93–94, 103.
28. Reichel-Dolmatoff, *The Shaman and the Jaguar*, pp. 118–19.
29. Ibid., pp. 169–71; see also "The Cultural Context of an Aboriginal Hallucinogen," pp. 107–9.
30. Ibid., p. 172.
31. Ibid., pp. 179–80; see also "The Cultural Context of an Aboriginal Hallucinogen," pp. 102–3.
32. Ibid., p. 181; see also "The Cultural Context of an Aboriginal Hallucinogen," p. 103.
33. Reichel-Dolmatoff, "The Cultural Context of an Aboriginal Hallucinogen," p. 102.
34. Reichel-Dolmatoff, *The Shaman and the Jaguar*, p. 181.
35. Ibid., p. 180.
36. Reichel-Dolmatoff, "The Cultural Context of an Aboriginal Hallucinogen," p. 103.
37. Ibid., pp. 103–4.

CHAPTER 6

1. Horst Kirchner, "Ein archäologischer Beitrag zur Urgeschichte des Schmanismus," *Anthropos*, vol. 47, 1952, p. 279 ff., as found in Eliade, *Shamanism*, p. 503.

2. Michel Lorblanchet, as found in "Behold the Stone Age," by Robert Hughes, *Time*, February 13, 1995, p. 60.

3. T. G. E. Powell, *Prehistoric Art* (New York: Praeger, 1966), p. 41.

4. See Leroi-Gourhan, *Treasures of Prehistoric Art*, pp. 513–14; Reichel-Dolmatoff, *The Shaman and the Jaguar*, pp. 168–81, and "The Cultural Context of an Aboriginal Hallucinogen," pp. 104–13.

5. Lewis-Williams and Dowson, "The Signs of All Times: Entoptic Phenomena in Upper Paleolithic Art," p. 213.

6. Ibid., p. 214.

7. Ibid., p. 215.

8. Ibid., p. 204, quoting in part R. K. Siegel, "Hallucinations," *Scientific American*, vol. 237, no. 4, 1977, p. 134.

9. Ibid., p. 204; Harner, *The Way of the Shaman*, pp. 25–39; Siegel, p. 134; R. K. Siegel and M. E. Jarvik, "Drug-induced Hallucinations in Animals and Man," in *Hallucinations: Behaviour, Experience, and Theory*, eds. R. K. Siegel and L. J. West (New York: Wiley, 1975), p. 139.

10. Eliade, "The Symbolism of Shadows in Archaic Religions," trans. Apostolos-Cappadonna and Adelman in *Symbolism, the Sacred and the Arts*, p. 4.

11. Clottes and Courtin, *The Cave Beneath the Sea*, pp. 155–56.

12. Ibid., pp. 71–76.

13. Ibid., pp. 156–58.

14. Ibid., pp. 157–60.

15. Ibid., p. 161.

16. Dale W. Ritter and Eric W. Ritter, "Medicine Men and Spirit Animals in Rock Art of Western North America," in *Acts of the International Symposium on Rock Art, Lecture at Hanko*, August 6–12 (Oslo, 1972), p. 101, citing Garrick Mallery, "Picture Writing of the American Indian," Tenth Annual Report of the Bureau of American Ethnology (1893), pp. 237, 463–64, 467, 773–74.

17. Lewis-Williams and Dowson, p. 214.

18. Campbell, *Historical Atlas of World Mythology*, vol. 1: *The Way of the Animal Powers*, p. 62; Leroi-Gourhan, *Treasures of Prehistoric Art*, p. 144.

19. Coomaraswamy, "Symplegades," pp. 524, ftnt. 10, 543.

20. Ruspoli, p. 89.

21. Leroi-Gourhan, *Treasures of Prehistoric Art*, p. 133.

22. Marshack, *The Roots of Civilization*, p. 236.

23. Chauvet, Deschamps, and Hillaire, p. 66.

24. Ibid., p. 46.

25. Ibid., pp. 42, 58.

26. Ibid. p. 41.

27. Jean Clottes, epilogue to Chauvet, Deschamps, and Hillaire, p. 96.

28. Coomaraswamy, "Medieval and Oriental Art," in *Traditional Art and Symbolism*, p. 47.

29. William Blake, *Complete Writings*, ed. Geoffrey Keynes (London: Oxford University Press, 1969), p. 576.

30. Plotinus, *The Enneads* V, 8, 1, p. 411.

31. Immanuel Kant, *Critique of Judgment*, trans. James Meredith (Oxford: Clarendon, 1964), pp. 77–79.

32. Campbell, *The Masks of God*, vol. 1: *Primitive Mythology*, p. 378.

33. *Black Elk Speaks*, as told through John Neihardt (Lincoln, Nebr.: Bison Books, University of Nebraska Press, 1988), p. 273.

34. Ibid., p. 43.

35. Ibid., p. 28.

36. William K. Powers, *Oglala Religion* (Lincoln, Nebr.: Bison Books, University of Nebraska Press, 1982), p. 97.

37. Eliade, *Shamanism*, pp. 480–81.

38. Ibid., p. 194, ftnt. 41.

39. Eliade, *Images and Symbols*, trans. Philip Mairet (New York: Sheed and Ward, 1969), p. 39.

40. Eliade, "Shamanism and Cosmology," in *Shamanism*, comp. Nicholson, p. 18.

41. Eliade, *Images and Symbols*, p. 40.

42. Ibid., p. 39.

43. Eliade, *Shamanism*, p. 271.

44. Ibid.

45. Wilbert, "Tobacco and Shamanistic Ecstasy Among the Warao Indians of Venezuela," p. 63.

46. Wasson, "What Was the Soma of the Aryans?" in *Flesh of the Gods*, p. 211.

47. Ibid., p. 213.

48. Eliade, *Shamanism*, p. 169.

49. Annette Laming-Emperaire, *Lascaux: Paintings and Engravings* (Baltimore: Penguin, 1959), trans. E. F. Armstrong, pp. 93–96, as found in Alexander Marshack, *The Roots of Civilization*, p. 278.

50. Lommel, *Shamanism: The Beginning of Art*, p. 111.

51. F. Kent Reilly III, "Art, Ritual and Rulership in the Olmec World," *The Olmec World*, pp. 39–41.

52. André Leroi-Gourhan, Résumé des Cours de 1975–76, *Annuaire du College de France*, 76th year, p. 430, as found in Jean Clottes and Jean Courtin, *The Cave Beneath the Sea*, p. 157.

53. Clottes and Courtin, p. 157.

54. Ibid., p. 159.

55. Eliade, *Shamanism*, p. 233; see also pp. 119–21, *Rites and Symbols of Initiation*, p. 93; Campbell, *The Masks of God*, vol. 1: *Primitive Mythology*, p. 256.
56. Halifax, *Shaman: The Wounded Healer*, p. 22.
57. Powers, p. 98.
58. Eliade, *Primitives to Zen*, p. 424.
59. Eliade, *Shamanism*, p. 160.
60. Clottes and Courtin, pp. 158–59.
61. Marshack, *The Roots of Civilization*, p. 206.
62. Ibid., p. 208.
63. Ibid., p. 274.
64. Ibid., p. 272.
65. Ibid., p. 237.
66. Ibid., p. 240, quoting Breuil, p. 238.
67. Chauvet, Deschamps, and Hillaire, p. 50.
68. Halifax, *Shamanic Voices*, pp. 110–11.
69. Ibid., p. 107.
70. Leroi-Gourhan, *Treasures of Prehistoric Art*, p. 474.
71. Ibid., pp. 123, 137, 474.
72. Marshack, *The Roots of Civilization*, pp. 238, 240.
73. Leroi-Gourhan, *Treasures of Prehistoric Art*, pp. 123, 137, 474.
74. Marshack, *The Roots of Civilization*, p. 238.
75. Lommel, *Shamanism: The Beginnings of Art*, p. 99.

BIBLIOGRAPHY

Apostolos-Cappadonna, Diane, ed. *Symbolism, the Sacred and the Arts*. New York: Crossroad, 1988.

Bahn, Paul G., and Jean Vertut. *Journey through the Ice Age*. Berkeley, CA: University of California, 1997.

Baring, Anne, and Jules Cashford. *The Myth of the Goddess: Evolution of an Image*. New York: Arkana, 1993.

Bassie-Sweet, Karen. *At the Edge of the World: Caves and Late Classic Maya World View*. Norman, OK: University of Oklahoma Press, 1996.

Bergson, Henri. *The Creative Mind: An Introduction to Metaphysics*. Trans. Mabelle L. Andison. New York: Citadel, 1946.

Biesele, Marguerite Anne. "Folklore and Ritual of !Kung Hunter-Gatherers." Ph.D. Dissertation, Harvard University, 1975.

Black Elk Speaks. As told through John Neihardt. Lincoln, NE: Bison Books, University of Nebraska Press, 1988.

Blake, William. *Complete Writings*. Edited by Geoffrey Keynes. London: Oxford University Press, 1969.

Bohm, David. *Wholeness and the Implicate Order*. New York: Ark Paperbacks, 1983.

Breazeale, Daniel, ed. *Philosophy and Truth: Selections from Nietzsche's Notebooks of the Early 1870s*. Atlantic Highlands, NJ: Humanities Press International, 1979.

Breuil, Abbé Henri. *Four Hundred Centuries of Cave Art*. Trans. Mary Boyle. Montignac, France: Centre d'Etudes et de Documentation Prehistoriques, 1952.

Bruno, David. "Rock Art and Inter-regional Interaction in Northeastern Australian History." *Antiquity*, vol. 64, no. 245, Dec. 1990, pp. 788–806.

Burkert, Walter. *Greek Religion*. Trans. John Raffon. Cambridge, MA: Harvard University Press, 1985.

———. *Structure and History in Greek Mythology and Ritual*. Berkeley, CA: University of California Press, 1982.

Campbell, Joseph. *The Hero with a Thousand Faces.* Princeton, NJ: Princeton University Press, Bollingen Series XVII, 1972.

———. *Historical Atlas of World Mythology.* Vol. 1, *The Way of the Animal Powers.* New York: Harper and Row, 1983.

———. *The Masks of God.* Vol. 1, *Primitive Mythology.* New York: Viking Press, 1970.

———. *The Masks of God.* Vol. 2, *Oriental Mythology.* New York: Viking Press, 1970.

———. *The Masks of God.* Vol. 3, *Occidental Mythology.* New York: Viking Press, 1970.

———. *The Masks of God.* Vol. 4, *Creative Mythology.* New York: Viking Press, 1970.

———. *The Mythic Image.* Princeton, NJ: Princeton University Press, Bollingen Series C, 1974.

———, ed. *Man and Time: Papers from the Eranos Yearbooks.* Vol. 3. Trans. Ralph Manheim. Princeton, NJ: Princeton University Press, Bollingen Series XXX, 1980.

———, ed. *Man and Transformation: Papers from the Eranos Yearbooks.* Vol. 5. Trans. Ralph Manheim. Princeton, NJ: Princeton University Press, Bollingen Series XXX, 1983.

———, and Maud Oakes, eds. *Where the Two Came to Their Father: A Navaho War Ceremonial.* Princeton, NJ: Princeton University Press, Bollingen Series I, 1991.

Capra, Fritjof. *The Tao of Physics: An Exploration of the Parallels Between Modern Physics and Eastern Mysticism.* Berkeley, CA: Shambhala, 1975.

Cassirer, Ernst. *Language and Myth.* Trans. Susanne K. Langer. New York: Dover, 1953.

———. *The Philosophy of the Enlightenment.* Trans. Fritz C. A. Koell and James P. Pettegrove. Princeton, NJ: Princeton University Press, 1951.

———. *The Philosophy of Symbolic Forms.* Vol. 2, *Mythical Thought.* Trans. Ralph Manheim. New Haven, CT: Yale University Press, 1955.

Chauvet, Jean-Marie, Eliette Brunel Deschamps, and Christian Hillaire. *The Dawn of Art: The Chauvet Cave.* Trans. Paul Bahn. New York: Harry N. Abrams, 1996.

C. G. Jung Speaking: Interviews and Encounters. Ed. W. McGuire and R. F. C. Hull. London: Pan Books, 1980.

Clarke, J. J. *In Search of Jung.* London: Routledge, 1992.

Clottes, Jean. Epilogue to *The Dawn of Art: The Chauvet Cave.* Jean-Marie Chauvet, Eliette Brunel Deschamps, and Christian Hillaire. Trans. Paul Bahn. New York: Harry N. Abrams, 1996.

———, and Jean Courtin. *The Cave Beneath the Sea: Paleolithic Images at Cosquer.* Trans. Marilyn Garner. New York: Harry N. Abrams, 1996.

Coe, Michael. *The Maya.* New York: Thames and Hudson, 1993.

————, ed. *The Olmec World: Ritual and Rulership.* Princeton, NJ: The Art Museum, Princeton University, in association with Harry N. Abrams, New York, 1996.

Cole, Sally J. *Legacy on Stone: Rock Art of the Colorado Plateau and Four Corners Region.* Boulder, CO: Johnson Books, 1990.

Coomaraswamy, Ananda. *Traditional Art and Symbolism.* Ed. Roger Lipsey. Princeton, NJ: Princeton University Press, Bollingen Series LXXXIX, 1986.

Curtis, Natalie. *The Indians' Book.* New York: Dover Publications, 1968.

Davidson, H. R. Ellis. *Gods and Myths of Northern Europe.* London: Penguin, 1990.

————. *Myths and Symbols in Pagan Europe: Early Scandinavian and Celtic Regions.* Syracuse, NY: Syracuse University Press, 1988.

Davies, Paul. *Superforce: The Search for a Grand Unified Theory of Nature.* New York: Touchstone, 1985.

Delluc, Brigette and Gilles. Comment on J. D. Lewis-Williams and T. A. Dowson, "The Signs of All Times: Entoptic Phenomena in Upper Paleolithic Art." *Current Anthropology*, vol. 29, no. 2, April 1988, p. 224.

Diószegi, Vilmos. *Tracing Shamans in Siberia.* Trans. A. R. Babo. Oosterhout, The Netherlands: Anthropological Publications, 1968.

Dodds, E. R. *The Greeks and the Irrational.* Berkeley, CA: University of California Press, 1951.

Dowson, Thomas A. *Rock Engravings of Southern Africa.* Johannesburg, South Africa: Witwatersrand, 1992.

Eliade, Mircea. *Australian Religions.* Ithaca, NY: Cornell University Press, 1973.

————. *From Primitives to Zen: A Thematic Sourcebook of the History of Religions.* New York: Harper and Row, 1977.

————. *A History of Religious Ideas.* Vol. 1, *From the Stone Age to the Eleusinian Mysteries.* Trans. Willard R. Trask. Chicago: University of Chicago Press, 1978.

————. *A History of Religious Ideas.* Vol. 2, *From Guatama Buddha to the Triumph of Christianity.* Trans. Willard R. Trask. Chicago: University of Chicago Press, 1982.

————. *A History of Religious Ideas.* Vol. 3, *From Muhammed to the Age of Reforms.* Trans. Alf Hiltebeitel and Diane Apostolos-Cappadonna. Chicago: University of Chicago Press, 1985.

————. *Images and Symbols.* Trans. Philip Mairet. New York: Sheed and Ward, 1969.

————. *Myth and Reality.* Trans. Willard R. Trask. New York: Harper Torchbooks, 1968.

————. "The Occult in the Modern World." In *Occultism, Witchcraft and Cultural Fashions.* Chicago: University of Chicago Press, 1976.

————. *Patterns in Comparative Religion.* Trans. Rosemary Sheed. New York: Meridian, 1974.

————. *The Quest: History and Meaning in Religion.* Chicago: University of Chicago Press, 1969.

———. *Rites and Symbols of Initiation: The Mysteries of Birth and Rebirth*. Trans. Willard R. Trask. New York: Harper Torchbooks, 1965.

———. *The Sacred and the Profane: The Nature of Religion*. Trans. Willard R. Trask. New York: Harper Torchbooks, 1961.

———. *Shamanism: Archaic Techniques of Ecstacy*. Trans. Willard R. Trask. Princeton, NJ: Princeton University Press, Bollingen Series LXXVI, 1972.

———. *The Two and the One*. Trans. J. M. Cohen. New York: Harper Torchbooks, 1965.

———. *Yoga: Immortality and Freedom*. Trans. Willard R. Trask. Princeton, NJ: Princeton University Press, Bollingen Series LVI, 1970.

Elkin, A. P. *Aboriginal Men of High Degree: Initiation and Sorcery in the World's Oldest Tradition*. Rochester, VT: Inner Traditions International, 1994.

Evens-Wentz, W. Y. *The Tibetan Book of the Dead*. London: Oxford University Press, 1960.

Fiedel, Stuart J. *Prehistory of the Americas*. Cambridge: Cambridge University Press, 1992.

Flood, Josephine. *The Riches of Ancient Australia: A Journey into Prehistory*. St. Lucia, Queensland: University of Queensland Press, 1990.

Forman, Robert K. C. *Meister Eckhart: Mystic as Theologian*. Rockport, MA: Element, 1991.

Freidel, David, Linda Schele, and Joy Parker. *Maya Cosmos: Three Thousand Years on the Shaman's Path*. New York: William Morrow, 1993.

Friedländer, Paul. *Plato: An Introduction*. Trans. Hans Meyerhoff. Princeton, NJ: Princeton University Press, Bollingen Series LIX, 1973.

Furst, Peter T., ed. *Flesh of the Gods: The Ritual Use of Hallucinogens*. Prospect Heights, IL: Waveland Press, 1990.

———, and Jill Furst. *North American Indian Art*. New York: Rizzoli, 1982.

Gimbutas, Marija. *The Language of the Goddess*. New York: HarperCollins, 1989

Goodchild, Peter, ed. *Raven Tales: Traditional Stories of Native Peoples*. Chicago: Chicago Review Press, 1991.

Graham, A. C. *Disputers of the Tao: Philosophical Argument in Ancient China*. La Salle, IL: Open Court, 1989.

Graziosi, Paolo. *Palaeolithic Art*. London: Faber and Faber, 1960.

Grove, David C. "Olmec Cave Paintings: Discovery from Guerrero, Mexico." *Science*, vol. 174, pp. 421–423, 1969.

———. *The Olmec Paintings of Oxtotitlan Cave, Guerrero, Mexico*. Studies in Pre-Columbian Art and Archaeology 6. Washington: Dumbarton Oaks, 1970.

Grube, G. M. A. *Plato's Thought*. Indianapolis, IN: Hackett Publishing Co., 1980.

Guthrie, W. K. C. *The Greeks and Their Gods*. Boston: Beacon Press, 1950.

Halifax, Joan. *Shaman: The Wounded Healer*. London: Thames and Hudson, 1982.

———. *Shamanic Voices: A Survey of Visionary Narrative*. New York: Arkana, 1991.

Halverson, John. "Art for Art's Sake in the Paleolithic." *Current Anthropology*, vol. 28, no. 1, 1987, pp. 63–71.

Handelman, D. "The Development of a Washo Shaman." *Ethnology*, vol. 6, 1967, pp. 444–64.

Harner, Michael. *The Way of the Shaman.* New York: Harper and Row, 1990.

Henderson, Joseph L., and Maud Oakes. *The Wisdom of the Serpent: The Myths of Death, Rebirth and Resurrection.* New York: Collier Books, 1972.

Hofstadter, Albert, and Richard Kuhns, eds. *Philosophies of Art and Beauty: Selected Readings in Aesthetics from Plato to Heidegger.* Chicago: University of Chicago Press, 1976.

Holmberg, Uno. *Finno-Ugric, Siberian Mythology.* Vol. 4. *The Mythology of All Races.* Boston: Marshall Jones, 1927.

Howitt, A.W. *The Native Tribes of South-East Australia.* London: MacMillan, 1904.

Hudson, Travis, and Georgia Lee. "Function and Symbolism in Chumash Rock Art." *Journal of New World Archaeology,* vol. 6, 1984, pp. 26–47.

Hughes, Robert. "Behold the Stone Age." *Time,* February 13, 1995.

Hultkrantz, Åke. "A Definition of Shamanism." *Temenos,* vol. 9, 1973, pp. 25–37.

———. *The Religions of the American Indians.* Trans. Monica Setterwall. Berkeley, CA: University of California Press, 1980.

Irwin, Lee. *The Dream Seekers: Native American Visionary Traditions of the Great Plains.* Norman, OK: University of Oklahoma Press, 1994.

Jaspers, Karl. *Kant.* From *The Great Philosophers.* Vol. 1. Trans. Ralph Manheim. San Diego, CA: Harvest/HBJ, 1962.

Jung, Carl G. *Collected Works.* Vol. 5, *Symbols of Transformation.* Trans. R. F .C. Hull. New York: Pantheon Books, Bollingen Series XX, 1956.

———. *Collected Works.* Vol. 7, *Two Essays on Analytical Psychology.* Trans. R. F. C. Hull. New York: Pantheon Books, Bollingen Series XX, 1953.

———. *Collected Works.* Vol. 8, *The Structure and Dynamics of the Psyche.* Trans. R. F. C. Hull. Princeton, NJ: Princeton University Press, Bollingen Series XX, 1969.

———. *Collected Works.* Vol. 9, *Part 1. The Archetypes and the Collective Unconscious.* Trans. R. F. C. Hull. Princeton, NJ: Princeton University Press, Bollingen Series XX, 1980.

———. *Collected Works.* Vol. 11, *Psychology and Religion: West and East.* Trans. R. F. C. Hull. New York: Pantheon Books, Bollingen Series XX, 1958.

———. *Collected Works.* Vol. 13, *Alchemical Studies.* Trans. R. F. C. Hull. Princeton, NJ: Princeton University Press, Bollingen Series XX, 1983.

———. *Collected Works.* Vol. 14, *Mysterium Coniunctionis.* Trans. R. F. C. Hull. Princeton, NJ: Princeton University Press, Bollingen Series XX, 1970.

———. *Collected Works.* Vol. 18, *The Symbolic Life.* Trans. R. F. C. Hull. Princeton, NJ: Princeton University Press, Princeton, NJ: Princeton University Press, Bollingen Series XX, 1980.

———. *Memories, Dreams, Reflections.* Trans. Richard and Clara Winston. New York: Vintage, 1989.

———. *Modern Man in Search of a Soul.* Trans. W. S. Dell and Cary F. Baynes. San Diego, CA: Harcourt Brace, 1933.

———, ed. *Man and His Symbols.* New York: Dell, 1968.

———, and Carl Kerényi. *Essays on a Science of Mythology.* Trans. R. F. C. Hull. Princeton, NJ: Princeton University Press, Bollingen Series XXII, 1969.

Kant, Immanuel. *Critique of Judgment.* Trans. James Meredith. Oxford: Clarendon, 1964.

Keyser, James D. *Indian Rock Art of the Columbia Plateau.* Seattle, WA: University of Washington Press, and Vancouver: Douglas & McIntyre, 1992.

Kofman, Sarah. *Nietzsche and Metaphor.* Trans. Duncan Large. Stanford, CA: Stanford University Press, 1993.

Ksenofontov, G.V. *Legendy i rasskazy o shamanach u. yakutov, buryat i tungusov.* Izdanie vtoroe. S. predisloviem S. A. Topkareva. Moscow: Izdatel'stvo Besbozhnik, 1930.

Kühn, Herbert. *Auf den Spüren des Eiszeitmenschen.* Wiesbaden, Germany: F. A. Brockhaus, 1953.

———. *On the Track of Prehistoric Man.* Trans. Alan Brodrick. New York: Random House, 1955.

La Barre, Weston. *The Ghost Dance: Origins of Religion.* New York: Doubleday, 1970.

Laming-Emperaire, A. *Lascaux: Paintings and Engravings.* Trans. E. F. Armstrong. Baltimore, MD: Penguin, 1959.

Larsen, Stephen. *The Shaman's Doorway: Opening Imagination to Power and Myth.* Barrytown, NY: Station Hill Press, 1988. Reprint, Rochester, VT: Inner Traditions International, 1998.

Lemonick, Michael D. "Stone Age Bombshell." *Time,* June 19, 1995.

Leon-Portilla, Miguel. *Aztec Thought and Culture.* Trans. J. E. Davis. Norman, OK: University of Oklahoma Press, 1990.

Leroi-Gourhan, André. *The Art of Prehistoric Man in Western Europe.* London: Thames and Hudson, 1967.

———. Résumé des Cours de 1975–76. *Annuaire du College de France,* 76th year, pp. 421–34.

———. *Treasures of Prehistoric Art.* Trans. Norbert Guterman. New York: Harry N. Abrams, 1967.

Lewis-Williams, J. David. *Believing and Seeing: Symbolic Meaning in Southern San Rock Paintings.* London: Academic Press, 1981.

———, and T. A. Dowson. "The Signs of All Times: Entoptic Phenomena in Upper Paleolithic Art." *Current Anthropology,* vol. 29, no. 2, April 1988, pp. 201–45.

Lommel, Andreas. *Die Unambal: Ein Stammin Nordwest-Australien.* Hamburg, Germany: Museum für Volkerkunde, 1952.

———. *Shamanism: The Beginnings of Art.* Trans. Michael Bullock. New York: McGraw-Hill, 1967.

———, and David Mowaljarlai. "Shamanism in Northwest Australia." *Oceania,* vol. 64, no. 4, June 1994, pp. 277–89.

Lorblanchet, Michel. "Spitting Images: Replicating the Spotted Horse of Pech-Merle." *Archeology,* vol. 44, no. 6, 1991, pp. 24–31.

Magee, Bryan. *The Philosophy of Schopenhauer.* Oxford: Oxford University Press, 1987.

Maringer, Johannes. *The Gods of Prehistoric Man*. London: Weidenfeld and Nicholson, 1960.

Marshack, Alexander. "Images of the Ice Age." *Archeology*, vol. 48, no. 4, July/ August 1995, pp. 28–39.

———. *The Roots of Civilization*. Mount Kisco, NY: Moyer Bell, 1991.

Matthews, Washington. "The Mountain Chant: A Navaho Ceremony." In *Fifth Annual Report of the Bureau of American Ethnology to the Secretary of the Smithsonian Institution, 1883–84*, Washington, D.C., 1887, pp. 379–486.

———. "The Prayer of a Navaho Shaman." *American Anthropologist*, Old Series vol. 1, 1888, pp. 147–70.

———, comp. *Navaho Legends*. Salt Lake City, UT: University of Utah Press, 1994.

Miller, Jay. *Shamanic Odyssey: The Lushootseed Salish Journey to the Land of the Dead*. Menlo Park, CA: Ballena Press, 1988.

Miller, Mary, and Karl Taube. *An Illustrated Dictionary of the Gods and Symbols of Ancient Mexico and the Maya*. New York: Thames and Hudson, 1993.

Myerhoff, Barbara G. *The Peyote Hunt: The Sacred Journey of the Huichol Indians*. Ithaca, NY: Cornell University Press, 1974.

Narr, Karr J. "Approaches to the Religion of Early Paleolithic Man." Trans. Nancy E. Auer. *History of Religions*, vol. 4, no. 1, Summer 1964, pp. 1–22.

Nicholson, Shirley, comp. *Shamanism*. Wheaton, IL: The Theosophical Publishing House, 1987.

Nietzsche, Friedrich. *The Birth of Tragedy*. Trans. Francis Golffing. Garden City, NY: Anchor Books, 1956.

———. "On Truth and Lies in a Nonmoral Sense." In *Philosophy and Truth*. Trans. Daniel Breazeale. Atlantic Highlands, NJ: Humanities Paperback Library, 1990.

Noll, Richard. "Mental Imagery Cultivation as a Cultural Phenomenon: The Role of Visions in Shamanism." *Current Anthropology*, vol. 26, no. 4, 1985, pp. 443–61.

———. "Shamanism and Schizophrenia: A State-specific Approach to the 'Schizophrenia Metaphor' of Shamanic States." *American Ethnologist*, vol. 10, 1983, pp. 443–59.

Opler, Morris Edward. *Apache Odyssey: A Journey Between Two Worlds*. New York: Holt, Rinehart and Winston, 1969.

Park, Willard Z. *Shamanism in Western North America*. Evanston, IL: Northwestern University Press, 1938.

Patterson, Alex. *A Field Guide to Rock Art Symbols of the Greater Southwest*. Boulder, Colorado: Johnson Books, 1992.

Peters, Larry G. "Trance, Initiation, and Psychotherapy in Tamang Shamanism." *American Ethnologist*, vol. 9, no. 1, 1982, pp. 21–30.

Pfeiffer, John E. *The Creative Explosion: An Inquiry into the Origins of Art and Religion*. New York: Harper and Row, 1982.

Plato. *Collected Dialogues*. Ed. Edith Hamilton and Huntington Cairns. Princeton, NJ: Princeton University Press, Bollingen Series LXXI, 1961.

———. *The Republic.* As found in *Plato's Thought*, G. M. A. Grube. Indianapolis, IN: Hackett Publishing, 1980.

Plotinus. *The Enneads.* Trans. Stephen MacKenna. New York: Penguin, 1991.

The Poetic Edda. Trans. H. A. Bellows. New York: American Scandinavian Foundation, 1923.

Popol Vuh. Trans. Dennis Tedlock. New York: Touchstone, 1985.

Popov, A. A. "How Sereptie Djaruoskin of the Nganasans (Tavgi Samoyeds) Became a Shaman." *Popular Beliefs and Folklore Tradition in Siberia.* Ed. Vilmos Diószegi, trans. Stephen P. Dunn. Bloomington, IN: University of Indiana Press, 1968.

———. *Tavgytsy, Materialy po etnograpfii i vedeyevskikh tavgytsev.* Moscow and Leningrad: Akademia Nauk Soyaza Sovetskik Sotzialisticheskikh and Trady Instituta Anthropologii i Etnografii I, 5, 1936.

Powell, T. G. E. *Prehistoric Art.* New York: Praeger, 1966.

Powers, William K. *Oglala Religion.* Lincoln, NE: Bison Books, University of Nebraska, 1982.

———. *Sacred Language: The Nature of Supernatural Discourse in Lakota.* Norman, OK: University of Oklahoma Press, 1986.

The Principal Upanisads. Trans. S. Radhakrishnan. I.4, 4–5. Atlantic Highlands, NJ: Humanities Paperback Library, 1992.

Progoff, Ira. *Jung, Synchronicity, and Human Destiny: C. G. Jung's Theory of Meaningful Coincidence.* New York: Julian Press, 1987.

Radin, Paul. *The Road of Life and Death: A Ritual Drama of the American Indians.* Princeton, NJ: Princeton University Press, Bollingen Series V, 1991.

Rasmussen, Knud. *Across Arctic America.* New York: G. P. Putnam's Sons, 1927.

———. *Intellectual Culture of the Iglulik Eskimos.* Trans. William Worster. Copenhagen: Gyldendalske boghandel, 1930.

Reichard, Gladys A. *Navaho Medicine Man.* New York: J. J. Augustin, 1939.

———. *Navaho Religion: A Study of Symbolism.* Princeton, NJ: Princeton University Press, Bollingen Series XVIII, 1990.

Reichel-Dolmatoff, Gerardo. *Amazonian Cosmos: The Sexual and Religious Symbolism of the Tukano Indians.* Chicago: The University of Chicago Press, 1971.

———. *Beyond the Milky Way.* Los Angeles: UCLA Latin American Center, 1978.

———. *The Shaman and the Jaguar: A Study of Narcotic Drugs Among the Indians of Colombia.* Philadelphia: Temple University Press, 1975.

Rhode, Erwin. *Psyche: The Cult of Souls and Belief in Immortality Among the Ancient Greeks.* Chicago: Ares Publishers, 1987.

Rilke, Rainer Maria. *Sonnets to Orpheus.* Trans. M. D. Herter Norton. New York: W. W. Norton, 1962.

Ripinsky-Naxon, Michael. *The Nature of Shamanism: Substance and Function of a Religious Metaphor.* Albany, NY: SUNY, 1993.

Ritter, Dale W., and Eric W. Ritter. "Medicine Men and Spirit Animals in Rock Art of Western North America." *Acts of the International Symposium on Rock Art, Lecture at Hanko*, August 1972, pp. 6–12.

Ruspoli, Mario. *The Cave of Lascaux: The Final Photographs.* Trans. Sebastian Wormwell. New York: Harry N. Abrams, 1987.

Safranski, Rudiger. *Schopenhauer and the Wild Years of Philosophy.* Trans. Ewald Osers. Cambridge, MA: Harvard University Press, 1990.

Sandner, Donald. *Navaho Symbols of Healing: A Jungian Exploration of Ritual, Image, and Medicine.* Rochester, VT: Healing Arts Press, 1991.

Schele, Linda, and David Freidel. *A Forest of Kings: The Untold Story of the Ancient Maya.* New York: Quill, 1990.

———, and Mary Ellen Miller. *The Blood of Kings: Dynasty and Ritual in Maya Art.* New York: George Braziller, 1986.

Schelling, F. W. J. *Philosophical Inquiries into the Nature of Human Freedom.* Trans. James Gutmann. La Salle, IL: Open Court, 1936.

———. *The Philosophy of Art* Trans. Douglas W. Stott. Minneapolis, MN: University of Minnesota, 1989.

———. *Sammtliche Werke.* Ed. K. F. A. Schelling. Vols. 11 and 12, *Philosophie der Mythologie.* Stuttgart and Ausburg: J. G. Cotta'scher Verlag, 1856–1861.

———. *System of Transcendental Idealism.* Trans. Peter Heath. Charlottesville, VA: University of Virginia Press, 1978.

Schiller, Friedrich. *On the Aesthetic Education of Man, in a Series of Letters.* Trans. Reginald Snell. New York: Frederick Ungar, 1965.

Schopenhauer, Arthur. *The Fourfold Root of Sufficient Reason.* Trans. E. F. J. Payne. La Salle, IL: Open Court, 1974.

———. *The World as Will and Representation.* Vols. 1 and 2. Trans. E. F. J. Payne. New York: Dover Publicatons, 1966.

Seidelman, Harold, and James Turner. *The Inuit Imagination: Arctic Myth and Sculpture.* New York: Thames and Hudson, 1994.

Settegast, Mary. *Plato, Prehistorian: 10,000 to 5,000 B.C. Myth, Religion, Archaeology.* Hudson, NY: Lindisfarne Press, 1990.

Shirokogoroff, S. M. *Psychomental Complex of the Tungus.* London: Kegan, Paul, Trench, Truebner, 1935.

Siegel, R. K. "Hallucinations." *Scientific American,* vol. 237, no. 4, 1977, pp. 132–40.

———, and L. J. West, eds. *Hallucinations: Behaviour, Experience, and Theory.* New York: Wiley, 1975.

Sieveking, Ann. *The Cave Artists.* London: Thames and Hudson, 1979.

Siikala, A. *The Rite Technique of the Siberian Shaman.* Helsinki: Academia Scientiarum Fennica, 1978.

Smith, Noel. *An Analysis of Ice Age Art, Its Psychology and Belief System.* New York: Peter Lane (American University Studies Series XX, Fine Arts, vol. 15), 1992.

Snow, Dean R. "Rock Art and the Power of Shamans." *Natural History,* vol. 86, no. 2, 1977, pp. 42–49.

Spencer, Baldwin, and F. J. Gillen. *The Native Tribes of Central Australia.* London: Macmillan, 1899.

Stone, Andrea. *Images from the Underworld: Naj Tunich and the Tradition of Maya Cave Paintings.* Austin, TX: University of Texas Press, 1995.

Strehlow, T. G. H. *Aranda Traditions*. Carlton, Australia: Melbourne University Press, 1947.

Tedlock, Barbara. *Time and the Highland Maya*. Albuquerque, NM: University of New Mexico Press, 1992.

Tedlock, Dennis. *Popul Vuh*. New York: Simon and Schuster, 1986.

Thompson, J. Eric. "Ethnology of the Mayas of Southern and Central British Honduras." *Field Museum of Natural History*, Publication 274, Anthropological Series, vol. XVII, no. 2, Chicago, 1930.

Ucko, Peter J., and Andre E. Rosenfeld. *Paleolithic Cave Art*. London: World University Library, 1967.

Vinnicombe, Patricia. *People of the Eland: Rock Paintings of the Drakensberg Bushman As a Reflection of Their Life and Thought*. Pietermaritzburg: University of Natal Press, 1976.

Walsh, Roger. *The Spirit of Shamanism*. Los Angeles: Jeremy P. Tarcher, 1990.

Weltfish, Gene. *The Lost Universe: Pawnee Life and Culture*. Lincoln, NE: Bison Books, University of Nebraska Press, 1977.

White, Alan. *Schelling: An Introduction to the System of Freedom*. New Haven, CT: Yale University Press, 1983.

Whyte, Lancelot Law. *The Unconscious Before Freud*. Garden City, NY: Anchor Books, 1962.

Winkelman, Michael. "Trance States: A Theoretical Model and Cross-Cultural Analysis." *Ethos*, vol. 14, 1986, pp. 174–203.

Wyman, Leland, and Bernard Haile. *Blessingway*. Tucson, AZ: University of Arizona Press, 1970.

Zammito, John H. *The Genesis of Kant's* Critique of Judgment. Chicago: The University of Chicago Press, 1992.

Zimmer, Heinrich. *Artistic Form and Yoga in the Sacred Images of India*. Trans. Gerald Chapple and James B. Lawson. Princeton, NJ: Princeton University Press, 1984.

———. *Myths and Symbols in Indian Art and Civilization*. Ed. Joseph Campbell. Princeton, NJ: Princeton University Press, Bollingen Series VI, 1972.

INDEX

The notation fig *following a page number indicates that the page contains an illustration.*